The Biblical Jubilee and the Struggle

❖ ❖ ❖ ❖ ❖ ❖ ❖

THE BIBLICAL JUBILEE AND THE STRUGGLE FOR LIFE

An invitation to personal, ecclesial, and social transformation

♦ ♦ ♦ ♦ ♦ ♦ ♦

Ross Kinsler and Gloria Kinsler

ORBIS BOOKS

Maryknoll, New York 10545

The Catholic Foreign Mission Society of America (Maryknoll) recruits and trains people for overseas missionary service. Through Orbis Books, Maryknoll aims to foster the international dialogue that is essential to mission. The books published, however, reflect the opinions of their authors and are not meant to represent the official position of the society. To obtain more information about Maryknoll and Orbis Books, visit our website at www.maryknoll.org.

Copyright © 1999 by Ross Kinsler and Gloria Kinsler

Published by Orbis Books, Maryknoll, NY 10545–0308.

Throughout the text all English translations of Spanish quotations are the work of the authors.

Queries regarding rights and permissions should be addressed to: Orbis Books, P.O. Box 308, Maryknoll, NY 10545–0308.

Manufactured in the United States of America

Library of Congress Cataloging-in-Publication Data

Kinsler, Ross.
   The biblical jubilee and the struggle for life : an invitation to personal, ecclesial, and social transformation / Ross Kinsler and Gloria Kinsler.
     p. cm.
   Includes bibliographical references and index.
   ISBN 1-57075-289-3 (pbk.)
   1. Distributive justice—Religious aspects—Christianity.
2. Human ecology—Religious aspects—Christianity. 3. Jubilee
(Judaism) 4. Sabbath—Biblical teaching. I. Kinsler, Gloria.
II. Title.
BR115.J8.K56 1999
263—dc21   99-37872
                                         CIP

Contents

Foreword

A commitment to justice and peace in a world like ours, marked by so many conflicts and intolerable social and economic inequalities, is a necessary condition for the preparation and celebration of the jubilee. Thus, in the spirit of the book of Leviticus (25:8–12), Christians will have to raise their voice on behalf of all the poor of the world.
—John Paul II, *Tertio Millenio Adveniente* (1994)

"We read the gospel as if we had no money," laments American Jesuit theologian John Haughey, "and we spend our money as if we know nothing of the Gospel." Indeed, the topic of economics is exceedingly difficult to introduce in most First World churches—more taboo than politics or even sex. Yet no aspect of our individual and corporate lives is more determinative of our welfare, and few subjects are more frequently addressed in our Scriptures.

The standard of economic and social justice is woven into the warp and woof of the Bible. Pull this strand and the whole fabric unravels. At the heart of this witness is the call to Sabbath and Jubilee, a tradition we might summarize in three axioms:

♦ The world as created by God is abundant, with enough for everyone— provided that human communities restrain their appetites and live within limits.
♦ Disparities in wealth are not "natural" but the result of human sin and must be mitigated within the community of faith through the regular practice of wealth distribution.
♦ The prophetic message calls people to the practice of such redistribution and is thus characterized as "good news" to the poor.

The Bible contends that this Sabbath theology of abundant grace and this Jubilee ethic of wealth and power redistribution is the only way out of our historical and persistent slavery to debt systems, with their competing theologies of meritocracy and alienating practices of wealth and power concentration.

"Sabbath economics" is an unfamiliar notion to North American churches because it has been marginalized by biblical interpreters, whose silence has helped to legitimate the very stratification of wealth that the Bible denounces. Skeptical of the Jubilee tradition as either irrelevant, utopian dreaming, or threatening, radical propaganda, these interpreters have not found evidence for its practice in either Testament because they have not been looking for it.. This is because, as theologian Douglas Meeks asserts in his excellent book *God the Economist*, "Our theological imaginations have long been captive to the market-driven orthodoxies of modern capitalism." Fortunately, Ross and Gloria Kinsler's thorough and accessible summary and rehabilitation of the Jubilee tradition for our time begins to redress this longstanding and scandalous suppression of "good news" for the poor.

The Kinslers are uniquely qualified for this task because they have come to their convictions through the fire of experience. Long-term Presbyterian missionaries in Central America, Ross and Gloria have lived through some of the worst of times in a region wracked over the past three decades by intensifying poverty and violence. The Kinslers have also witnessed first-hand—and been contributors to—the survival and resurgence of popular movements of faith and liberation, despite the repressive conditions. Over the years they have faithfully labored to interpret Central American realities to the North American church and have facilitated many a visit to the region. Gloria is legendary as an exposure tour leader and organizer, while Ross has traveled throughout Latin America spreading the vision and practice of popular theological education.

These reflections, then, arise not from abstract musing but from the heart of a social movement of faith, hope, and love. The Kinslers stand in a tradition of solidarity work that has offered sanctuary to refugees, borne witness against the violence of military regimes, and through it all, kept reading the Scriptures. This movement is part of the "subversive memory" of Jubilee justice that has periodically erupted throughout church history. It animated early monks, medieval communitarians, and radical reformers. It was given voice in the tracts of eighteenth-century "Levelers" and in nineteenth-century African slave spirituals. Today, at the turning of the millennium, this vision of "release from the bondage of debt" is again firing the imaginations of faith-based activists. We can see this in groups such as the international "Jubilee 2000" Campaign, which is educating and organizing in support of debt relief for impoverished Third World countries. We can also see it in the many local experiments with small-scale and alternative business practices, technologies, land uses, financial systems, trade patterns, consumption habits, and income distribution schemes.

To be sure, these are hard times for those trying to find alternatives to the triumphal march of a global capitalism that leaves in its wake ever-increasing disparities between rich and poor. The authors of *The Biblical Jubilee and the Struggle for Life* rightly understand this historical moment as a unique opportunity for the church to renew its spirituality and its mission to the world by rediscovering the radically different vision of economic and social practice found at the heart of its own story.

This book is the ideal resource for churches to nurture commitment and creativity by promoting "Jubilee literacy," a spirituality of forgiveness and reparation, and practical economic disciplines for individuals, households, and congregations. However, the Kinslers are clear that with this hope for renewal also comes a warning: Any theology that refuses to reckon with the realities of the increasingly unequal distribution of wealth and power in the human family today is both cruel and irrelevant. We Christians *must* talk about economics, and talk about it in light of the gospel.

"Who, then, can be saved?" (Mark 10:26). The evangelist Mark's epilogue to the infamous story of Jesus and the rich man, so troublesome for our North American churches, anticipates our incredulous resistance. Does Jesus *really* expect the "haves" (that is, us) to participate in wealth redistribution as a condition for discipleship (10:21–22)? Can we imagine a world in which there are no rich and poor? To the disciples' skepticism, and to ours, Jesus replies simply, "I know it seems impossible to you, but for God all things are possible" (10:27). In other words, economics is ultimately a theological issue.

We owe a debt of gratitude to the Kinslers for their faithful labor, which has borne fruit for all of us in this volume. May this ancient biblical vision indeed animate new possibilities for our history, as invoked in the prayer of the nineteenth-century abolitionist William Lloyd Garrison:

> God speed the year of jubilee, the wide world o'er!
> When from their galling chains set free,
> Th' oppressed shall vilely bend the knee
> And wear the yoke of tyranny, like brutes, no more—
> That year will come, and Freedom's reign
> To all their plundered rights again, restore.

Ched Myers

Preface

The word "Jubilee" has gained wide use with the approach of the year 2000, which by all accounts will be a rare anniversary. This is a special time to celebrate but also to ponder over the past and future direction of humankind and planet Earth. For Jews and Christians it is an opportune time to return to our biblical roots, to rediscover the divine mandates regarding Jubilee.

Our own interest in the biblical Jubilee goes back some years. For us it has become an indispensable key to the whole biblical message. It epitomizes the struggle for fullness of life for all God's people, which is, we believe, our legacy as heirs of the Torah and the Prophets and as followers of Jesus. It responds powerfully to the primary concerns facing all of us as we enter the new millennium.

Having lived and worked among the peoples of Central America for twenty-five years, we know first hand that the struggle for life is painfully urgent there and around the world. We know also that many advocates of the poor have been martyred for proclaiming the very same principles set forth in the Sabbath Year and Jubilee mandates of the Hebrew Scriptures. Having served all these years as mission workers of the Presbyterian church (USA), we know how difficult it is for relatively affluent Christians of the north, including ourselves, to comprehend and practice those mandates. We are deeply indebted to friends and colleagues both north and south for enabling us to pursue our journey into Jubilee and for permitting us to share with them what we have learned along the way. This book is our attempt to repay our debt.

Our first mission assignment took us to Guatemala, where we served for thirteen years as that land and people entered the most violent period of their long history of marginalization, dehumanization, and oppression. We taught at the Presbyterian Seminary there, but we were slow learners. Only gradually did we come to understand the social, economic, racial–ethnic, military, political, gender, and religious dimensions of domination at work there and around the world. Only gradually did we begin to understand what "good news to the poor" and "liberation of the oppressed" must mean. Among those who enabled us to see what is now so obvious are Julia, Nelly, Chepe, Moisés, Celestino, Rigoberta, Juana, Manuel, Juan, and many others. Among the peoples of Guatemala who bore the brunt of brutal repression and gave their lives so that we all might join their struggle for life are Ladinos, Quiches, Mames, Cakchiqueles, Kekchies, and others.

Our current assignment brought us to Costa Rica in 1987 and here, too, we have continued to learn about this world we live in and the faith we share "from the underside." As the Cold War came to a close and its ideology was cleared away, we could see ever more clearly how the logic of the dominant, market-centered, economic order is driving hundreds of millions of people to the limits of survival and depriving hundreds of millions more of their fundamental rights to dignity and full participation in life as God intended it to be. The Latin American Biblical University (Seminary), where we now teach, gathers mature students from different parts of the region each year for intensive periods of study, and it reaches out through a network of centers and institutions to many more who carry out their theological studies in their local contexts while they support their families and exercise leadership in their churches, communities, and diverse occupations. Together we struggle to find deeper understanding of the gospel in the face of this global crisis. We have used the Jubilee as the theme for our 75th anniversary celebration in 1998, and we continue to work together on the roots and implications of the biblical Jubilee as guidance for our mission into the new millennium.

Among those who have been our mentors in the study of the biblical roots of Jubilee are Thomas Hanks, former professor of this institution, and Elsa Tamez, its current president. Among those who have generously and patiently worked with us on this manuscript are two very good friends who have made major contributions in this area. Sharon Ringe's book, *Jesus, Liberation, and the Biblical Jubilee: Images for Ethics and Christology*, is the current classic. In recent years, she has taken time from teaching at Wesley Seminary in Washington to come to Costa Rica for special assignments. She has dedicated precious time to counsel us in the writing of this book.

Ched Myers is another extraordinary biblical person, most known for his ground breaking commentary, *Binding the Strong Man: A Political Reading of Mark's Story of Jesus*. He combines his biblical work with social activism, challenging church people and others to build a movement for social justice, ecological integrity, and spiritual wholeness. In recent months he has focused increasingly on Jubilee as an invaluable and perhaps incomparable key to the biblical message for our time. He has contributed generously and patiently to the whole process of bringing this manuscript to its present form.

We want readers to know that this work on the biblical Jubilee really is a work in process. We have only begun to trace its roots and explore its implications. So we want to encourage many others to take up the challenge, engage in the process, discover new dimensions and implications of the vision, and share the fruits of their experience. The task is urgent. We must intensify our efforts, multiply our forces, broaden our movement.

Introduction

"Proclaim liberty throughout the land to all its inhabitants." Those words, taken from Leviticus, one of the least-known books of the Bible, may contain the spark that can ignite spiritual fires capable of bringing about the personal, ecclesial, and social transformation that today's world so urgently needs. The original Jubilee mandate was announced on the Day of Atonement, the holiest day of the year. It was accompanied by the sound of trumpets. The words are inscribed on the Liberty Bell in Philadelphia, which was rung in 1776 to declare the independence of the Thirteen Colonies.

We believe that the Sabbath–Jubilee mandates speak directly to the primary predicaments of our time: the destruction of the biosphere, the crushing burden of national and personal debts, the oppression of meaningless labor and the threat of unemployment, basic economic and social insecurity, and the spreading plague of consumerism, which is the motor that drives us all away from life as God intended it to be. Can it be that by digging into these mandates from ancient times we can find fundamental guidelines for the central concerns of our own time? Why did Luke choose that special Jubilee text, Isaiah 61:1–2a, to explain the mission of Jesus in his inaugural sermon? Can it be that we too will find there the central meaning of our faith and vocation in today's world? What in fact does the Bible have to say about the critical problems of daily living and human survival as we close the most violent century of our history and begin a new and very uncertain millennium? Can the biblical Jubilee offer us vital signposts through which we can identify and experience God's reign in our own lives and in our world here and now?

We should have found the answers to these questions over thirty-five years ago, when we were completing research in Scotland on the mission of Jesus in the synoptic Gospels. However, it wasn't until years later in Guatemala, during one of the terrible periods of military repression, that a participant in one of our extension seminary courses pointed out that the biblical Jubilee is still perhaps the most pertinent proposal for agrarian reform and social justice that we can find anywhere. It responds to the most urgent needs of poor peasants throughout Central America and much of the Third World—debt relief and access to the land. The central mandates of the Sabbath Day, the Sabbath Year, and the Jubilee Year have become ever more urgent for all of us during the 1990s because of the globalization of market-oriented economics, the pervasive socioeconomic polarization of humankind, and the threat of what some are calling "planetary death."

It was probably inevitable that many would pick up the Jubilee theme as an apt way to consider the end of the second millennium, whether from an apocalyptic, institutional, or philosophical perspective. We often use anniversaries to review our goals, evaluate our progress, and make plans for the future. The Sabbath Day was intended to break the cycle of daily work—always in danger of degeneration into exploitation or drudgery—to offer rest and restoration for humans and animals alike, and to recall the divine purpose of liberation from slavery for building an alternative social possibility in which all would have enough and none would have more than enough. The Sabbath Year called for concrete actions every seven years and the Jubilee every fifty years to rectify serious inequities in the socioeconomic order and overcome the tendency toward the accumulation of wealth and power for a few and marginalization and poverty for many. It sets forth these mandates in the context of spiritual renewal and faithfulness to the God who liberated the Hebrew slaves from Egypt and gave them the Promised Land.

We have approached this study out of our concern for the churches in North America and Latin America and more specifically out of our experience in Central America. In the 1970s and 1980s it was all too evident that the suffering of the peoples of Central America was directly related to U.S. foreign policy, so this had to be our concern. With the signing of peace accords, the media have turned to other regions, but the ongoing economic struggles of the peoples of Central America are just as tragic, producing more malnutrition, disease, and death than ever before. These conditions are directly related to the "New World Order" so proudly proclaimed by U.S. presidents and legislators and dominated by U.S. economic interests, so this too must be our concern. The resultant "war against the poor" generated by this new economic order demands our utmost attention, serious biblical–theological reflection, and critical social analysis beyond anything we have yet attempted in our churches. We will have to deal with these realities in the new millennium. The biblical Jubilee offers vital clues for an understanding of the problems we face and the options we must consider. It provides a spiritual foundation for commitment and action.

Our primary concern here is this biblical material. We want to explore in some depth the Sabbath–Jubilee mandates and vision because they are so central to the overall biblical message, and yet they are so little understood in our churches. They are so relevant to our human-ecological predicament, and yet they are so rarely developed in our personal, ecclesial, and social life. We do not presume to know the full extent and implications of this biblical strand, but we can begin to provide some of its historical-literary-social-cultural background. As we pursue these concerns, we are increasingly surprised by the emergence of Sabbath–Jubilee images and echoes in so many biblical texts.

This study is only a beginning; we want to encourage others to continue to explore and share this exciting dimension of God's marvelous provision for life in God's realm. Together we face a monumental pedagogical task, as complex as the global context in which we live. We have organized each chapter around the three dimensions of what many call "the hermeneutical circle." The first section considers some salient aspects of "Today's World," beginning with socioeconomic and going on to political–ideological and religious–spiritual realities that pose challenges for our faith and our lives. The second section, "Biblical Faith," turns to the Bible and considers materials surrounding the Sabbath–Jubilee mandates and the Jubilee vision of God's reign among God's people—beginning with the Hebrew Scriptures (Chapters 2 through 4) and then going on to the Christian Scriptures (Chapters 5 through 7). The final section considers the challenge of "Responsible Discipleship" in today's world in faithfulness to the Jubilee vision in terms of personal, ecclesial, and social transformation. The first and last sections are necessary to provide a context for the biblical material in terms of our own realities, but they are only introductory and suggestive. Each reader or group will of course work out their own analysis of today's world and make their own conclusions regarding responsible discipleship in their own contexts.

The most critical dimension of this entire process is no doubt the question of commitment and action. Without commitment there will be no action, and without action there will probably be no real commitment or even understanding. This leads us back to pedagogy. Our strongest recommendation is to undertake this study with a partner and, if at all possible, with a small group that will share mutual responsibility and accountability for both study and action. Each session, on a weekly or biweekly basis, can then generate meaningful and even life-changing participation, as all share concerns, reflections, and experiences as agents of Jubilee in the struggle for fullness of life for all people. At the end of Chapter 4, which concludes the Old Testament studies on the Jubilee, we pose a series of questions for personal and group reflection about our responsibility for transformation as Jubilee people in today's world.

Our goal in gathering and sharing these resources is to promote personal, ecclesial, and social transformation. We and our world need conversion if we are not only to survive but to achieve our full humanity in God's image. Out of our Judeo-Christian tradition, we speak of *personal transformation* as a task that we can only approach in prayer, in profound respect for the Bible, and with deep concern for others near and far and for all God's creation. Each reader personally, from the outset and throughout this process, will want to reflect on his or her own pilgrimage. In fact the opening session of any study group might well be dedicated to sharing personal journeys, particularly in terms of growing commitment to God's justice in this unjust world, to full humanity in our dehumanizing societies, and to the integrity of God's creation which is on the verge of collapse.

We speak of *ecclesial transformation* because we know that as isolated individuals we can do little. This is not to say that any particular form of church is essential but rather to recognize that "church" may be experienced in many different ways, formal and informal. At the institution where we teach we often recall the words of a colleague who said that our seminary is not *the* church; it is not *a* church; but it is *church*. To sustain processes of personal transformation and to promote processes of social transformation, we all need some form of church, and this expression of church will itself need to engage in ongoing transformation if it is to contribute to personal and social transformation. In our experience it has been the progressive incorporation and full participation of people from the periphery—the poor, women, the laity, racial and ethnic minorities, refugees, the differently abled—that has provided the greatest stimulus to the renewal of the churches. Theologies of liberation emerging from their experiences are bringing home to all of us fuller understanding of the gospel and of our own humanity.

Finally we speak of *social transformation* as the ultimate goal of God's reign and our discipleship. We recommend a continuing, radical critique of the dominant socioeconomic system, which we learn from the various liberation theologies, north and south, and a continuing focus on micro-efforts toward social transformation, to which all of us can relate. The Bible itself represents the perspective of oppressed peoples and their struggles for fullness of life according to God's will, as set forth so incisively in the Sabbath–Jubilee vision. The Bible leads us into a radical, fundamental critique of domination systems at every level, systems in which we ourselves and our traditions have been immersed, and it calls for prophetic action and coherent lifestyle for the well-being of all God's people and all God's creation. We are called to deal with macro-questions as we take micro-steps in response to the Jubilee challenge. We are not alone. The unprecedented awakening of marginalized and excluded sectors of humankind in this generation offers diverse and ample venues for the practice of Jubilee.

Scattered throughout the book are data, quotations, and other materials that can serve as liturgical resources for reflection, meditation, and prayer. Our final chapter, Chapter 8, will focus directly on "liturgy as world-making" and the biblical Jubilee as celebration of our life together as God's people. The dimension of celebration and the affirmation of life should run throughout the entire process for each reader and group. The following prayer, which appears at the conclusion of Enrique Bermúdez' book, *Death and Resurrection in Guatemala* (1986, pp. 74–75), may be a useful place to start.

> ### *Prayer for a People in the Throes of Martyrdom*
> Lord, may your Gospel be for me not a book,
>   but Good News, lived and shared.
> May I not be embittered by oppression.
> May I speak more of hope than of calamities.

May my denunciations be first subjected to discernment,
 in community,
 brought before you in profound prayer,
 and uttered without arrogance,
 not as an instrument of aggression,
 but neither with timidity and cowardice.
May I never resign myself to the exploitation of the poor,
 in whatever form it may come.
 Help me to be subversive of any unjust order.
 Help me to be free,
 and to struggle for the freedom of the oppressed.
May I never become accustomed to the suffering of the martyrs
 and the news that my brothers and sisters are enduring
   persecution,
 but may their lives and witness ever move me to conversion
 and to the greatest loyalty to the Kingdom.
May I accept my church with an ever growing love
 and with Christian realism.
May I not reject it for its faults,
 but feel myself committed to renew it,
 and help it to be what you, Lord, want it to be.
May I fear not death, but infidelity.

1 ❖ ❖ ❖ ❖ ❖ ❖

The Jubilee Challenge—
Fullness of Life for
All God's People

This opening chapter will provide a general overview of the Jubilee challenge. Our intention is to

❖ articulate a beginning analysis of the central predicament of today's world: the spiraling polarization of rich and poor locally and globally, a predominant ideology that not only accepts but justifies this reality, and the dehumanization that this reality and this ideology are generating all around us.

❖ give an initial overview of the biblical message in response to this predicament, using the Jubilee teachings as a key to that message running through the Old and New Testaments.

❖ begin to explore both general and specific implications of this analysis of today's world and this reading of the biblical message for responsible discipleship in our personal lives, in our churches, and in society.

We will sharpen and deepen these three dimensions of our study in each succeeding chapter, focusing on critical elements of each.

Today's World ❖ ❖ ❖ ❖ ❖

The Champagne Glass Analogy

The diagram shown in Figure 1 appeared in the 1992 report of the United Nations Program on Development. It presents graphically what we have called the central predicament of our time—the spiraling polarization of rich and poor—which has horrendous implications for the entire human family. Each of us is invited to consider his or her place in this reality, to imagine what life is like for those who find themselves in the different socioeconomic levels. We must ask how we have come to such a dramatic situation and consider what is being done to correct the egregious inequality.

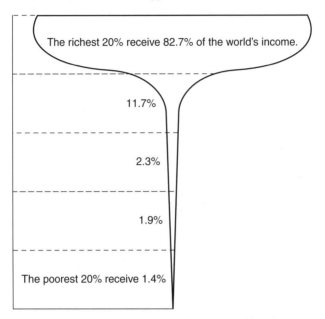

The richest 20% receive 82.7% of the world's income.

11.7%

2.3%

1.9%

The poorest 20% receive 1.4%

Figure 1. The Champagne Glass Analogy. Each horizontal band represents one-fifth of the world's population.

There are many ways to work with these data. The richest 20% of the world's population enjoys 82.7% of the world's annual income, which is more than four times the total income of the other 80% of the world's population. One might have known that there were a few extremely rich people in the world, but this suggests that there are now a billion people, including the large U.S. middle class, who enjoy enormous benefits from the existing socioeconomic system and will probably do everything they can to maintain their advantages or even to improve them. In the United States, virtually every city has wealthy suburbs and is building new luxury housing, thereby increasing the investment of this sector of the population in the very system that is marginalizing their fellow human beings locally and worldwide.

At the other end of the scale—that is, at the bottom of the champagne glass—20% of the world's population, the poorest one billion people, receive annually just 1.4% of the world's income, about one-fourteenth of their share. The poorest 40%, two billion people, receive 3.3%; and the poorest 60%, three billion people, a total of 5.6%. We have all known poor people who are healthy and happy and who even have certain cultural and family values that we might envy. But what are the implications of these data in terms of the daily struggle to put enough food on the table, to pay the rent and utilities and purchase other bare essentials, to clothe their children and keep them in school, to meet emergency medical needs, and so on?

What do these realities mean in terms of basic human dignity and security for those billions of people at the bottom, and what do they mean for the basic humanity of those at the top who are monopolizing and consuming so much of the world's wealth?

Perhaps the most worrisome aspect of the United Nations report is the fact that this polarization is not diminishing but growing. U.N. research indicates that in 1960 the ratio of income between the richest 20% and the poorest 20% was 30:1. In 1990 it had grown to the level of 60:1. But when in 1992 U.N. researchers adjusted their data to compare not just rich countries and poor countries but rich and poor within each country, the result was even more dramatic. The wealthiest 20% of the world's population was actually receiving annually 150 times as much as the poorest 20%. Evidently that trend is not only continuing but accelerating! (Mulligan, 1992, p. 36).

One might consider that this is all very good for those at the top of the champagne glass, including the majority of U.S. church members. It is also easy to see that this glass is exceedingly unstable. It has no base and can fall over and shatter, endangering all of the world's people. Those at the top may well use their resources to maintain their position of power and privilege, but the great majority may, as has happened in the past, rebel, claim a more just portion, and destroy the structures and institutions that deprive them of the essentials as well as the luxuries of life. Or they may, as we have already seen, give up the struggle to "make it" in the world and turn to alcohol and drugs, delinquency, or suicide.

Harper's Magazine recently (October, 1997) reported that since 1986, the United States has reduced its food aid worldwide by 29%, and it is estimated that 240,183 people could be fed for one year with the food that the U.S. population wastes in one day. No doubt many U.S. churches contribute to hunger programs, especially in response to emergency appeals, but these efforts pale into insignificance in comparison to our government's policies and our level of food waste.

Globalization of the "Free Market"

The preeminence of today's socioeconomic system, if not all its results, is justified through ideology, as with any system. What is striking now is the degree to which the current dominant ideology has an economic thrust rather than political. In Latin America we call this "neoliberalism," which we usually translate as "free market" ideology. This worldview affirms that free markets, free trade, and competition unfettered by governments and international organizations offer the best solution to the world's needs and thus justify the current difficulties faced by some sectors and nations.

One of the authors we have found most helpful because of his comprehensive analysis and biblical critique of this ideology is Ulrich Duchrow. His book, *Alternatives to Global Capitalism: Drawn from Biblical History, De-*

signed for Political Action, is published in association with the European Kairos movement. He explains how since the 1960s there has been a power shift away from the Keynesian balance of economic and social interests under government regulation, with a commitment to a wide range of social welfare concerns, toward a primary commitment to profit and wealth accumulation through deregulation, government withdrawal, and increasing submission to the dictates of the marketplace. "The result is that the accumulation of money assets is now the absolute, immutable yardstick for all economic, social, ecological, and political decisions. It is no longer just an aim but a concrete mechanism" (Duchrow, 1995, p. 71).

This power shift is justified by an ideology that is founded upon a peculiar understanding of and commitment to "freedom." It is a superficial commitment to political democracy—specifically, the freedom to vote in elections—and a primary commitment to the freedom to own and accumulate private property—specifically, private enterprise and the freedom of the market. This ideology is advocated as the freedom of everyone, every social sector, every enterprise, and every country to compete in the marketplace. The assumption is that all will become more efficient producers and all can effectively gain prosperity. The overwhelming evidence is, however, that this ideology leads rather to the strong becoming stronger and the weak weaker, the rich richer and the poor poorer. As globalization progresses, we are witnessing economic and social polarization beyond any previous period in human history.

In future chapters we will examine the roots of these developments in order to confront them with our biblical mandates and seek effective ways to respond to the emerging human and ecological results. As Duchrow writes, "Our point of departure and reference is human beings, most of whom nowadays are living in increasing misery, and nature, the basis of all life on our planet and now in danger" (ibid., p. 19). We believe that ultimately every political and ideological system must be judged not so much on what it affirms but on what it actually contributes to the integral well-being of humankind and nature.

What we now see is not only the transcendence of economics over politics but the rule of money through the transnationalization of financial markets and the deregulation of those markets. With the accumulation of wealth as the primary goal, other economic and social concerns become secondary and thus diminished or eliminated. At the national level we have seen the demise of organized labor as a significant factor in economic decisions, thus reducing concern for workers and their families. The concern for profit leads easily to downsizing, layoffs, automation, plant closings, and the transfer of jobs to Third World centers of cheap labor. More recently we have seen the progressive dismantling of the welfare system and a growing condemnation of the most vulnerable and marginalized social sectors based on virulent use of neoliberal rhetoric. Almost no one denies that there have been abuses in the labor movement and in the welfare system, but these have become excuses to abandon the human concerns of our economic system.

At the international level, the free flow of loans to Third World countries has created an enormous debt crisis that now ensures a massive flow of capital from the poor countries of the south to the rich countries of the north. Because of their absolute dependence on funding from the north, especially through the International Monetary Fund (IMF) and the World Bank, these poor countries must submit to the economic policies dictated by these international monetary organizations. These organizations are ruled by the wealthy countries, whose overall concern is to continue extracting profits through interest payments. In the face of insistence that development can only be achieved through market-centered free enterprise, this arrangement is in fact draining capital from the poor countries, increasing poverty, and reducing public and social services. Between 1982 and 1988 the poor countries paid the rich countries $236.2 billion net, but the debtor nations still owed $1,500 billion. In recent years they have transferred to the north approximately $50 billion per year through interest payments. The United Nations estimates that the total transfer, south to north, due to debts plus unfavorable trade arrangements, comes closer to $500 billion per year in what has been called "reverse development" or subsidies for the rich nations by the poor peoples of the world (ibid., pp. 77–78).

This analysis will require further study, but certain elements are already clear. There has been an important shift away from the concern for human development and well-being to the concern for the accumulation of wealth. The primacy of economics and more specifically of money is having widespread effects on the lives of people worldwide, and this situation is particularly evident in the creation and management of debts.

Spiritual Alienation, Insolidarity, and Religious Proliferation

Our concern is not simply economic or monetary. The champagne glass analogy provides data about income and reveals starkly the extent to which the current world economic order is producing a vast sea of poverty. As Duchrow describes,

> Income, however, is only one aspect of poverty, even if it is the deciding factor. Alongside income (as we learn from poverty research), one has to take into account a number of other factors. These include work, education, housing, health, and social relations, and also personal considerations such as emotional satisfaction, or loneliness, depression, and anxiety. At issue is the uncertainty of being able to meet one's basic human needs. (ibid., p. 13)

Furthermore, our concern is not merely for the poor. The social and ideological world that we have identified is producing a general climate characterized by our colleagues in Latin America as *"sálvese quien pueda"* or "save yourself if you can" without regard for anyone else. It is the old lifeboat analogy: "Every man/woman for himself/herself." This predominance of selfishness is fundamentally a spiritual predicament.

The decade of the 1990s is characterized by various kinds of alienation, basic self-centeredness, and a growing array of religious/spiritual symbols. These phenomena may well be explained by the great uncertainty that has overtaken our society. The lack of job security, which now reaches from the least-skilled employees to corporate vice presidents, inevitably engenders great anxiety. Many of us are but a paycheck or two away from bankruptcy and homelessness. The resultant scramble to gain some security in such an insecure economic world fosters unhealthy competition with and alienation from others in the workplace. The need to hoard all possible resources for oneself and one's family makes solidarity with others in need more and more difficult. These factors militate against our basic humanity and contribute to the hunger for spiritual resources to fill the emptiness and transcend the insecurity.

Certainly we can welcome the popular demand for transcendent answers to our human predicaments, but we must examine these answers to see whether in fact they not only fill empty hearts but respond effectively to the major predicaments of our socioeconomic and political–ideological realities. Do they genuinely resolve our economic anxiety? Do they enable us to relate as human beings with our neighbors? Do they show us how to work for a more just world, to look out for those who are more vulnerable, to share ourselves and our material resources with others?

Biblical Faith ◆ ◆ ◆ ◆ ◆

We intend now to explore the biblical message in response to the issues just raised and to focus on the Jubilee as the primary key for this exploration. We begin with the assertion that the Exodus is the foundational paradigm for the history of salvation in the Old Testament and that the ministry and message of Jesus provide the foundational paradigm for the history of salvation in the New Testament. Any attempt to get to the heart of the biblical message must deal with these two essential paradigms, which in turn must form one integrated history of salvation.

The Exodus and the Logic of Liberation

Walter Brueggemann has a special way of capturing the essence of major biblical themes and movements. His little book, *Hope within History*, summarizes the essence of the Exodus experience for the people of Israel. He puts forward three important dimensions of the Exodus experience as foundational for the formation and renewal of Israel's faith throughout its history:

◆ Critique of the dominant ideology
◆ Public processing of pain
◆ Release of new social imagination

The story of Moses and the liberation of the Hebrew slaves from Egypt, narrated in Exodus 1–15, was and continues to be a powerful model for resistance and for hope not only for the original actors in the story but their descendents throughout the Old Testament and later for Christians and other concerned people down to our own time. This is subversive literature, however we may evaluate its historical accuracy.

As Brueggemann points out, the Exodus experience begins as *a critique of the dominant ideology*. As slaves under the thumb of one of the world's great empires, the Hebrews would normally assume that the power of Pharaoh was absolute and the possibility for freedom nonexistent. But these Hebrew slaves—and after them the Israelites under successive oppressive kings and empires—developed their own identity, which did not belong to Pharaoh's world and was not subject to the dominant ideology.

1. The Israelite knows that he or she lives in a contrived world. Egyptian arrangements are not thought to be either absolute or worthy of trust and respect.
2. The contrivance is not a matter of accident or indifference. It is quite intentionally designed to serve the special interests of some at the expense of others.
3. Because this technological–ideological world is a contrivance and not a given, it may be undone and dismantled—deconstructed. The world may then be arranged in an alternative way if one has the courage and wits to do so.
4. The agent of such dismantling, deconstruction, and delegitimization is known by name—Yahweh. (ibid., p. 12)

Throughout their history the people of Israel maintained this subversive memory through liturgy, the great festivals, the Torah, the Prophets, and regular teaching in their homes and later in the synagogues.

The second foundational dimension of the Exodus story is *the public processing of pain*. The key texts are Exodus 2:23–25 and 3:7–8a:

After a long time the king of Egypt died. The Israelites groaned under their slavery, and cried out. Out of the slavery their cry for help rose up to God. God heard their groaning, and God remembered his covenant with Abraham, Isaac, and Jacob. God looked upon the Israelites, and God took notice of them.

Then the Lord said, "I have observed the misery of my people who are in Egypt; I have heard their cry on account of their taskmasters. Indeed, I know their sufferings, and I have come down to deliver them from the Egyptians."

Not only did Israel question the dominant ideology and refuse to accept their miserable reality as final, but the people gave voice to their suffering communally and publicly. This was revolutionary and empowering!

Brueggemann calls this "an irreversible act of civil disobedience."

> The outcry is an announcement for all to notice that the peasants would no longer conform to the system, silently meet production quotas, and go home at night exhausted. The outcry is an announcement that Israel would no longer bow before the imperial ideology, because the slaves had noticed that the ideology did not square with the reality of pain in their own lives which no amount of ideology could lead them to deny. (1987, p. 17)

It was precisely in the context of this outcry, this public processing of pain, that Israel came to know Yahweh—the Lord, the God of Abraham, Isaac, and Jacob—by name. At the burning bush, as he received God's mandate to go to Pharaoh and bring the Israelites out of Egypt, Moses asked by what name he was to follow these instructions. And God answered, "I AM WHO I AM. . . . This is my name forever, and this my title for all generations" (Exodus 3:14–15).

Israel's faith was formed in the crucible of slavery in Egypt, in the experience of crying out to God, in learning that God's name is Yahweh and that this God hears the cry of the people and comes down to deliver them. This public processing of pain, together with the critique of the dominant ideology, became an essential element in the faith of Israel as each generation discovered its identity. It was the foundation for survival and resistance under every subsequent experience of oppression, whether domestic or foreign. "The cry of pain begins the formation of a counter-community around an alternative perception of reality" (Brueggemann, 1987, pp. 17–18).

The third dimension of Israel's experience of the Exodus is *the release of new social imagination*. Having critiqued the dominant ideology and having cried out publicly in their pain, Israel went on to dream of a new possibility, a Promised Land where all would prosper under the blessing of Yahweh.

> *I have come down to deliver them from the Egyptians, and to bring them up out of that land to a good and broad land, a land flowing with milk and honey.*   Exodus 3:8

Brueggemann underlines three aspects of this new social imagination. The first is *liturgical* and appears especially in the Song of Moses and the Song of Miriam in Exodus 15. The liberated slaves danced, sang, and celebrated their freedom and Yahweh's victory over Pharaoh. If their God was more powerful than Pharaoh, they could hope for a future social existence that would defend and articulate that freedom. The second aspect of this social imagination is *political*. At Sinai the Hebrews committed themselves to Yahweh as their king, to the construction of a new social reality utterly different from the slavery they had experienced in Egypt and instead consistent with God's liberating act. The third aspect of this social imagination is *legislative*. Israel undertook the weighty task of elaborating in the Torah a way to live as people of Yahweh in contrast to the peoples around them (Brueggemann, 1987, pp. 21–23).

It was precisely in the context of the experience of the Exodus that the logic or the spirituality of liberation emerged—at Sinai and at every subsequent stage of Israel's history. The Exodus was not simply an experience of liberation and the ongoing memory of that liberation. Israel was to incarnate that critique of dominant ideologies, that public processing of pain, and that release of new social imagination in its ongoing life as the people of Yahweh. Liberation from slavery, from Egypt, must lead to responsible living in social relationships that are liberating and just. Yahweh would reign not only in Israel's liturgies but also in Israel's daily life; not only in the Tabernacle but also in their homes, fields, communities, tribes, and nation. This spirituality of liberation is what gave birth to the vision of Jubilee.

The Jubilee Vision—The Seventh Day, the Seventh Year, the Fiftieth Year

Strangely, Christians have given little attention to the Sabbath cycles that are articulated so prominently in the Old Testament and carried forward strategically in the New Testament. We shall consider here in summary fashion key passages from the Old Testament, particularly the main traditions of the Pentateuch, and then explore the mission and message of Jesus. We shall find in the Sabbath and Jubilee cycles important clues to the ongoing vocation of Israel as people of God, people who had been liberated from slavery in order to create an alternative economic-social-spiritual order.

Sabbath Day. Exodus 16 narrates one of the first experiences of Israel in the wilderness after its deliverance from Egypt. It has special importance as the first testing, the first lesson, for their new life as a liberated people. It gives us an important clue as to the meaning and purpose of the Sabbath Day and also by implication of the Sabbath Year and the Jubilee.

According to the narrative, the Israelites had been in the wilderness only a short time when they began to complain for lack of food. The Lord responded by sending bread from heaven each morning and quails each evening with the explicit commandment that they were to gather each day only the portion necessary for the members of each household and to leave nothing over. Mysteriously, "those who gathered much had nothing over, and those who gathered little had no shortage" (v. 18). All had as much as they needed. When some tried to hoard or hold over an extra amount, it went bad, and they incurred the wrath of Moses. On the sixth day they were to gather an amount sufficient for two days and then rest on the seventh day. Moses told them, "This is what the Lord has commanded: 'Tomorrow is a day of solemn rest, a holy Sabbath to the Lord' " (v. 23). In this case, what was put aside did not go bad, and those who went out to gather food on the seventh day found none. Moses then said, "See! The Lord has given you the Sabbath, therefore on the sixth day he gives you food for two days; each of you stay where you are; do not leave your place on the seventh day." (v. 29). So the people rested on the seventh day. Thus even before the giving of the Ten Commandments at Mount Sinai the people of Israel learned that they were to enjoy rest regularly on the seventh day. And the Lord commanded them to keep a daily measure of manna in the ark of the Covenant as a memorial of their deliverance from Egypt, of their dependence on the Lord in the wilderness, and as an example of God's intention that all should have enough.

As twentieth-century Christians, we are most familiar with the Sabbath Day as one of the Ten Commandments, but we are perhaps not so clear about the theological foundations and the ethical implications of this mandate. In Exodus 20 the Decalogue begins with the foundational memory of the Exodus, which sets forth for all time that Israel's faith is not legalistic. The Law itself is based on God's grace, God's liberating intervention in history on behalf of an insignificant, enslaved people.

> *I am the Lord your God, who brought you out of the land of Egypt, out of the house of slavery.* Exodus 20: 2

In this version of the Ten Commandments, the Fourth Commandment reads as follows.

> *Remember the Sabbath Day, and keep it holy. Six days you shall labor and do all your work. But the seventh day is a Sabbath to the Lord your God; you shall not do any work—you, your son or your daughter, your male or female slave, your livestock, or the alien resident in your towns. For in six days the Lord made heaven and earth, the sea, and all that is in them, but rested the seventh day; therefore the Lord blessed the Sabbath Day and consecrated it.*
> Exodus 20:8–11

In our Western church history this commandment took on a primarily religious significance. The assumption was that no work should be done on the Sabbath Day so that people could go to church, meditate on God, and engage in religious or spiritually uplifting exercises. On rereading the text, it becomes evident that this commandment is really concerned primarily about rest and the de-absolutization of work—that is, with breaking the cycle of work on a regular, weekly basis so that all, people and animals, including slaves and aliens, might rest. This is therefore a concern for the health and well-being of the entire household, which might otherwise be exploited to the point of exhaustion. The theological foundation of this commandment is here stated as the creation, for even God rested the seventh day and therefore blessed the Sabbath Day and consecrated it (Genesis 2:3). The concern for laboring people and animals is thus given divine sanction.

In Exodus 23:12, we find another version of the Sabbath Day mandate together with the Sabbath Year mandate, which we will consider later.

> *Six days you shall do your work, but on the seventh day you shall rest, so that your ox and your donkey may have relief, and your homeborn slave and the resident alien may be refreshed.*

This text explicitly expresses the concern for the health of beasts of burden, slaves, and aliens—those most likely to be worn out through exploitation. No religious function is expressed or implied.

The Deuteronomic tradition offers another version of the Ten Commandments in Deuteronomy 5. As in Exodus 20 it begins with the foundational memory of the Exodus.

> *I am the Lord your God, who brought you out of the land of Egypt, out of the house of slavery.*   Deuteronomy 5:6

This affirmation is set in the context of the giving of the Law at Mount Horeb/Mount Sinai, and the entire Book of Deuteronomy is set in the context of Moses' final instructions to his people before his death and before their entrance into the Promised Land. The Ten Commandments are the cornerstone for the fulfillment of the process of liberation from Egypt and the establishment of God's people as an alternative social reality.

The Third Commandment here reads as follows.

> *Observe the Sabbath Day and keep it holy, as the Lord your God commanded you. Six days you shall labor and do all your work. But the seventh day is a Sabbath to the Lord your God; you shall not do any work—you, or your son or your daughter, or your male or female slave, or your ox or your donkey, or any of your livestock, or the resident alien in your towns, so that your male and female slave may rest as well as you. Remember that you were a slave in the land of Egypt, and the Lord your God brought you out from there with a mighty hand and an outstretched arm; therefore the Lord your God commanded you to keep the Sabbath Day.*
> Deuteronomy 5:12–15

Here again the intention is clearly rest and recuperation for laboring persons and animals. Neither slaves nor aliens nor animals would be interested in Israel's religious practices. And here the reference to slaves is repeated, so as to underline concern for them. Most important of all, the theological foundation here is not the fact that God rested on the seventh day of creation, but rather the explicit reference to Israel's original status as slaves and their liberation from Egypt. "Therefore the Lord your God commanded you to keep the Sabbath Day." The Sabbath Day commandment is holy precisely because it is a logical and necessary fulfillment of God's liberating act on behalf of God's people. It poses for Israel these alternatives: Sabbath or slavery.

Sabbath Year. We turn now to the Sabbath Year. The first reference is found in Exodus 23, which is a series of instructions concerning justice for all the people—false witness, your enemy's animals, false charges and bribes in lawsuits, oppression of aliens. The rationale is:

> *You know the heart of an alien, for you were aliens in the land of Egypt.* Exodus 23:9

The Sabbath Year mandate then follows:

> *For six years you shall sow your land and gather in its yield; but the seventh year you shall let it rest and lie fallow, so that the poor of your people may eat; and what they leave the wild animals may eat. You shall do the same with your vineyard, and with your olive orchard.* Exodus 23:10–11

Here again, as in the Sabbath Day mandate, the concern is to provide rest for laborers and animals, but now is added rest for the land, the need for it to lie fallow for one year in seven. And this mandate includes explicit concern for the poor and even the wild animals, who evidently would be allowed to gather produce from the unattended fields and vineyards during the Sabbath Year.

Our next reference to the Sabbath Year is found in Deuteronomy 15:1–18, at the heart of the Deuteronomic Code. We find here two new and extensive mandates for the ordering of the alternative socioeconomic order in the Promised Land. As we go through this passage, we will want to note not only the specific mandates but also their intention and their theological–spiritual foundations. (Underlining with different colors may be helpful in this regard.)

> *Every seventh year you shall grant a remission of debts. And this is the manner of the remission: every creditor shall remit the claim that is held against a neighbor, not exacting it of a neighbor who is a member of the community, because the Lord's remission has been proclaimed. Of a foreigner you may exact it, but you must remit your claim on whatever any member of your community owes you. There will, however, be no one in need among you, because the Lord is sure to bless you in the land that the Lord your God is giving you as a possession to occupy, if only you will obey the Lord your God by diligently observing this entire commandment that I command you today. When the Lord your God has blessed you, as he promised you, you will lend to many nations, but you will not borrow; you will rule over many nations, but they will not rule over you.*

> *If there is among you anyone in need, a member of your community in any of your towns within the land that the Lord your God is giving you, do not be hard-hearted or tight-fisted toward your needy neighbor. You should rather open your hand, willingly lending enough to meet the need, whatever it may be. Be careful that you do not entertain a mean thought, thinking, "The seventh year, the year of remission, is near," and therefore view your needy neighbor with hostility and give nothing; your neighbor might cry to the Lord against you, and you would incur guilt. Give liberally and be ungrudging when you do so, for on this account the Lord your God will bless you in all your work and in all that you undertake. Since there will never cease to be some in need on the earth, I therefore command you, "Open your hand to the poor and needy neighbor in your land."*
>
> *If a member of your community, whether a Hebrew man or a Hebrew woman, is sold to you and works for you six years, in the seventh year you shall set that person free. And when you send a male slave out from you a free person, you shall not send him out empty-handed. Provide liberally out of your flock, your threshing floor, and your wine press, thus giving to him some of the bounty with which the Lord your God has blessed you. Remember that you were a slave in the land of Egypt, and the Lord your God redeemed you; for this reason I lay this command upon you today. But if he says to you, "I will not go out from you," because he loves you and your household, since he is well off with you, then you shall take an awl and thrust it through his earlobe into the door, and he shall be your slave forever.*
>
> *You shall do the same with regard to your female slave.*
>
> *Do not consider it a hardship when you send them out from you free persons, because for six years they have given you services worth the wages of hired laborers; and the Lord your God will bless you in all that you do.*

This remarkable passage provides several important clues to God's intention for God's people. We have noted that Deuteronomy presents itself as Moses' last exhortation to his people as they prepare to enter the Promised Land. It refers to the giving of the Law at Sinai. In later chapters we will see that the Book of Deuteronomy was probably formulated in several stages, beginning with the fall of Samaria in 722 B.C. and the reform of King Josiah in 622 B.C., and ending in the exile following the fall of Jerusalem in 587 B.C. In any case it contains very specific ethical mandates within the Deuteronomic vision for God's people at critical moments in their history. As such it merits careful attention for God's people today, as we too face critical realities for our own well-being.

Deuteronomy 15:1–18 is concerned with two dimensions of a central problem of ancient peasant societies: debts and slavery. Originally and ideally, every family of Israel, with the exception of the Levites, had its own parcel of land as the basis of its economic well-being and social security. Sooner or later, however, families faced natural disasters, violent intervention by local, national, or international exploitation, or even faulty administration. If they lost their crops, they needed access to loans in order to have enough to eat and also to plant seed the following spring. If adversity continued or if loans were provided at high interest, the borrowers might not be able to pay them back, and they might lose their land, which was the only security for their loans. If they lost their land, they might become day laborers or share croppers, or they could fall into slavery. This would lead to increasing poverty, breakup of the family, loss of dignity, and, very likely, malnutrition, illness, and even death. So the Deuteronomic Code required that every seventh year debts should be canceled and slaves freed, halting the "normal" process of socioeconomic marginalization and impoverishment. The express intention is that "there will be no one in need among you" (v. 4). In fact this mandate is incorporated into the Law precisely because "there will never cease to be some in need on the earth" (v. 11). The commandment of Yahweh is, "Open your hand to the poor and needy neighbor in your land" (v. 11).

These economic requirements are divine mandates. The forgiving of debts every seventh year is called "the Lord's remission." If it is followed, "The Lord is sure to bless you in the land"; in fact the land itself is "the land that the Lord your God is giving you as a possession to occupy" (v. 4). The Lord not only provides the land but also its bountiful fruit. Therefore those Hebrews who fall into slavery are to be freed in the seventh year, and they are not to be sent away empty-handed. They are to be given liberally out of the flocks, the grains, and the wine that they labored to produce. Above all, "Remember that you were a slave in the land of Egypt, and the Lord your God redeemed you; for this reason I lay this command upon you today" (v. 15). This subversive memory is reinforced by the warning "your neighbor might cry to the Lord against you, and you would incur guilt," just as the slaves in Egypt had cried out and were liberated (v. 9).

Critical questions remain regarding the practice of slavery and the application of these Sabbath mandates to non-Hebrews. What we have found, however, is a radical confrontation with the principal mechanisms of marginalization and alienation. Further, these remarkable mandates are founded upon the spirituality of liberation emerging out of the Exodus experience. God freed the Hebrew slaves in order to create an alternative social order in which all God's people might continue to enjoy fullness of life, even in the face of natural disasters and human injustice.

Finally we turn to references to the Sabbath Year that are intertwined with the central Jubilee text in Leviticus 25. The portions that refer to the seventh year are verses 1–7 and 18–22. The emphasis is on rest for the land and for those who work the land. The first portion also indicates that, during the Sabbath Year, all may eat what the land yields—"you, your male and female slaves, your hired and your bound laborers who live with you; for your livestock also, and for the wild animals in your land all its yield shall be for food" (v. 6–8). The second portion is also concerned with what they will eat during the seventh year and during the eighth year and until next harvest. The promise is that by keeping these ordinances they "may live on the land securely" (v. 18).

Jubilee Year. The primary passages dealing with the Jubilee Year are Leviticus 25:8–17 and 23–55. As we shall be examining these passages more closely in another chapter, we will include here only certain portions and mention briefly the main mandates and their theological foundations and ethical implications. The Jubilee is like a super-Sabbath Year, coming after seven Sabbath Years or seven weeks of years. It is to be proclaimed with the sound of a trumpet (*yobel*—probable origin of the word Jubilee) on the Day of Atonement, the holiest day of the year, when expiation is made for the sins of the high priest, the priesthood, and the people, when all that might separate them from Yahweh is removed. The Jubilee is proclaimed as "liberty throughout the land to all its inhabitants" (v. 10). This passage is based on the socioeconomic–spiritual vision of the tribes of Yahweh before the formation of the monarchy, is set in the context of the giving of the Law at Mount Sinai, and reaches its final form at the time of the return from exile, when critical questions about the distribution of the land and the shape of Israel's life as people of God had to be discussed.

The first mandate for the Jubilee Year is that during the fiftieth year every family of Israel, except the Levites, will have the right to recover and return to their land.

> *And you shall hallow the fiftieth year and you shall proclaim liberty throughout the land to all its inhabitants. It shall be a Jubilee for you: you shall return, every one of you, to your property and every one of you to your family. That fiftieth year shall be a Jubilee for you: you shall not sow, or reap the aftergrowth, or harvest the unpruned vines. For it is a Jubilee; it shall be holy to you: you shall eat only what the field itself produces.*
>
> *In this Year of Jubilee you shall return, every one of you, to your property.*   Leviticus 25:10–13

It goes on then to indicate that the land should be valued not for its intrinsic or speculative value but simply in terms of the number of crops it will yield before the next Jubilee, when it will be returned to its original owner.

The theological foundation for this mandate is found in verse 23:

> *The land shall not be sold in perpetuity, for the land is mine; with me you are but aliens and tenants.*

For any peasant culture, as we have noted, dependence on the land is fundamental for food, survival, security, and present and future well-being. When disaster strikes, debts are incurred leading to loss of the land, liberty, and even life itself. In Deuteronomy 15 we found important solutions in the remission of debts and freedom for slaves every Sabbath Year. Here we find the ultimate solution to the problem of exploitation, poverty, and marginalization, every fifty years, through the redistribution of the land to all the families of Israel. It is a proposal for periodic, perpetual land reform such as the world has never seen. It was meant to provide hope to all the people, even to those in the worst circumstances, that their lives would be reestablished in the Year of Jubilee with all that the land could provide with the blessing of Yahweh. It was not simply a socioeconomic plan; it was a divine mandate, a holy obligation in keeping with God's rule. "You shall fear your God; for I am the Lord your God" (v. 17).

The rest of Leviticus 25 includes instructions concerning the redemption of lands and houses by those forced to sell or by relatives and concerning the treatment of Hebrew slaves and their families and their liberation at the Jubilee. By assumption, the Jubilee mandates include the remission of debts so that slaves might be freed and all families might return to their lands and houses. Within these portions we find that the fundamental foundation for the Jubilee Year, as for the Sabbath Year and the Sabbath Day, is the experience of the Exodus, which we have called the logic or spirituality of liberation. God's people are to treat each other, even those who fall into slavery, in ways radically different from the way people of other nations treat one another, because

> *I am the Lord your God, who brought you out of the land of Egypt, to give you the land of Canaan, to be your God.* Leviticus 25:38

> *For they are my servants, whom I brought out of the land of Egypt.* Leviticus 25:42

We will not at this point consider the other scattered references and allusions to the Jubilee Year in the Old Testament but rather turn to the key passage that links this tradition most directly with Jesus' proclamation of Jubilee as his own mission: Isaiah 61:1–2a. This is the text that Jesus read for his "inaugural sermon," according to Luke's Gospel (4:18–19), which is somewhat different.

> *The spirit of the Lord God is upon me,*
> *   because the Lord has anointed me;*
> *he has sent me to bring good news to the oppressed,*
> *   to bind up the brokenhearted,*
> *to proclaim liberty to the captives,*
> *   and release to the prisoners;*
> *to proclaim the year of the Lord's favor.*

The specific reference to the Jubilee is of course the final phrase, "the year of the Lord's favor." The previous phrases do not repeat explicitly the four cardinal elements we have identified in the Sabbath and Jubilee texts—cancellation of debts, freeing of slaves, return to family lands, and rest for the land and for workers. They do however point directly to the essence of the Jubilee mandates in that they promise to overcome oppression and suffering. This passage has been called, in fact, a radicalization of the Jubilee in that it goes beyond the specific mandates of the earlier texts and proclaims a general, comprehensive response to oppression and poverty as God's intention. This text thus serves as a summary of the various Isaiah traditions, which speak concretely to the various oppressions, sufferings, and illnesses of God's people with promises of liberation, hope, and healing.

The year of the Lord's favor thus focuses on liberation as God's primary intention for God's people. Liberation here is a fundamentally spiritual matter, for it comes from "the Spirit of the Lord God." But it cannot be "spiritualized" into a pietistic or religious matter. As with the Jubilee and Sabbath texts that we have considered previously, it is concerned with socioeconomic oppression, which in ancient times was primarily manifest in the distribution of the land, debt servicing, and labor relations. Throughout its history Israel was tempted to follow the "natural" tendencies of neighboring peoples to allow some to become rich and many to become poor through the practice of usury, the accumulation of land, and slavery. The Sabbath Day, the Sabbath Year, and the Jubilee provided divine mandates to resist and reverse these tendencies so that all God's people might enjoy fullness of life.

Jesus and the Jubilee

Essential to any overview of the biblical Jubilee is a consideration, however cursory, of its relation to Jesus' message and ministry and crucifixion. By the same token we believe that a consideration of the Jubilee is essential for any understanding of Jesus' message and ministry and crucifixion. We shall be making a more careful study of these areas in Chapters 5 and 6. At this time we will deal primarily with the passages in the synoptic Gospels that deal with the beginning of Jesus' ministry.

Luke's Gospel has a rather long introduction, ending with Jesus' baptism by John and temptation in the wilderness. It then gives a brief, general statement about Jesus' return to Galilee and the beginning of his teaching in the synagogues (Luke 4:14–15). Then follows the first event of Jesus' ministry—his appearance at the synagogue in Nazareth, his home town. He reads the Jubilee text from Isaiah 61:1–2a, and he declares, "Today this scripture has been fulfilled in your hearing" At first his hearers were "amazed at the gracious words that came from his mouth," but later, on hearing his further explanations, they "were filled with rage" and tried to throw him off a cliff. Luke goes on to narrate Jesus' casting out a demon and healing at Simon's house, and he concludes this first section of Jesus' ministry with these words of Jesus: "I must proclaim the good news of the kingdom of God to the other cities also, for I was sent for this purpose" (Luke 4:16–43).

It thus becomes clear that in Luke, as in Mark and Matthew, the central theme of Jesus' message and ministry is the good news of the reign of God. It is also clear that for Luke the essential content of this message about the reign of God is contained in the biblical Jubilee as summarized by Isaiah. The use of Isaiah 61:1–2a at the outset of Luke's narrative of Jesus' ministry thus becomes a central clue to the entire Gospel of Luke.

Mark is the shortest and considered to be the oldest Gospel, for it provides the basic outline used by Matthew and Luke. It has a very short introduction, summarizing Jesus' baptism and temptation in the wilderness, then begins the story of Jesus' ministry with a brief paragraph about his return to Galilee and his message: "The time is fulfilled, and the kingdom of God has come near; repent, and believe in the good news" (Mark 1:14–15). Mark then goes on to narrate Jesus' calling of the first disciples, the cleansing of the man with an unclean spirit, and the healing of Simon's mother and others. It then concludes this first section with words similar to Luke's: "Let us go on to the neighboring towns, so that I may proclaim the message there also; for that is what I came out to do" (Mark 1:38). Mark's Gospel contains many references to the Sabbath Day, many expressions of Jesus' concern for the poor and marginalized, and many confrontations with those in authority. The very first phrase in this opening section introduces Jesus' ministry with a reference to the arrest of John the Baptist, which suggests that Jesus' own ministry will be surrounded by conflict and lead to his death. Such an ending would of course be more than likely for anyone who would proclaim the cancellation of debts, freeing of slaves, and redistribution of the land.

Matthew's Gospel, like Luke's, has a long introduction ending with Jesus' baptism and temptation. Like Mark, it begins the story of Jesus' ministry with a general paragraph telling of John's arrest and indicating that Jesus came to Galilee proclaiming this message: "Repent, for the kingdom of heaven has come near" (Matthew 4:12–17). This is followed by the calling of the first disciples and another paragraph summarizing Jesus' ministry as "teaching in their synagogues and proclaiming the good news of the kingdom and curing every disease and every sickness among the people . . . various diseases and pains, demoniacs, epileptics, and paralytics" (Matthew 4:18–24).

Then comes the first of several major teaching discourses, the Sermon on the Mount. This discourse begins with the Beatitudes, which are good news for the poor in spirit, those who mourn, the meek, those who hunger and thirst for righteousness, the merciful, the pure in heart, the peacemakers, and those who are persecuted for righteousness' (justice's) sake (Matthew 5:3–10). Here, as in Mark, there is no direct reference to the Jubilee, but the content is similar. The coming of God's reign brings good news to the poor and liberation for the oppressed.

For centuries the tendency has been to "spiritualize" these passages; but the evident meaning, as we have seen in our study of the Jubilee, is holistic, socioeconomic as well as religious. At the very least we are challenged to consider more carefully the meaning of the teachings and actions of Jesus in light of the Jubilee.

Responsible Discipleship ◆ ◆ ◆ ◆ ◆

No one should presume to offer a panacea for the woes of today's world, but it is our belief that we all must strive to find ways to live and act conscientiously. The dominant socioeconomic order, which is becoming global at an alarming rate and in apparently irresistible ways, may overwhelm and immobilize us. On the other hand, we remember that the biblical history of salvation begins with supposedly powerless slaves, aliens living at the heart of one of the world's greatest empires. Surely the God who liberated them can guide us too into responsible action for personal, ecclesial, and social transformation. At least we can learn how others are making spaces and creating times for resistance and liberation.

Personal Transformation

Jubilee spirituality may draw upon and incorporate experiences and perspectives from diverse sources. It may include traditional spiritual exercises, but it will relate them organically with the real world and the grave socioeconomic and ecological problems of life for our own and future generations. Evely Laser Schlensky, who chairs the Commission on Social Action of Reform Judaism, puts it this way: "Torah study to me is even more engaging than prayer. It offers ways of thinking about how we are to rework the world." In an interview for *The Witness* (October 1977, pp. 8–10) she explains,

> Spirituality is not a word I'm particularly drawn to. I know that it's very much in vogue now. But there is a traditional Jewish notion of how we're supposed to be in the world which is much more meaningful to me—that is the concept of holiness. There's a deeper word for it, *kedusha*. Probably the best way to understand what is meant by holiness is to refer to Leviticus 19, which is called the Holiness Code. It starts out, "You shall be holy, for I the Lord your God am holy." It goes on to detail many specific behaviors. While some are ritual behaviors like keeping the Sabbath and not making idols, others are—in fact most are—in the realm of an ethical mandate, instructing how you're supposed to treat the poor and the stranger. (ibid.)

How are we to practice Sabbath in order to "remake the world"? We can begin by recovering times and spaces in our personal and family lives. We found such a philosophy expressed in the introduction to a cookbook, *The New Laurel's Kitchen* (Robertson et al., 1986). The authors write about "the potential value of the Inhabited Kitchen" in which "cooking can be a high-status occupation. So can raising your own food. So is the teaching of our children," not only through schools but also through the examples we set.

> Nurturant work is not only for mothers, not only for parents even; it is the birthright of every man, woman, and child. Without it, we never grow to our full stature. This is an easy truth to discover when you start living it out. The only reason it is obscured from view in today's world is that supporting life is not a value on which our culture is based. . . . Instead of fighting for a bigger share of the cake, women are concurring, let us see whether we can't bake a better cake. *All* of us, men and women alike. Let's make a world that has a place for every one of us, and that must surely start within our homes. (Robertson et al., 1986, p. 36)

The Sabbath Day, the Sabbath Year, and the Jubilee are certainly concerned about resisting the endemic processes of economic polarization. But they are also concerned fundamentally about human spirituality and lifestyle as they are impacted by the economy. Bob Goudzwaard and Harry de Lange, in their book, *Beyond Poverty and Affluence: Toward an Economy of Care*, point out that

> the appeal to alter our lifestyle does not consist of urging us to make painful sacrifices for the sake of others. On the contrary, our appeal is fundamentally different in principle. It involves the realization that because of our collective drive for more and more, we directly damage our own well-being. We require another vision of life, a vision in which the word enough plays a positive role. The implementation of such a vision will create new possibilities for neighborliness, for demonstrating care for our surroundings, and for having more time available in our harried lives. Such a vision will help to liberate not only the poor but also the rich. (Goudzwaard, 1995, p. 159)

Ecclesial Transformation

In her book, *Proclaim Jubilee! A Spirituality for the Twenty-First Century*, Maria Harris points out that Jubilee means not only rest and reverence for the land but also rest and reverence for that other land, "the land of ourselves, the tiny country each of us comprises, whose geography we know so well. We are to let that land, the land of our bodies, our blood, our breath, and our bones, lie fallow too" (1996, p. 25). In ways that we must discover for ourselves and our families, we can learn to practice Sabbath, to break the frenetic pace of our daily, weekly, monthly, yearly lives, in order to renew our health holistically.

This is not so much a matter of being religious on Sunday. In fact the demands of church activities may make that day as frenetic as any other day. Rather the Sabbath concern is to recall who we are and to recover our humanity, so that we may continue to live in the world without succumbing to the reigning ideology and mechanisms of production and consumption, so that we may live less in competition and more in community with those around us. The Sabbath–Jubilee mandate for rest might lead us to consider the whole range of factors that are causing stressful lifestyles, various kinds of overconsumption, and patterns of overwork, which can undermine our physical and emotional health, our families, and our social life. It might enable us to consider the other Sabbath–Jubilee mandates concerning debts and slavery and the distribution of economic resources for the life of all. And it might help us to understand why so many are so poor and not blame them for being poor. Our churches and synagogues can become Jubilee communities, small laboratories in which we can practice alternative economic possibilities, try new forms of solidarity, and experience Jubilee spirituality together.

Walter Brueggemann's marvelous book, *Israel's Praise*, develops the concept of liturgy as remembering, enacting, and hoping for liberation. Its intention is not to escape or withdraw from the world; it is a process of "world-making." So it should be in the celebration of the Sabbath Day, the Sabbath Year, and the Jubilee. These or equivalent cycles in our church life today are opportunities to celebrate what God has done, beginning with the liberation of the Hebrew slaves from Egypt and continuing through the Bible and the entire history of salvation. Our liturgies are opportunities to dramatize and experience—through music and prayer, preaching and communion, Scripture and testimony—our present, ongoing liberation from all oppression and alienation and dehumanization. Worship is of course expectation and empowerment for living witness and service that will bring liberation to those around us and to ourselves.

Earlier we cited Brueggemann's book, *Hope within History*, in which he probes the meaning of the Exodus in terms that can vitalize our understanding and experience of church today. We may even consider the need to recreate church in each place and generation and culture in these same terms. How do we collectively—as church—call into question the dominant ideology of our nation and world, which is polarizing humankind to such a degree that one billion people enjoy barely 1.4% of the income while another billion enjoy 84.6%? How do we gather and process publicly the enormous pain of our own people and the peoples of the world, so that their cry, as it becomes our cry, will rise up to God and empower us all to work for change? How are we to awaken a new social imagination that will mobilize not only our families but also our neighbors, not only our churches but also our communities, to join movements for liberation and full humanity of all people?

Social Transformation

In the process of this study, we will want to look at some of the current pro-
posals for the celebration of Jubilee now and in the coming years. Many
church groups, indigenous movements, and others began to organize and
make pronouncements around the 500th anniversary of the European conquest of the Americas in 1992. That anniversary should have been a great
opportunity to carry out a super-Jubilee by recognizing the terrible injustices
and atrocities committed against native peoples, African Americans, and
women; by canceling the enormous debts that continue to oppress the Latin
American and Caribbean nations; by rectifying the trade relations that continue slave-like conditions to satisfy the demand for cheap commodities; by
redistributing the agricultural lands to those who work them, especially the
indigenous peoples whose lives and culture depend on the land; and by re-
versing some of the ecological devastation now threatening the Western
Hemisphere. During 1992, little was achieved in terms of these biblical
mandates, but various social sectors of Latin America were mobilized as
never before—especially indigenous peoples, women, and African Latin
Americans—and their awakening cannot be reversed.

At the Seoul, Korea, Convocation of the World Council of Churches
on "Justice, Peace, and the Integrity of Creation" in 1990, some of the participants, largely people of color, began to organize a process that was later
called "1992/Kairos USA." Recognizing the contributions of earlier *Kairos*
documents coming out of South Africa, Central America, and an interre-
gional group, these participants developed a network of some 125 groups to
oppose the official celebration of the 500 years of imperialism and oppression. Their document was completed and published in 1994. Its title is *On
the Way: From Kairos to Jubilee.* The introduction to that document, which
we will consider later, ends with these words.

> We who participated in Kairos USA are Christian people and part of
> the church in the United States. We believe the church is being chal-
> lenged by God to interpret the signs of this time and place. As descen-
> dants of those who embody the pain and privilege of our collective
> history over the past 500 years, we now see signs of extreme crisis and
> rare opportunity. We feel compelled to join the path of those who have
> resisted over the centuries. From our diverse places and life situations
> we have written this document in an attempt to speak together to a
> common crisis. We invite you to join your voice with ours in defining
> and living out a response to this time of kairos. (p. 2)

Our intention in this opening chapter has been, as we stated at the
outset, to give an overview of the Jubilee challenge in response to our current local, national, and global human predicament, which is characterized
increasingly by the concentration of wealth by a few and the spiraling impoverishment and marginalization of the many. Each of us will have to

make his or her own analysis of this tragic context and examine the biblical message for guidance in his or her own faith and vocation. As responsible followers of Jesus Christ, we are compelled to get involved in today's struggle for life where we find ourselves and around the world. The biblical Jubilee, along with the Sabbath Day and the Sabbath Year, offers critical insight into this same predicament down through human history, and it gives us divine mandates for action. Let us pray that God's Spirit will lead us into deeper understanding and more faithful living as we continue to confront and explore this challenge so that all God's people might have fullness of life.

2 ◆ ◆ ◆ ◆ ◆ ◆ ◆

The Promised Land—
An Alternative Social
Possibility

Chapters 2, 3, and 4 will examine more closely what the Hebrew Scriptures propose for human well-being under God's reign. In Chapter 1 we made a quick overview of the Exodus logic of liberation and of the principal Sabbath–Jubilee texts of the Old and New Testaments. Chapter 2 will provide more background on the meaning of the land for the people of Israel, then focus on the formative experience of the tribes of Yahweh prior to the monarchy, and reinforce our understanding of the Sabbath–Jubilee mandate to give rest to the land and to all who work the land. We will set these biblical concerns within the context of our modern world's suicidal abuse of nature and human labor in the name of capital accumulation. Rather than focus on these negative realities, however, we will try to find positive contemporary alternatives that might confirm and reinforce the biblical mandate for Sabbath–Jubilee rest and renewal. These concerns can be expressed in the following questions:

◆ What current experiments and movements offer hope for the adequate care of both the human family and its natural environment for our own and future generations?
◆ What biblical mandates offer guidance as to how the human family and its natural environment might be sustained for present and future generations?
◆ What recommendations can we make for ourselves, our churches, and our societies on the bases of the previous answers?

These questions and answers may serve for discussion at the conclusion of this chapter and for dialogue in our homes, faith communities, and elsewhere.

Today's World ◆ ◆ ◆ ◆ ◆

A World Council of Churches document, *Christian Faith and the World Economy Today*, sets the current ecological crisis firmly in the context of the world's economic realities:

> The cumulative threats of global warming, the destruction of the protective ozone layer, land degradation through deforestation, erosion, desertification, salinization and pollution of water, air, and land must be traced more or less directly back to industrial processes which human beings have undertaken with a view to wealth creation. (WCC, 1993, p. 23)

The document cites the WCC Assembly at Canberra as follows:

> It is shocking and frightening for us that the human species on this earth, which came on the scene somewhere around 80,000 years ago, in the 4.5 billion year long history of this earth, has been able to threaten the very foundations of life on our planet in only about 200 years of industrialization. (ibid.)

Behind these economic developments, so destructive to the environment, lie fundamentally flawed views of nature. The dominant economic forces have given themselves unlimited license to exploit the Earth's resources and abuse the environment as they wish. Until relatively recently, these forces have acted as if the Earth's resources were inexhaustible and human beings had every right to do with them as they wish. The words of Genesis 1:26, "have dominion over," have been interpreted to mean "to exploit" the fish of the sea, the birds of the air, and all the animals of the Earth. There has been little sense of responsibility for the stewardship of animal and plant life. The words of Genesis 1:28, "fill the earth and subdue it," have been used to justify the destruction of forests and jungles and the removal of all apparent obstacles to human life. The manifest destiny of human beings was, to intellectuals and popular belief alike, to rise up and flourish at the expense of nature.

Latin America holds 23% of the world's forests, including 60% of the tropical rain forests, which are irreplaceable. In Latin America deforestation has in recent years taken almost ten million acres per year and along with it hundreds of species of animals. Fifty years ago 75% of Costa Rica, a small country with more biodiversity than the entire United States, was covered with lush forests; now it is less than 20% forest-covered. Brazil loses the equivalent of Costa Rica's entire national territory to deforestation each year. All of this is due to economic factors, such as profiteering by corporations and desperation of landless peasants, which overrule all the environmental rhetoric and protective legislation that these nations are devising. The lungs of the world are being sacrificed at an astonishing rate on the altars of economic gain, legally or illegally, for the benefit of a few.

Over against this gloomy, pessimistic picture of our dominant Western economic–ecological reality, we shall consider signs of hope that come out of alternative experiences and point toward alternative possibilities. First, a Mayan friend shares his particular vision of reality. Second, we shall take another look at the Sandinista experience in the 1980s. And third, we shall consider the Earth Charter, a proposal coming out of the meeting of non-governmental organizations at Rio de Janeiro in 1992. These examples should bring to mind many other signs of hope.

A Mayan Cosmogony

We turn now to one particular expression of the cosmovision and praxis of the Native American peoples. There is great diversity in the beliefs and practices of the various American peoples whose roots pre-date Columbus by millennia, but there are remarkable, fundamental similarities as well. We shall concentrate our attention here on Daniel Matul's book, *Somos un Solo Corazón: Cultura Maya Contemporánea* (*We Are All One Heart: Contemporary Mayan Culture*).

When reading Matul's book or hearing him speak, one is struck first and foremost by his profound, almost mystical sense of respect—for those he is addressing, for those whose beliefs and practices he expounds and shares personally, for all of creation, and especially for the elders of his people in the distant past and today. His purpose is to share the Mayan vision, which is inclusive, respects the universe, and calls for its periodic renewal, after the fashion of the biblical Jubilee.

> Our cosmogonic vision, contemplating the multiple expressions of the cosmos, discovers the most intricate guidelines for the renewal of life, and also its laws of expansion and contraction, of aging and death. Therefore we consider that the universe calls for periodic reparation, renewal, and strengthening. (Matul, 1994, p. 19)

To respect and renewal he adds integrity. Human beings find maturity in relation to themselves, to others, and to God.

> We come to unify science and religion, recognizing that secular life and religious life are indivisible. Then out of this wealth emanates something so real and so profound: cosmos and creature are two sides of the same weaving; they remain united by indestructible bonds. (ibid., p. 19)

Social organization should likewise reflect the cosmic equilibrium, social plurality within the cosmic unity, social justice over against centralized power. The inner struggle over ego and passion is linked to the encounter with the universe.

"Thus *Chomb' al Juyub Tak'aj* (ecology) links, ties together, and harmonizes primary aspects of existence—the cosmic, the physical, and the spiritual—until they become one" (ibid., p. 22). Heaven and earth are joined; humanity is in itself the universe. These are the grounds for building relationships, solidarity, and understanding among different cultures, philosophies, religions, and powers. They provide the basis for unity in plurality, even unity between nature and culture. The ancient book of the Mayan people, *Pop Wuj*, provides this mystical, mythic identity for humankind. Salvation cannot be a merely personal, individual act of decision. To be human is to be concerned with the brother or sister at our side. We are together the hope for a real and profound human existence.

Of special importance to the Mayans is Mother Earth, humanity's primary tie with nature and with the universe and with God. The following sentences taken from Matul's book are not just affirmations but invitations to meditation. They resonate deeply with biblical Jubilee–Sabbath spirituality.

> Mother Earth belongs to God, and only the fruits of our work belong to us. (Matul, 1994, p. 45)

> No one owns the land. It has only been loaned to us to be used as a dwelling place in the world, and it also serves as a material symbol of continuity among the generations. (ibid., p. 48)

> Humankind must be like a grateful child and love the world as a mother or father; humankind should pay tribute to the Earth, for from her we receive all that we have in life, and she even opens her body to receive our bodies when we die. (ibid., p. 41)

> To abuse nature would be like committing suicide, making us enemies of ourselves. (ibid., p. 39)

> A tree gives life to the people, so when one cuts a tree, first one asks permission from the Heart of Heaven-Heart of Earth. (ibid., p. 43)

> The dream of every Mayan is to have a piece of land in order to plant corn, for corn gives us spiritual satisfaction, physical strength, vigor, health. Consequently material and spiritual life come essentially from CORN. (ibid., p. 49)

> Before clearing the land and wounding Mother Earth one fasts and makes offerings to the Earth. Each phase of the agricultural process is a religious ceremony, so agriculture–religion are intimately related. (ibid., p. 49)

The Sandinista Experience

The modern, industrial heritage, which is driven by the primary motive of wealth accumulation, leads not only to the destruction of nature but also to a disregard for vast sectors of human life as well. Economic value has been reduced to short-term monetary value and overridden other values such as justice, solidarity, community, and sustainability. The logic of the market takes precedence over all the rest: Without competitive prices there will be no sales; without sales there will be no profit; without profit there will be no continuing investment; without investment there will be no production; without production there will be no employment. So labor costs must be depressed as much as possible, and ecological considerations, which increase costs rather than profits, must necessarily be disregarded.

When the armed conflicts ended in Nicaragua and El Salvador and later in Guatemala, no doubt many of us thought that the economic situation and the prospects for the life of the peoples of Central America would improve. What we should have understood—what is now evident—is that the war behind these conflicts was always an economic war against the poor; that is, the struggle of the rich—land holders and business, national and transnational companies, foreign investors and banks—to maintain an economic system that favors the enrichment of a few and the perpetual impoverishment of the large majorities. Jesuit theologian Jon Sobrino explained this years ago with these words:

> When death by wars in Central America ends, the other death, the more fundamental death, the death by hunger, will continue. That this death is the result of robbery makes it a crime equal to the crime of violent homicide. It will be necessary to struggle against that crime with the same vigor and the same determination, because this is what violent death itself, the death by war, was all about from the beginning. (Not published.)

We do well to remember that the struggles of the Central American peoples were from the beginning concerned primarily with the basic economic realities that were and still are producing extreme poverty, malnutrition, and marginalization, and only secondarily with politics and ideology and military power. We must also recognize, now that the Cold War is over, what Nicaragua's Sandinista Revolution of 1979 actually achieved before it was violently undermined by the *contra* war financed and directed by Washington, D.C. During the first year, rising from the rubble of the Somoza family's desperate last stand against virtually the entire population, the new government launched a literacy campaign that achieved more in six months than the other countries of Central America, except Costa Rica, had achieved in 100 years. It was an outpouring of public fervor for the building of a new nation founded on equality, fraternity, and solidarity. Schools and universities dispersed faculty and students throughout the countryside under mostly primitive conditions. Their consciousness was transformed even as they contributed to the conscientization and training of the poor and long-forgotten members of their national family. Illiteracy dropped dramatically from 53% to 13% of the population, itself a modern social miracle, and the people learned that fundamental changes in their personal and national life were possible.

With substantial help from Russia, Eastern and Western Europe, and Cuba, similar progress was made in health care, housing, formal education, arts and crafts, and labor relations. Rural and urban communities organized to care for special needs, distribute essential foods, voice needs and complaints before higher authorities, and later to protect themselves against *contra* attacks. Great efforts were made at all levels to change the logic of wealth accumulation to a "logic of the majority," so that the economy would serve the basic needs of all the people. Lands recovered from the Somoza family and absentee landlords were distributed among poor farmers individually and in cooperatives, and this was accompanied by access to necessary small loans and technical services and basic infrastructure. Many errors were committed by the young and inexperienced leadership, but in general they served, as they had fought, with deep commitment to their cause. During the early years of the Sandinista Revolution those of us who had the privilege of witnessing the annual celebration of the July 19th triumph over Somoza could not help but be overcome, along with the enormous crowd in Carlos Fonseca Stadium overlooking Lake Managua, not only by the memory of that victory and the martyrs who had made it possible but also by the surge of pride for their own socioeconomic achievements and visionary hope for the future.

Given the power realities and strategic priorities of the United States, that revolution could not be allowed to continue. The embargo and the *contra* war and the propaganda finally achieved their goal, which was not simply to overthrow the Sandinista regime but also to destroy the dream of an alternative socioeconomic and cultural or spiritual way of life. As many said, the reigning empire could not let this colony go free, because many others would demand freedom as well. President George Bush announced publicly on the eve of the February 1990 Nicaraguan election that the *contra* war would continue if the Sandinistas won, and so an exhausted people gave their votes by a small but significant majority to Violeta Chamorro. As a result Nicaragua is now the second poorest country in Latin America, most of the social and economic reforms have been reversed, progress is again measured not in terms of human development but simply in terms of GNP, and unemployment stands at about 70%.

The Earth Charter

While the United Nations Conference on the Environment and Development was being held in Rio de Janeiro (June 1992), 20,190 people representing 9,358 nongovernmental organizations (NGOs) in 171 countries met nearby for their own Global Forum. One outcome was the launching of the Earth Charter Action Plan, a campaign to gather worldwide support by individuals, NGOs, corporations, governments, and ultimately the United Nations for the Earth Charter, which they began to draft at the Rio meeting. It happens that the coordinating office has been established in San José,

Costa Rica, so we have had the opportunity of taking groups there to learn about the process.

A draft of the Preamble of the Earth Charter, which is still evolving, contains the following affirmations:

1. We are Earth, the people, plants and animals, rains and oceans, breath of the forest and flow of the sea.
2. We honor Earth as the home of all living things.
3. We cherish Earth's beauty and diversity of life.
4. We welcome Earth's ability to renew as being the basis of all life.
5. We recognize the special place of Earth's Indigenous Peoples, their territories, their customs, and their unique relationship to Earth.
6. We are appalled at the human suffering, poverty, and damage to Earth caused by inequality of power.
7. We accept a shared responsibility to protect and restore Earth and to allow wise and equitable use of resources so as to achieve an ecological balance and new social, economic, and spiritual values.
8. In all our diversity we are one.
9. Our common home is increasingly threatened.
10. We thus commit ourselves to the following principles, noting at all times the particular needs of women, indigenous peoples, the South, the disabled, and all those who are disadvantaged. (Earth Council)

The document then continues with principles that deal with the protection and renewal of the environment and also with the eradication of poverty, military force, and economic oppression in the struggle for social justice and economic, spiritual, cultural, and ecological well-being. The final section is an action plan that urges adoption of the spirit and principles of the Earth Charter and concrete actions that include the commitment of a percentage of all operating budgets and profits for "the restoration, protection, and management of Earth's ecosystems and the promotion of equitable development."

Although it is encouraging to see so many organizations concerned enough to launch such a comprehensive and idealistic campaign, it is difficult to see how they can achieve sufficient political will to overcome the dominant economic forces and their motivation for naked profit over against ecological and human concerns. Such a vision can be effective only if enough people all over the globe organize with determination not only to demand different values and conditions in their own communities but to live under them.

Biblical Faith ◆ ◆ ◆ ◆ ◆

We turn now to the Sabbath–Jubilee traditions in order to explore God's declared will for humankind in relation to ecological well-being and social justice, both of which are profoundly spiritual concerns. As a first step, we shall consider the meaning of the land in the Hebrew Scriptures. This is, we believe, necessary for our understanding of the Sabbath and Jubilee mandates. As we found in Chapter 1, liberation from Egypt necessarily led to the awakening of a new social possibility. The people of Yahweh were delivered from slavery and given the Promised Land in order to establish a different lifestyle in keeping with their liberation. Secondly, we shall consider the formation of the tribes of Yahweh as an alternative society, founded not on bloody conquest, as portrayed in the Book of Joshua, but rather on Sabbath–Jubilee principles. We believe that these principles took shape precisely in the premonarchy period of Israel's history. Finally, we shall consider the meaning of "Sabbath rest" and "Sabbath economics" as care for the well-being of the entire household, in contrast with ancient and contemporary economics of wealth accumulation.

The Land as Gift, Temptation, Responsibility, and Threat

Once again we will make use of Walter Brueggemann's incisive Old Testament studies, this time his book, *The Land: Place as Gift, Promise, and Challenge in Biblical Faith.* Brueggemann states at the outset, "Land is a central, if not *the central theme* of Biblical faith" (1977, p. 3). In Chapter 4, he reviews the basic theological meanings of the land as expounded in Deuteronomy. After liberation from Egypt, the giving of the Law at Mount Sinai, and forty years of wilderness wanderings, Israel stands at the river Jordan, ready to enter the Promised Land. This is one of the most critical moments in the entire history of salvation. How are the people of God to understand and fulfill their vocation in this new land?

Land as Gift.   For Israel the land is, first, a gift of Yahweh. The God who delivered them from Egypt, by grace, gave them the Promised Land, also by grace.

> *For the Lord your God is bringing you into a good land, a land with flowing streams, with springs and underground waters welling up in valleys and hills, a land of wheat and barley, of vines and fig trees and pomegranates, a land of olive trees and honey, a land where you may eat bread without scarcity, where you will lack nothing, a land whose stones are iron and from whose hills you may mine copper. You shall eat your fill and bless the Lord your God for the good land that he has given you.*   Deuteronomy 8:7–10

Israel could be assured even into the future insofar as they continued to recognize and trust in the Lord as their liberator and giver of the land, insofar as they continued to hear and obey the Word of the Lord, insofar as they continued to live that alternative social possibility required by their liberation from slavery. "The gifted land is covenanted land. It is not only nourishing space. It is also covenanted place. The Jordan is entry not into safe space but into a context of covenant" (Brueggemann, 1977, p. 52).

Land as Temptation.   For Israel the land is also temptation. It can be seductive. For the land may give the people a sense of security so that they no longer remember their identity as people of Yahweh, delivered from slavery in Egypt, covenanted with the Lord who delivered them. Thus Moses warns them as they are poised to cross the Jordan and occupy their new land:

> *Therefore, observe diligently the commandment—the statutes and the ordinances—that I am commanding you today.*
>
> *If you heed these ordinances, by diligently observing them, the Lord your God will maintain with you the covenant loyalty that he swore to your ancestors; he will love you, bless you, and multiply you; he will bless the fruit of your womb and the fruit of your ground, your grain and your wine and your oil, the increase of your cattle and the issue of your flock, in the land that he swore to your ancestors to give you.*   Deuteronomy 7:11–13

On entering the Promised Land, Israel would be tempted to forget Yahweh and Yahweh's ways. They might even adopt the very practices that had enslaved them in Egypt, and they might look for other gods that would approve of these practices. "Remembering Yahweh is not simply an act of religious devotion. . . . Remembering Yahweh is for Israel the source of the qualities of humanness and humaneness which are its distinctive heritage" (Brueggemann, 1977, p. 55). The possibility remains that Israel might lose the land if they forget and abandon their covenant, their history, their foundation.

Land as Responsibility.   For Israel the land is, thirdly, responsibility. It is precisely at the entrance to the Promised Land—likewise at the time of King Josiah's reform and at the time of the return from exile—that they must review the Law given to them at Sinai, for it is in the Law that they can find the necessary guidance for their life. The keeping of the Law is not simply to please the Lord or even to ensure continuing blessing and prosperity but rather to maintain their roots and identity as liberated slaves, so that all might enjoy fullness of life. Central to this responsibility are the Sabbath Day (Deuteronomy 5:12–15) and the Sabbath Year (Deuteronomy 15:1–18), which provide for rest, forgiveness of debts, concern for the poor, and freedom of slaves. In these two texts, the theological foundation is the memory that the Hebrews were once slaves in Egypt.

Land as Threat.   Finally, for Israel the land is threat. Given the new security of possessing their own land, Israel might forget her real identity as a liberated people gifted with this land and fail to trust in Yahweh. Granted the possibility of organizing their society to gain power and wealth, they might abandon their covenant with Yahweh and its Sabbath obligations toward debtors, the poor, and slaves. This new power and wealth might even lead them to adopt other gods more in keeping with their aberrant life in the land and also in keeping with their pagan neighbors. Thus the people of Israel might lose their faith, their identity, their social experiment, and the land, which normally would mean that they would lose their very lives and existence as a people.

The Tribes of Yahweh

One of the most exciting and edifying developments in Old Testament studies in recent years has been the rereading of the "conquest" of Canaan and the formation of the tribes of Yahweh. In the past, one of the most difficult problems for scholars and believers in general was the Joshua story of violent conquest under the divine mandate to kill every man, woman, and child. Archaeological research has revealed that there was no such systematic conquest of Canaan, and the Book of Judges itself indicates that the process of settlement and conquest took place over a long period of time. Under the leadership of George Mendenhall and Norman Gottwald, a new understanding has emerged that can be summarized as "social revolution and retribalization," a complex analysis of social, economic, political, and religious elements present in thirteenth-century (B.C.) Palestine. We will make use of the excellent summary found in Anthony Ceresko's book, *Introduction to the Old Testament: A Liberation Perspective.*

At the time when the Israelites made their way from Egypt to the Promised Land, the city-states of Canaan were themselves in turmoil due to a weakening of Egypt's hegemony on the one hand and the alienation of peasant farmers and other disaffected groups on the other. Technological innovations, especially the introduction of iron for tools to clear the wooded hills and plows to work the rockier upland soil, were opening up the possibility for these disaffected groups to build larger settlements in the hill country, beyond the reach of the chariots of the dominant city-states. When the Hebrews arrived from Egypt, they were able to join with this population of peasant farmers, herdsmen, and others fleeing the oppressive city-states and settling the hill country, thus making common cause for freedom and self-determination. This social revolution in turn found among the former Hebrew slaves socioeconomic ideals and a religious faith in support of their movement.

> The Moses group, in rejecting both the physical and psychic bondage of the Egyptian socio-political and economic system, had also abandoned the religious ideology that legitimated and reinforced that system. In replacing the Egyptian gods, whose son the Pharaoh claimed to be, they chose, or claimed to have been chosen by, Yahweh, the god of the oppressed, a god who stands by the poor and frees those

enslaved. The religious cult they began to develop would also serve as a binding and legitimating force for the new people now being created in the hill country of Canaan. (Ceresko, 1992, p. 97)

This new social order was built through a process that has been called "retribalization." The predominant socioeconomic system at that time was for urban elites to control and to extract as much as possible from the surrounding agricultural areas and villages so as to leave only a minimum for their subsistence. This has been called the Asiatic mode of production. The aim of the tribes of Yahweh was to resist the Asiatic mode centered in the city-states and to create a decentralized, egalitarian, tribal mode of life so that all the clans and families might have enough. None would become wealthy and powerful and oppress and exploit the rest, and surpluses produced would not be siphoned off through tributes to urban elites. They turned back from the dominant state paradigm to a tribal paradigm.

The tribes of Yahweh found important foundations for this alternative way of life through the public worship of Yahweh and through the covenant. The covenant required that each extended family have access to the basic resources for survival, particularly through the spirituality and practice of the Sabbath Day, the Sabbath Year, and the Jubilee. The Tenth Commandment was a clear prohibition of the accumulation of property, so that they should not even desire the houses and lands of their neighbors. Periodic assemblies provided opportunities for families and clans to meet and handle disputes, name their representatives, and maintain a wide base of power. Periodic festivals provided opportunities for the people to "affirm, strengthen, and celebrate their unity and identity as Yahweh's 'chosen' people. For they were a people who, in adverse and trying circumstances, had found a way to come together and as a people seize control of their destiny, their future, their history" (ibid., p. 101).

Yahwism developed then, in the words of Ceresko, as "the religion of the social revolution." The Hebrew story of liberation from slavery in Egypt takes on new meaning in the struggle of oppressed Canaanite peoples "to free themselves from their former bondage and establish themselves in a situation in which they could maintain that freedom" (ibid., p. 103).

> The origins of Israel are most authentically read not as the inexplicable result of an arbitrary choice by a God who intervenes into the history of an ethnically and racially homogeneous people by miraculous works in a "top-down" model of divine action. Rather, our view sees how Israel emerged as the result of one of many movements within human history of groups of people at the bottom or on the margins struggling to achieve and maintain a more just, peaceful, and free human community. Israel was one of the few groups successful in its efforts, and part of that success is the record of the struggle, which is left as a heritage for future generations, a sign and beacon of hope to all those who long for liberation. In this struggle, the people were re-

sponding to the call of the Spirit of God in their midst, a Spirit who invites all human beings to free themselves from every kind of bondage. (ibid., p. 103)

Yahwism was an alternative way of life—social, economic, political, religious. It gave a transcendent dimension to the struggle of diverse, marginalized peoples to overcome the dominant mechanisms and ideologies of oppression and to create a new social order in which all would have enough.

Alicia Winters describes this egalitarian, peasant way of life in her article, "El Goel en el Antiguo Israel" (1994, pp. 19–29). Even without the burden of tributes and forced labor imposed by the city-states of Canaan, daily life in the Canaanite hill country was arduous—subject to droughts, insects, bandits, and loss of crops that could lead to hunger, disease, and premature death. The tribal peoples were able to counteract these dangers through networks of solidarity for mutual support and protection. Extended families (*bet-abot*) formed the base, living in close proximity and reaching 50 to 100 people of various generations and relations. Access to the land was the primary basis for subsistence, identity, and self-determination. These extended families were gathered into associations or clans (*mispajah*) for mutual support and protection at the level of villages or neighborhoods, insuring the survival of each family against military intrusion, providing wells and terraces and communal lands for grazing, offering loans without interest, organizing work teams, and celebrating festivals. These associations together formed tribes for mutual defense and aid at yet another level as regional alliances to protect their independence and meet internal crises, and they in turn formed the Israelite intertribal confederation or alliance.

> By means of this alliance, Israel achieved political self-government, economic development, military defense, and a cultural identity that gave prominence to their religion as the ideological base of the system and the source of its legitimacy and efficacy. Israel's egalitarian tribalism functioned as an alternative to the centralized and hierarchical state. (Winters, 1994, p. 23)

The main concerns of this alternative socioeconomic system were to resist the accumulation of debts, the concentration of land in the hands of a few, and slavery. To ensure the long-term security of the families of Israel, provision was made to rescue or restore (*goel*) their land and release family members from bond service. As we find in Leviticus 25, the key Jubilee passage, specific rights and responsibilities were established for emergency response by close relatives to impoverished members who lost their land or their freedom. Similarly we find in Numbers 35:19–21 provision for justice toward the family of victims of homicide, and in Deuteronomy 25:5–10 for marriage of widows to ensure descendants for the deceased.

> The solidarity evidenced in the action of the *goel* in these four situations was not just a sentimental response or an expression of good

will but a manifestation of the values that unified and motivated the people of Israel in their struggle to ensure for each family the control of and access to their own resources, above all the land. The Israelites were basically peasants, farmers dedicated to the cultivation of small plots and the raising of cattle for family subsistence. The arduous struggle to ensure viable communities came down to the need for children and productive land. As depressed and marginal peasants in Canaan, they had been recruited as forced laborers on large *latifundios* or as tenant farmers on leased lands. They longed for full right to the land as the source of life. (ibid., pp. 25–26)

It is not altogether clear how fully the tribes of Yahweh were able to carry out their vision or even to what extent this vision itself was a later mythical idealization. No doubt the Sabbath–Jubilee mandates are rooted in this vision as an ongoing challenge among the people of Yahweh. They naturally returned again and again to this vision in the face of national oppressors and external empires and their systems of social, political, and economic domination.

The blessing of Yahweh came down to this: the formation of a solidary people who sheltered and restored the needy, providing the necessary elements to maintain their integrity and subsistence. To be an Israelite meant to belong to this solidary people, and to commit oneself to Yahweh meant to commit oneself to the solidary structures that Yahweh had established—to the point of acting as *goel* if needed. (ibid., p. 27)

Sabbath Rest

The mandate to give rest to the land and to those who work the land goes back to the Covenant Code (Exodus 20–23), the oldest strand of law in the Pentateuch. In Exodus 23:10–13 we find both the Sabbath Year and the Sabbath Day, and both command rest, *shabat*, stopping of work so that both humans and working animals and the land itself may be released regularly from the demands of labor and production—"rest," "have relief," "be refreshed." Here, and in the Decalogue of Exodus 20 and Deuteronomy 5, the Sabbath Rest mandate is tied to the giving of the Law at Sinai and posed as an essential part of Israel's covenant with Yahweh, a necessary expression of Israel's identity as a people liberated from slavery. It provides an ancient basis for what may be considered today as the two primary concerns of God and God's people: social justice and ecological integrity.

The practice of a periodic fallow year was not unknown among the peoples of the ancient Near East, and there are various references to this practice in the history of Israel through the time of Jesus. Exodus 23:10–11 expresses concern specifically for the poor and the wild animals, who are to be allowed to gather what the land yields during the fallow year. Exodus

21:2–6 provides for the release of Hebrew slaves after six years of service, which seems to be applied individually. Exodus 23:10–11 does not state clearly whether all lands were to be left fallow individually or simultaneously. On the other hand Leviticus 25:1–7 and 18–22, which were probably composed late in the redaction of the Pentateuch, indicate that the fallow year was to be practiced simultaneously—that is, all lands lay fallow in the same year—so that provision for food during that year must be made.

The Priestly Tradition of the Pentateuch, which includes the Holiness Code (Leviticus 17–25), mandates the Sabbath Day, the Sabbath Year, and the Jubilee Year. This tradition, which played a decisive role in the final redaction of the Pentateuch in the exilic and post-exilic period, begins the story of salvation in Genesis 1:1–2, 4a with the story of creation, thus linking Israel and Israel's God with the whole of nature. The Priestly Tradition centers on the worship of God at the Jerusalem Temple, but it boldly affirms that the world itself was created by Israel's God. It traces the story of salvation from creation through the Patriarchs, the Exodus, Sinai and the desert, into the Promised Land. It links God's act of creation with the seventh day.

The Priestly story of creation, Genesis 1:1–2, 4a, begins and ends with summary statements:

In the beginning . . . God created the heavens and the earth. (1:1)

Thus the heavens and the earth were finished, and all their multitude. (2:1)

Evidently the whole of creation is conceived as a unity, including the human race. Yet humankind is given a special place.

"Let us make humankind in our image, according to our likeness; and let them have dominion over the fish of the sea, and over the birds of the air, and over the cattle, and over all the wild animals of the earth, and over every creeping thing that creeps upon the earth."
So God created humankind in God's image . . . male and female he created them. (1:26–27)

At the very least, these words indicate that humans are to reflect the nature and will of God in their stewardship of creation and in their social life. They are not to exploit but to care for all of nature so that it will continue to reproduce life and provide food for all. God labored for six days and saw that all of creation was "very good."

And on the seventh day God finished the work that he had done, and he rested on the seventh day from all the work that he had done. So God blessed the seventh day and hallowed it, because on it God rested from all the work that he had done in creation.
These are the generations of the heavens and earth when they were created. (2:2–4a)

God rested the seventh day, blessed it, and hallowed it. And so the Sabbath Day became a permanent memorial and covenant for God's people, who are to regard that day and all of creation as a holy responsibility. We are to serve and worship God through the preservation of planet Earth for the life of all its inhabitants.

Sabbath Economics

We return now to a key Sabbath text, Exodus 16, keeping in mind the significance of Israel's land as gift, temptation, responsibility, and threat and the founding experiences of the tribes of Yahweh as social revolution and re-tribalization. The story of manna in the wilderness is now clearly much more than an incident out of Israel's history, more than a spiritual allegory of God's care for God's people in time of need. As the first major narrative following the story of liberation from Egypt, it provides an important revelation of Israel's mandate to become a different socioeconomic community.

The story begins with the complaint of the people against Moses and Aaron, because they were hungry. They apparently thought they were going to die of hunger in the wilderness. Already they longed for the old ways of Egypt, even though they had been slaves. They were not ready for this new experience in the wilderness. So the Lord told Moses that he would provide bread and meat, but with a test, in order to begin to instruct them in a different way of living. They were to gather only enough for each person in each household, an *omer* per person, and no more. If some gathered more and others less, each only had just enough. They were not to keep any for the next day, except that they were to gather a double amount on the sixth day, two *omers* per person. The seventh day would be a holy Sabbath to the Lord.

What then was the first lesson for Israel after their liberation from Egypt? The text provides the answer at the beginning and at the end.

> *So Moses and Aaron said to all the Israelites, "In the evening you shall know that it was the Lord who brought you out of the land of Egypt, and in the morning you shall see the glory of the Lord, because he has heard your complaining against the Lord."*
>
> Exodus 16:6–7

> *Moses said, "This is what the Lord has commanded: 'Let an omer of [manna] be kept throughout your generations, in order that they may see the food with which I fed you in the wilderness, when I brought you out of the land of Egypt.'"* Exodus 16:32

Israel must learn to recognize God's mighty acts on their behalf. They were to rely on the Lord. But there is much more here than that. Israel was to live by an economy of enough for all and reject the economy of excess accumulation for some and hunger and humiliation for others. Israel was to remember that they were once slaves in Egypt, so as never to repeat that experience in their new life in the Promised Land. For Egypt and Canaan, then Assyria and Babylon (and later Rome), all practiced socioeconomic systems of wealth accumulation and centralized power and of resultant poverty and marginalization. Israel's later rulers fell into the same evil pattern again and again. To remember the Lord and the Lord's deliverance from Egypt was necessarily to practice justice, to care for the needy and vulnerable, to make sure that all God's people had enough. Israel's vocation was to create an alternative social possibility.

Sabbath practices are therefore fundamentally economic. That is not to say that they are not spiritual. They are divine mandates, and they are linked directly to the foundational events in the history of salvation. The separation of religion from economics, spirituality from materiality, is a later development that has plagued God's people down through history. As we shall see, in the time of the monarchy, Israel's leaders and people thought they could please God by being religious without practicing justice, and the prophets had to denounce their infidelity repeatedly, even to the point of rejecting Temple worship.

In other chapters we shall examine other Sabbath–Jubilee texts, already mentioned in Chapter 1, that add important mandates for the alternative social possibility in the Promised Land. In Chapter 3 we shall consider what happens when God's Sabbath economy is rejected. Chapter 4 focuses more directly on the Sabbath and Jubilee texts. All along the way we shall ask ourselves what these mandates can and should mean in our own cultural and social contexts today.

Responsible Discipleship ◆ ◆ ◆ ◆ ◆

Simple Lifestyle—The Logic of Enough

In recent decades there has been a growing consciousness among people of faith and others that we must establish limits to our lifestyle personally and collectively at every level. This concern is expressed through slogans and titles such as, "enough is enough," "live simply so that others may simply live," and "more with less." It is a concern both for those who have too little and for those who have too much. It is a matter of personal well-being, and it is a global concern for the human family and the ecosystem. It is fundamentally a concern for the fair distribution of all the world's resources, not just for food for survival but also for education and health care, funds and technology for development, information and communication systems, arts and recreation and culture, family counseling and community organization, humanitarian values and human rights. It is a concern for the spiritual, emotional, physical, and social health of those who have too much as well as those who have too little. It is all too evident, however, that our ecosystem cannot sustain the current level of consumption even for the most privileged 20% of the world's population, much less extend that level of consumption to the other 80%, which simple justice would require.

The logic of enough set forth clearly in the Exodus 16 story is the central mandate of the Sabbath. It could once again become a basic commitment of Jews and Christians and others concerned about the state of the world and of their own lives. It could draw on the contributions of other faiths and traditions, such as the Mayan cosmogony that we looked at earlier. It could explore social, economic, and political experiments of the past and present, such as the Sandinista Revolution of the 1980s, even though such experiments have often been maligned and misunderstood precisely because they deviate from the dominant ideologies and powers. It could provide important motivation and grounding for local and global campaigns such as the Earth Charter.

While recognizing the necessity of facing global needs, we suggest here that every concerned person, family, and group give primary attention to their own lifestyle, not because it is more important, but because it will give validity and credibility to our efforts regarding the wider dimensions of our human predicament. Sooner or later we have to demand of ourselves what we know to be necessary for the well-being of others. Our lifestyle is directly and indirectly related to those wider concerns.

One of the most obvious and basic dimensions of our personal lifestyle that needs attention is food. We have all seen statistics on obesity and unhealthy eating habits. We know what our bodies need and what we should avoid. We have all felt the temptation to eat too much of one thing or another. In this area of our lives clearly enough is enough. In fact it is far better for us, for those who depend on us, and for our world. So careful, responsible eating is a good starting point for a simple, responsible lifestyle.

Perhaps the most current and complex dimension of our lifestyle and work style is the matter of technology. In one short generation we have jumped from simple telephones and postal services to cellular phones, voice mail, fax, electronic mail, pagers, and two-way visual conferencing. Even the specialists in this area are now beginning to warn us of the dangers of being overwhelmed with information far beyond what we can absorb, of being seduced by these accelerating innovations, as if they were an end in themselves, and of being chained twenty-four hours a day to our work and other demands. The level of stress continues to rise, and some say that our "productivity" may be falling rather than rising. On the other hand, the rapid advance of technology continues to disadvantage people and nations with fewer resources, and it may entice them to neglect more basic needs and abandon more essential values in their efforts to "catch up."

Covenanting for Life

On April 30, 1973, a group of directors and personnel from several retreat centers met in a town near Lexington, Kentucky, historically connected with the Shaker movement. They began to share their personal commitments in response to the already alarming global panorama of vast human needs, of enormous waste, of rapidly diminishing resources, and of terrible injustice in their distribution. The participants wrote down their commitments, and they called the document "The Shakertown Pledge." They made these commitments personally and as a group, and they extended an invitation to other interested persons and groups. They suggested that others adapt the pledge in terms appropriate to their own confessional background and to their understanding of the call to justice and peace and the integrity of creation in today's world. The document attempts to integrate devotional life, social conscience, and simple lifestyle as essential elements for faithfulness.

This example may serve to challenge us, twenty-five years later, to consider our commitments to God and to others in the face of even greater and more urgent needs of today's world. The points put forward by the original authors are simple, clear, elementary. We may want to follow their example, as we try to respond to the imperative challenges of our reality today—to the comprehensive call of God in our respective contexts. Whatever else we choose to include, we cannot leave out the demands of God's economy and God's creation, as they are expressed in the Sabbath and Jubilee texts of the Bible.

The Shakertown Pledge

Recognizing that the earth and the fullness thereof is a gift from our gracious God and that we are called to cherish, nurture, and provide loving stewardship for the earth's resources, and recognizing that life itself is a gift and a call to responsibility, joy, and celebration, I make the following declarations:

1. I declare myself to be a world citizen.
2. I commit myself to lead an ecologically sound life.
3. I commit myself to lead a life of creative simplicity and to share my personal wealth with the world's poor.
4. I commit myself to join with others in the reshaping of institutions in order to bring about a more just global society in which all people have full access to the needed resources for their physical, emotional, intellectual, and spiritual growth.
5. I commit myself to occupational accountability, and so doing I will seek to avoid the creation of products which cause harm to others.
6. I affirm the gift of my body and commit myself to its proper nourishment and physical well-being.
7. I commit myself to examine continually my relations with others and to attempt to relate honestly, morally, and lovingly to those around me.
8. I commit myself to personal renewal through prayer, meditation, and study.
9. I commit myself to responsible participation in a community of faith. (Finnerty, 1977, p. 97)

We may want to encourage our faith communities, our working groups, and our families to reflect with us on these matters. As our churches come to the end of the twentieth century and we prepare ourselves for the third millennium, it may be important to consider individually, within our respective traditions, and globally what are our commitments under our covenant with the God of the Exodus. We stand at a crossroad, at the border, like Israel preparing to enter the Promised Land. We must be clear about our real goals and foundations if we are going to try to build an alternative world in which there will be enough, and not too much, for all God's people.

Ecofeminism

In her book, *Women Healing Earth: Third World Women on Ecology, Feminism, and Religion*, Rosemary Radford Ruether has gathered contributions from Latin American, Asian, and African women in an effort to increase communication between themselves and with First World women around the issues of feminism, ecology, and religion. She draws out the connection between domination of women and domination of nature in patriarchal culture, which identifies women "with body, earth, sex, the flesh in its mortality, weakness, and sin-proneness, vis-à-vis a masculinity identified with spirit, mind, and sovereign power over both women and nature as the property of ruling class males" (Ruether, 1996, p. 3). Patriarchal societies exploit women's bodies and work, and they exploit nature. Women and nature are colonized to produce wealth for men, especially those of the dominant classes. "Religion then comes in to reinforce this domination of women and nature as reflecting the will of God and the relation of God as supreme deified patriarchal male to the world that he created and rules" (ibid., p. 3).

Third World women are especially helpful in maintaining the connection between ecofeminism and socioeconomic and racial–ethnic domination. Northern ecofeminists are especially concerned about solidarity with nature, about resistance to the violence against nature and against themselves, about healing nature and society. Surely all of these connections are essential for humankind and nature in the struggle for fullness of life for all. They raise essential questions about the roots of social justice and the integrity of nature in our still largely patriarchal world.

The experience and perspective of women is likewise essential for our understanding and critique of religion.

> There is a deeper truth to the link between women and nature that has been distorted by patriarchy to exploit them both. Women are the life-givers, the nurturers, the ones in whom the seed of life grows. Women were and often remain the primary food gatherers, the inventors of agriculture. Their bodies are in mysterious tune with the cycles of the moon and the tides of the sea. It was by experiencing women as the

life-givers, the birthers of children, the food-providers, that early humans made the image of the female the first personification of the divine, as the Goddess, the source of all life. (ibid., p. 4)

Later patriarchal societies imposed a concept of God as "patriarchal warrior and ruler, outside of and disconnected with nature, which they used to suppress the earlier concept of the Goddess as immanent life within nature" (ibid., p. 4).

The dialogue among northern and southern ecofeminists will help all of us to understand and to work together against the oppression of women, the destruction of nature, and the growing devastation of poverty, which affects all people but especially women and children. All impoverishment—of women, of nature—is clearly interrelated in fundamental ways. These are primary concerns of the God of the Jubilee.

We have considered various socioeconomic possibilities in keeping with the Sabbath principles of providing enough for all God's people and protecting the environment. But the overwhelming reality of our modern world is the globalization and centralization of an economic system that ignores and abuses those very principles. We will therefore have to examine further the foundations of this economic system and also the nature and foundations of Sabbath economics and what we might call Jubilee spirituality. We know that there are many attempts to find alternatives within and outside the dominant system. We remember that, from the time of the Exodus, the wilderness wanderings, and the "conquest" of Canaan, the people of Yahweh faced incredible odds, and so today their spiritual descendents cannot but continue on their journey into hope, into the Promised Land.

3 ◆ ◆ ◆ ◆ ◆ ◆ ◆

Abuse of Land, Labor, and Life

Our task in this chapter will be to dig more deeply into the predicament of our world, into the understanding of the human predicament in the Hebrew Scriptures, and into our responsibility as people of faith to use that ancient understanding to guide us into faithful response to our contemporary predicament. The Sabbath–Jubilee tradition running through the Bible is a helpful key to open up the whole history of salvation even in diverse circumstances. It presents divine mandates so urgent that they point the way to life or death for peoples and nations and even the Earth itself. Our intention is not to dwell on the well-known abuses of our time or biblical times but rather to explore the roots of these abuses then and now in order to deepen our understanding of and commitment to God's rule for the life of all God's creation. The following questions sum up our concerns in this chapter:

◆ What are the critical dimensions of humankind's war against the poor and collective rush toward economic and ecological suicide?
◆ What were the critical dimensions of Israel's deviation from God's rule for life that led to whole-scale injustice and national disaster under the monarchy?
◆ What are people of faith doing today to expose our human and ecological predicament and to call us to change before it is too late?

Chapter 4 will build on the results of our work in this chapter with a focus on Sabbath economics, Jubilee spirituality, liberty for all.

Today's World ◆ ◆ ◆ ◆ ◆

Economic and Ecological Suicide

Bob Goudzwaard and Harry de Lange, in their book, *Beyond Poverty and Affluence: Toward an Economy of Care*, offer an interesting analysis of what has been happening among the industrialized nations in terms of six paradoxes:

1. The Scarcity Paradox: Our society, a society of unprecedented wealth, experiences unprecedented scarcity.
2. The Poverty Paradox: Poverty is rising sharply in the midst of wealthy societies.
3. The Care Paradox: In the midst of more wealth, we have fewer opportunities to practice care than before.
4. The Labor Paradox: Our society's need for more labor is becoming critical even as unemployment rises.
5. The Health Paradox: Even though our level of health care has increased, our level of disease is rising.
6. The Time Paradox: Despite substantially more wealth, we have less and less time in our lives. (1995, pp. 2–5)

Goudzwaard and de Lange are concerned about the socioeconomic roots of these paradoxes in supposedly successful First World nations. In particular, they are concerned about global poverty, which according to UNICEF, takes the lives of 40,000 children each day, about 17 million a year "from lack of necessities and from exhaustion." Bread for the World's Institute on Hunger and Development stated in its report, *Hunger 1992*, that one third of the children in the developing countries are permanently impaired due to poor nourishment (ibid., p. 8).

Theologian–economist Xabier Gorostiaga, then-president of Regional Coordination of Economic and Social Research (CRIES) and president of the University of Central America in Managua, offered an important analysis of the regional and global socioeconomic and cultural crisis in a speech before the Conference of the Latin American Sociology Association in May, 1991. His title was "Latin America in the New World Order," and his concern was to reflect on the new realities following the collapse of socialism and the end of the Cold War. Following are some theses from that memorable discourse that are still relevant today.

Never before in history has there been such a concentration and centralization of capital in so few nations and in the hands of so few people. . . . This concentration of capital corresponds to the character of the new technological revolution in which the cycle of capital accumulation depends less and less on intensive use of natural resources and labor, or even of productive capital, and more on an accumulation of technology based on the intensive use of knowledge. This concentration and centralization of technological knowledge is more intense and monopolistic than other forms of capital, and only increases the gap between North and South. (Gorostiaga, 1991, p. 32)

The automatization and robotization of production means that labor loses value relative to capital, in both the North and South. Both processes lead to a permanent structural deterioration of value relative to what are supposedly the South's comparative advantages in production and world trade. (ibid., p. 32)

The transnationalization of systems of production, financing, and marketing . . . for the first time permits a truly global market. (ibid., p. 32)

The revolution in telecommunications, transportation, and informatics has produced management innovations that have further facilitated mergers of capital and technology, whereby private business in Latin America and the South in general is increasingly incorporated in a dependent way into the logic of centralized capital. National business, both private and state-run, is increasingly marginalized and in an asymmetric position vis-à-vis transnational industry, and thus more and more isolated from the logic of the domestic market and the survival of the large impoverished majority. (ibid., p. 32)

The crisis is not only one of distribution and equity, it is a crisis of values and the direction humanity is taking. For this reason we can call it a crisis of civilization. Society worldwide is neither sustainable nor stable under these conditions. Democracy is not possible for the majority of the world's population, and this fact is leading to increasing ungovernability in many nations of the world. (ibid., p. 35)

The South is portrayed as a den of evil goings-on, a dangerous place for citizens from the North. In this vision, the threats of drugs, immigration, and political instability, along with regional conflicts, all come from the South. The objective structural gap between North and South is widened with this subjective ideologization, which has deep and racist roots. Instead of confronting the causes of the crisis, this ideological view looks at the consequences and seeks to lay blame there. (ibid., p. 35)

Debt has substituted the direct investment of the 1970s as a mechanism to extract net financial transfers out of Latin America. It puts the state and even private enterprise into a submissive position with its denationalizing effect. (ibid., p. 36)

Bretton Woods—Foundations of Our World Economy

Julio de Santa Ana explains the origin of this now-global economic situation in his book, *La práctica económica como religión: crítica teológica a la economía política* (*Economic Practice as Religion: Theological Critique of the Political Economy*). In 1944, representatives of the countries allied against national socialism met at Bretton Woods, New Hampshire, to plan together their future economic development. Concerned about the tremendous damage caused by the economic depression of the 1930s and the destruction of World War II, which ended the year after the meeting, these representatives proposed the creation of a free world market that would, supposedly, contribute to the growth and well-being of all nations and also foster peace among them. They decided to use the dollar as the international monetary base, and they established the International Monetary Fund (IMF), the World Bank (WB), and later the General Agreement on Tariffs and Trade (GATT) as instruments to manage this new economic order. During the following decades there was much economic growth, but the wealth generated was concentrated in those countries and sectors with the greatest power. And there were many more wars, all in the Third World.

During the 1970s the U.S. dollar was freed from the gold standard and became abundant with the enormous profits being generated in petroleum. The Third World countries, which already had enormous economic and technological disadvantages, were pressed to receive more loans at low interest in order to invest and compete more in the world market, but interest rates skyrocketed, trapping these countries with debts they could never repay. The countries of the north have used these arrangements to their advantage, maintaining the dependence and exploitation of the countries of the south even to the point of dictating the latter's internal economic policies.

During recent years, the countries of Central America and the rest of Latin America have had to submit to the "structural adjustment plans" imposed by the IMF, World Bank, Inter-American Development Bank, and U.S. Aid for International Development. Under the mandate of "free" market economics and the weight of their foreign debts, these countries are being forced to orient their economies toward a hemispheric market dominated by the First World; privatize government businesses, banks, and services; eliminate subsidies; reduce the public sector; repress unions; increase agro-exportation of nontraditional products; and provide an ongoing supply of cheap labor. It has been necessary that the real value of salaries in some countries drop 34%, so that the gross national product would increase. It has been necessary that level of employment, standard of living, education, health, and life expectancy fall so that the economic capacity of these peoples could be placed at the service of the market, producing profits for investors, paying interest on the debt, and providing bananas, coffee, flowers, and broccoli at very good prices for the supermarkets of the north.

In his book, *The Politics of Rich and Poor*, Kevin Phillips describes in great detail the results of this system in the United States during the 1980s. The administration of Ronald Reagan openly proclaimed its neoliberal ideology, which some have called savage capitalism, and applied it recklessly. Taxes for the rich were reduced markedly, and fiscal and commercial controls were also reduced, with the illusion that the rich would invest their new wealth and produce a wave of prosperity that would benefit all. This economic policy did in fact increase enormously the wealth of the elites; it also hurt the large middle class and it increased poverty. That decade, which saw the scandal of homeless men, women, and children sleeping in the streets of major U.S. cities, ended with three million millionaires, 100,000 deca-millionaires, 1,500 centa-millionaires, and 54 billionaires. Equally serious, the United States, which began the 1980s as the world's biggest creditor, became the most indebted, with an external debt of $500 billion and a total debt of $8 trillion.

The Commodification of Land, Labor, and Life

Ulrich Duchrow, whose book, *Alternatives to Global Capitalism*, we referred to in Chapter 1, traces the roots of this economic system to the philosophies of Thomas Hobbes, John Locke, and John Law in the seventeenth century. According to Hobbes, human beings are naturally driven to accumulate property and wealth in competition with each other. Since Hobbes's time, advocates of the capitalist market economy have insisted that accumulation of wealth is a natural law and that "anyone claiming the opposite must be an ideologist, at best an idealist not to be taken seriously" (Duchrow, 1995, p. 52). Thus "capitalism itself gives the impression of being the source of everything productive. Its distinctive mechanism of self-generation is presented as the source of life" (ibid., p. 41). He goes on:

> John Locke provided the theological and philosophical legitimation for the accumulation of wealth and property, while John Law invented a new system of paper money, thus providing the economic basis for extending the monetary economy. The transformation of working people, the land, and money, as a means of exchange, into the fiction of being commodities left society at the mercy of the capitalist market, dividing it, destroying nature, and allowing money to become a fetish, as Karl Marx showed. (ibid., p. 43)

Locke used the divine mandate to subdue the Earth (Genesis 1:28), as a justification for the mechanism of wealth accumulation. The accumulation of wealth was considered rational. In his *Second Treatise of Government*, he states that the chief end of civil society "is the preservation of property" (ibid., p. 44). Ownership is the right to use and consume property, so Locke "is concerned with actually justifying unrestricted accumulation, amassing possessions via the unrestricted money-accumulation mechanism" (ibid., p. 45). This thinking led to the full flowering of capitalist theory with Adam Smith's *Wealth of Nations* in 1776.

> Smith regarded human beings as automatons striving to make a profit. The difference here is, however, that the state is no longer required to regulate the market. Under the liberal conception of industrial capitalism, the market regulates itself. . . . Smith uses the concept of the "invisible hand," keeping the market working harmoniously to the greatest common good. (ibid., p. 55)

Smith did assume, however, that the economic system would be held in check by the natural human concern for others, and he allowed for the intervention of government when selfish employers became excessively exploitative.

> Smith's philosophy and the mechanistic traditions on which it was based sowed the seed of the view that the economy has autonomous laws, and therefore also of the assumption that scientific economics and its techniques are essential in recognizing and controlling economic processes and interpreting human behavior within the economy. (ibid., p. 55)

We all know how this system works today. The market-oriented economy drives investors, businesses, and producers not to focus on the limited needs of all for survival but rather to stimulate and satisfy the unlimited desires, real and artificial, of those who have purchasing power, so as to accumulate more and more wealth. The ownership of property is considered to be a natural right, and the motivation to increase one's wealth is considered to be right and necessary. Extreme levels of income and consumption are viewed as valid achievement through competition, and extreme levels of poverty are viewed as the result of failure to compete or to work hard. The far-reaching power of this socioeconomic system lies to some degree in its appeal not only for the very rich or even for the middle classes but for all of us, because we all want more and are constantly encouraged by the system to seek more for ourselves. In the slums of every city from New York to Buenos Aires, Los Angeles to Seoul, the poor are encouraged to buy television sets that will ensure constant bombardment with the illusions of material prosperity without regard for their neighbors and without any serious analysis of their own exclusion from that material prosperity.

So all of life is reduced to commodities for and from the marketplace. The land is essential insofar as it provides raw materials for the machines of production. The preservation and renewal of nature is secondary to the demand for profit. Labor is also essential insofar as it is necessary for production. The cost of labor must be reduced as far as possible or eliminated for the maximization of profit. And so life itself is defined by monetary considerations, in terms of commodities, in the calculus of the market economy. "The commodity description of labor, land, and money is entirely fictitious. Nevertheless, it is with the help of this fixation that the actual markets for labor, land, and money are organized" (Karl Polanyi, cited by Duchrow, 1995, p. 31).

While working on this manuscript in the United States, we have followed with interest the national debate about tobacco. For many years we marveled at the fact that the surgeon general could announce year after year that smoking was causing 200,000, then 300,000 annual deaths from lung cancer, perhaps a total of 500,000 annual deaths from all effects including secondary exposure, without any more serious demand than warnings on tobacco products and in advertising. Over the years, the overall rate of smoking has fallen significantly in the United States, which has been very encouraging. But now we learn that the tobacco companies have been targeting our youth with advertising campaigns in order to capture future smoking generations. Rates may actually be going up among youth, women, and minorities. And there are reports of alleged manipulation of nicotine content among tobacco growers in Brazil in order to increase addiction, sales, and profits. Years ago, when it first became evident that smoking would fall in the United States, the tobacco companies began to increase their propaganda abroad, without the surgeon general's warning, and at least in one case they were able to pressure Third World countries to allow free entry of their products through free market policies of the U.S. government. This is just one example of the primacy of profits over people.

Biblical Faith ◆ ◆ ◆ ◆ ◆

We turn now to the Old Testament to examine what happened to the people of Israel after the initial period of settlement in the Promised Land. We shall consider first the dynamics and results of the formation of the monarchy, which we shall refer to as the logic of centralization. Then we shall look at the prophets' denunciations of Israel's unfaithfulness, above all the nation's failure to fulfill their vocation as an alternative, just, socioeconomic order. Finally we shall observe the tragic consequences of that disobedience—destruction and exile—and the prophets' reading of those events as divine judgment and the emergence of a new message of hope. These studies build upon our previous studies of the centrality of the Exodus experience of liberation and the foundational experience of settlement in the Promised Land as an alternative social possibility. They will lead directly to a deeper analysis of the Sabbath–Jubilee mandates in response to the experience of wealth and power accumulation of Israel's elites at the expense of the larger population.

The Monarchy and the Logic of Centralization

Anthony Ceresko warns against "an overly simplistic view of the shift from tribal league to monarchy under David . . . as a kind of fall from grace or return to paganism or betrayal of the revolution," and he also warns against "a naive acceptance of the view garnered from a superficial reading of the Bible—that the move to a monarchy was somehow willed by God" (Ceresko, 1992, p. 150). The historical situation was complex. Israel faced the threat of the Philistines to the southwest and of other potential enemies on all sides. The loosely federated tribes were not well equipped to defend against organized military powers, and apparently they were not willing to continue trusting in Yahweh. So they demanded a king against the advice of aging prophet and judge Samuel. Saul reigned from 1020 to 1000 B.C., followed by David, 1000 to 962 B.C., and Solomon from 962 to 922 B.C. The monarchy brought with it not only a more centralized defense force but also a centralization of the worship of Yahweh in Jerusalem. It enabled Israel to defend itself but also to extend its borders. But with these developments, especially under Solomon, came a costly central administration, elite courtiers, luxurious palaces, and even foreign gods.

When Samuel was first faced with this challenge, he prayed to the Lord, and the Lord responded, reminding the people of their deliverance from Egypt and warning them with these words, first to Samuel and then to the people directly, as reported in 1 Samuel 8:7–9 and 11–18.

> *"Listen to the voice of the people in all that they say to you; for they have not rejected you, but they have rejected me from being king over them. Just as they have done to me, from the day I brought them up out of Egypt to this day, forsaking me and serving other gods, so also they are doing to you. Now then, listen to their voice; only—you shall solemnly warn them and show them the ways of the king who shall reign over them."*

> *"These will be the ways of the king who will reign over you: he will take your sons and appoint them to his chariots and to be his horsemen, and to run before his chariots; and he will appoint for himself commanders of thousands and commanders of fifties, and some to plow his ground and to reap his harvest, and to make his implements of war and the equipment of his chariots. He will take your daughters to be perfumers and cooks and bakers. He will take the best of your fields and vineyards and olive orchards and give them to his courtiers. He will take one-tenth of your grain and of your vineyards and give it to his officers and his courtiers. He will take your male and female slaves, and the best of your cattle and donkeys, and put them to his work. He will take one-tenth of your flocks, and you shall be his slaves. And in that day you will cry out because of your king, whom you have chosen for yourselves; but the Lord will not answer you in that day."*

This warning came to full fruition with King Solomon, whose wisdom, wealth, power, fame, and errors are described at length in 1 Kings, of which this is a small sample:

> *Thus King Solomon excelled all the kings of the earth in riches and in wisdom. The whole earth sought the presence of Solomon to hear his wisdom, which God had put into his mind. Every one of them brought a present, objects of silver and gold, garments, weaponry, spices, horses, and mules, so much year by year.* 1 Kings 10:23–25

Solomon loved many foreign women, and they brought their gods, and he set up holy sites for them, thus departing from Israel's covenant with

Yahweh. Israel's enemies began to mobilize against Solomon, and the people of Israel suffered under the weight of his sumptuous rule. So when Solomon died, his kingdom was divided. The tribes of the north carried on the kingly tradition from 922 to 722 B.C., when Samaria was destroyed by Assyria and many Israelites were deported, never to be heard of again. Judah to the south carried on its monarchy from 922 to 587 B.C., when Jerusalem was finally destroyed and many of her people deported to Babylon.

The socioeconomic and theological–spiritual significance of these developments cannot be overemphasized. The ever-greater concentration of wealth and power by royalty and the ruling class required ever-greater exploitation of rural peasants and urban workers. Increasing taxes, forced labor, and land expropriation impoverished the common people, broke down family and community life, and increased malnutrition, disease, and death, especially among the very young and the very old. The rich and powerful accumulated large estates through the debt system, with high interest rates, and slavery. The socioeconomic–spiritual values that Israel had learned from the Exodus and the wilderness wanderings and the gift of the Promised Land were undermined. Israel's faith commitment to Yahweh was violated, provoking the denunciations of the prophets.

> The conflicts between prophet and king are described in the biblical record as mainly religious conflicts between Baalism and Yahwism. But in fact they represent a much broader and more pervasive conflict involving two contrasting visions of how to organize and maintain human community and society. Thus most of the kings of both Israel and Judah were criticized for "failing to walk in the ways of Yahweh." They were presented in the Deuteronomistic historical sources as erring principally by theological failures, for example, in cultic matters such as the proper sanctuary where worship of Yahweh was supposed to take place.
>
> But this conflict of theologies represents only the tip of the iceberg. Baalism and Yahwism constituted, in fact, the ideological elements of much broader visions and practice. Baalism favored and promoted a community and society based on hierarchy and social stratification. Yahwism, by contrast, represented the more egalitarian ideals of the older tribal confederation, traditions still clung to and practiced among the majority of Israelites in the villages and countryside. The prophets were the most eloquent and aggressive defenders and promoters of these older ideals. They were innovative and creative in the way they promoted and expressed these ideals in new ways adapted to the new circumstances. At the same time they were radically conservative in the sense of their challenge to return to the ideals of justice and egalitarian communal practices of former days. (Ceresko, 1992, p. 153)

Prophetic Denunciation of Religion without Justice

The prophets went to great lengths to declare the centrality of the practice of justice for Israel's faith and faithfulness. They did so in direct confrontation with kings and princes, priests, false prophets, and the people when they strayed from their covenant with Yahweh. When King David took Bathsheba and then tried to cover up his deed by causing her husband Uriah to be killed in battle, the prophet Nathan denounced him with terrible words of judgment from the Lord God. When King Ahab connived with his wife Jezebel to kill Naboth and take his vineyard, thus violating the ancient patrimony of the land, the prophet Elijah announced the terrible sentence of the Lord: "Have you killed and also taken possession? . . . In the place where dogs licked up the blood of Naboth, dogs will also lick up your blood" (1 Kings 21:19). Later prophets were ever more explicit in their denunciations of socioeconomic sin as the breaking of Israel's covenant with Yahweh and the cause of God's wrathful judgment.

> Almost invariably, whether the messages are words of consolation and comfort, or words of challenge, warning, and doom, they do not involve purely personal or exclusively religious matters. Rather, they concern the life of the entire people and the shape and character of Israelite society, whether the messages are delivered to an individual such as the king or proclaimed to the people as a whole. (Ceresko, 1992, p. 172)

The eighth-century prophet Amos preached to the Northern Kingdom. Apparently his messages were revised later for the Southern Kingdom after the fall of Samaria (722 B.C.); and they were again adapted at the end of the exile or after the return (538 B.C.). Amos was deeply concerned about the breakdown of earlier egalitarian economics, which the Sabbath and Jubilee mandates sought to maintain, leading to the accumulation of property by the rich and powerful.

> *Thus says the Lord:*
> *For three transgressions of Israel,*
> *   and for four, I will not revoke the punishment;*
> *because they sell the righteous for silver,*
> *   and the needy for a pair of sandals—*
> *they who trample the head of the poor into the dust of the earth,*
> *   and push the afflicted out of the way.*   Amos 2:6–7

So strong was the Lord's judgment upon Israel's disobedience that their entire religious system—festivals, sacrifices, liturgies, music—was condemned.

> *I hate, I despise your festivals,*
> *   and I take no delight in your solemn assemblies.*

Even though you offer me your burnt offerings and grain offerings,
*   I will not accept them;*
and the offerings of well-being of your fatted animals
*   I will not look upon.*
Take away from me the noise of your songs;
*   I will not listen to the melody of your harps.*
But let justice roll down like waters,
*   and righteousness like an ever-flowing stream.*   Amos 5:21–24

Israel was called to create and maintain an alternative social reality unlike Egypt, unlike Canaan, unlike the other nations. This was the significance of the giving of the Law at Sinai and the giving of the Promised Land. Amos reminded his people of their roots, and he himself was driven by a powerful and empowering encounter with their true God.

> Israel's foundational vision had been that of a people joined together in the common project of building a just and peaceful community guided by and animated by their covenant loyalty to their common God, Yahweh. That vision had been grounded on the right of access to the sources of life's basic necessities and the provisions for mutual aid. Both of these foundation stones were being crushed and thrown by the wayside. Motivated by greed and a lust for power, and intent on aping the elegant and arrogant trappings of the court and ruling classes of imperial powers like Assyria, the nobility and rich merchant classes of the Northern Kingdom ignored the covenant obligations toward their fellow Israelites. Instead of low or no-interest loans to help a family through a period of economic hardship brought on by drought, for example, they charged exorbitant interest rates, often 50 percent or more. When people could not pay, they seized the land and either evicted the occupants or reduced them to a state of near slavery as tenant farmers. (Ceresko, 1992, p. 181)

Amos himself understood by personal experience the importance of Israel's calling. Growing up as a shepherd and farmer in the rural village of Tekoa, he was no doubt brought up with the traditional values of mutual care, social justice, and economic equality. He could see and feel the suffering of his people due to the injustice and corruption of the ruling class. He was called to speak for Yahweh in denunciation of those in power, to call his people to remember and return to their covenant with the God who had liberated them from such abuse, and to announce the coming judgment.

Destruction and Exile, Judgment and Rebirth of Hope

The prophet Jeremiah also grew up in a small village, Anathoth, not far from Jerusalem, and he was called by God to carry out his vocation during the last forty years of the Southern Kingdom, 627 to 587 B.C., and into the succeeding exiles. He was appointed "over nations and over kingdoms, to pluck up and to pull down, to destroy and to overthrow, to build and to plant" (Jeremiah 1:10). He began his ministry during the reign of King Josiah, but apparently he had a jaundiced view of Josiah's reform in 622 B.C. The rest of his time in Jerusalem was spent in unheeded calls to repentance, vitriolic denunciation of the sins of the people and their rulers, persecution by the authorities and ridicule by his friends, and agonizing announcement of impending destruction. His prophecies and narratives bare his very soul, as he struggled on God's behalf with his wayward people and on their behalf with a wrathful God.

On one special occasion, probably a national festival, perhaps the coronation of a new king, the Lord placed Jeremiah at one of the Temple gates. The Lord gave him this message:

> *Hear the word of the Lord, all you people of Judah, you that enter these gates to worship the Lord. Thus says the Lord of hosts, the God of Israel: Amend your ways and your doings, and let me dwell with you in this place. Do not trust in these deceptive words: "This is the temple of the Lord, the temple of the Lord, the temple of the Lord."* Jeremiah 7:2–4

Evidently the people were singing or chanting and certainly trusting in the great Temple of Jerusalem with the traditional belief that God was present and would never abandon the chosen people. Perhaps it was a time of crisis as Assyrian or Babylonian armies were advancing toward Judah, and they wanted to reassure themselves that they would not be overcome. The word of the Lord through Jeremiah tries to set them straight with the declaration that they are deceiving themselves. The Lord is not concerned with the Temple or with Temple worship but with their "ways." Then the Lord explains clearly what they must do.

> *For if you truly amend your ways and your doings, if you truly act justly one with another, if you do not oppress the alien, the orphan, and the widow, or shed innocent blood in this place, and if you do not go after other gods to your own hurt, then I will dwell with you in this place, in the land that I gave of old to your ancestors forever and ever.* Jeremiah 7:5–7

Again the Lord warns them of their false trust in the Temple, even to the point of allowing the destruction of the Temple, as he had allowed the Philistines to take the ark of the Covenant, which was based at Shiloh, and defeat Israel's army because of their disobedience (1 Samuel 4:10–11).

> *Here you are, trusting in deceptive words to no avail. Will you steal, murder, commit adultery, swear falsely, make offerings to Baal, and go after other gods that you have not known, and then come and stand before me in this house, which is called by my name, and say, "We are safe!"—only to go on doing all these abominations? Has this house, which is called by my name, become a den of robbers in*

> *your sight? You know, I too am watching, says the Lord. Go now to*
> *my place that was in Shiloh, where I made my name dwell at first,*
> *and see what I did to it for the wickedness of my people Israel. And*
> *now, because you have done all these things, says the Lord, and*
> *when I spoke to you persistently, you did not listen, and when I*
> *called you, you did not answer, therefore I will do to the house that*
> *is called by my name, in which you trust, and to the place that I gave*
> *to you and to your ancestors, just what I did to Shiloh. And I will*
> *cast you out of my sight, just as I cast out all your kinsfolk, all the*
> *offspring of Ephraim.*   Jeremiah 7:8–15

According to Jeremiah 26, which evidently refers to the same event, Jeremiah's preaching that day provoked the priests and the prophets and all the people to such a degree that they called for his death. No doubt his words about the Temple were considered the ultimate sacrilege, worthy of the death penalty. A judicial proceeding was launched immediately by the princes of Judah, with declarations against Jeremiah by the priests and prophets, but others came to his defense, and he was set free.

Ironically it was precisely Jeremiah's relentless words of judgment, even in the face of total failure to bring his people to repentance, that ultimately became the basis for hope. The false prophets of the day, no doubt to please their hearers and gain support, were proclaiming "peace, peace" as the war clouds approached the gates of Jerusalem, encouraging that false trust in the Temple and the god of their false Temple worship. So when destruction came, these prophets and their god and the Temple worship were discredited. On the other hand, Jeremiah's prophecies were confirmed in all their devastation. By the same token, if Yahweh was in fact the author of this destruction, Yahweh could also bring hope out of this same judgment. Jeremiah's God did offer a word of hope:

> *The days are surely coming, says the Lord, when I will make a new*
> *covenant with the house of Israel and the house of Judah. It will not*
> *be like the covenant that I made with their ancestors when I took*
> *them by the hand to bring them out of the land of Egypt—a cove-*
> *nant that they broke, though I was their husband, says the Lord. But*
> *this is the covenant that I will make with the house of Israel after*
> *those days, says the Lord: I will put my law within them, and I will*
> *write it on their hearts; and I will be their God, and they shall be my*
> *people. No longer shall they teach one another, or say to each other,*
> *"Know the Lord," for they shall all know me, from the least of them*
> *to the greatest, says the Lord; for I will forgive their iniquity, and re-*
> *member their sin no more.*   Jeremiah 31:31–34

We find a similar irony at the end of the Holiness Code after the presentation of the Sabbath Year and the Jubilee Year in Leviticus 25. The code ends with various penalties for disobedience to the commandments given, that is, for breaking the covenant with Yahweh. In terms as brutal as those of Jeremiah, the Lord promises terrible, almost unspeakable punishment. Then, as if to underline the centrality of Sabbath economics and Jubilee spirituality, the Lord goes on to say:

> *Then the land shall enjoy its Sabbath years as long as it lies desolate, while you are in the land of your enemies; then the land shall rest, and enjoy its Sabbath years. As long as it lies desolate, it shall have the rest it did not have on your Sabbaths when you were living on it.*
> Leviticus 26:34–35

It concludes, like Jeremiah, with a word of hope, founded on the Lord's covenant with Israel, which in turn is founded on the Lord's act of liberation from Egypt:

> *Yet for all that, when they are in the land of their enemies, I will not spurn them, or abhor them so as to destroy them utterly and break my covenant with them; for I am the Lord their God; but I will remember in their favor the covenant with their ancestors whom I brought out of the land of Egypt in the sight of the nations, to be their God: I am the Lord.*   Leviticus 26:44–45

The period of the Babylonian captivity can be calculated from the destruction of Jerusalem in 587 B.C. to the initial return under the decree of Cyrus in 538 B.C. as fifty years, equivalent to the cycle of Jubilee mandated in Leviticus 25.

Responsible Discipleship ◆ ◆ ◆ ◆ ◆

We have considered some aspects of our contemporary world that explain the unprecedented polarization between rich and poor and its effects. We have found that, during the period of the monarchy, Israel experienced a similar polarization with similar effects. We must now consider what God calls us to do about our current situation on the basis of our reading of God's judgment on Israel's social behavior during the monarchy. Such interpretation and application should not be undertaken simplistically or carelessly—neither should it be avoided or neglected. Insofar as we consider ourselves heirs of Israel's faith, we must take very seriously God's judgment upon God's people and their leaders then and now. Following are some suggestive options by North American and Central American people of faith.

A Call for Repentance

Repentance is a common word in our religious vocabulary, but it has generally been used in a personal, pietistic, intimate way. It is written into our liturgies and read rather perfunctorily during worship with varying degrees of seriousness and sincerity. It rarely takes on its root meaning: to turn around, to change direction in one's life, to be converted or transformed. In any case, as this repentance is personal and intimate, there is no way of confirming the supposed changes.

We suggest that one important starting point for all of us is to adopt and apply a more biblical, holistic understanding of repentance. As we have considered throughout our study thus far, God is not interested simply in religious practices but rather in alternative living in consonance with our liberation from "slavery" in "Egypt." Therefore we must examine, personally and collectively, to what extent we are caught up in the dominant socioeconomic system and its ideology. Whether we are rich or poor or somewhere between, we need to examine very seriously the temptations and attractions of this system and compare them with the biblical mandates for justice. We must recognize, even as we go to church, that God is concerned about our lifestyle more than our worship style.

Perhaps we need to create new prayers of confession in which we share and hold ourselves personally and collectively accountable for our social and economic behavior and ideological commitments. We certainly will need to help each other resist the ubiquitous pressures of consumerism on ourselves and our families. We will need to find ways to link these concerns meaningfully with the larger political world. This will require a new understanding of spirituality more in keeping with the call to Israel to become an alternative people of Yahweh.

The people of the United States are "good people" generally. But ours is the wealthiest and most powerful nation in the world. If we consider our political system to be democratic, then we are responsible for what our government does. We must then repent of, reject, and turn away from those policies and decisions that enable our country to continue practicing injustice of all kinds. We must question and call to account our leaders and our people and ourselves for consuming far more nonrenewable resources than the rest of the world, for producing more ecological damage, for practicing structural and personal racism, for denying equal rights to women, for denigrating the poor. We also have much to celebrate and encourage—many changes have been made over the years to enhance participation and enable steps toward justice. Yet there is much for which we must repent, especially as we consider the fate of other peoples around the world whom our economic system has exploited or neglected or ignored.

On the Way: From Kairos to Jubilee

As mentioned in Chapter 2, the Kairos USA movement released a document entitled *On the Way: From Kairos to Jubilee* to express convictions about the present reality of our country and our world and to call our churches to interpret the signs of this time and place and to act responsibly in the face of the current crisis of our civilization and our planet. It begins with a statement of purpose, which includes the following paragraphs.

> The empire in which we dwell
> serves the idols we are forbidden to worship.
> Systemic injustice and perverse values,
> social evil and personal irresponsibilities
> permeate the fabric of our lives.

The crisis in our nation is far greater than the sum of our many social ills. It strikes deeply into the heart of all that identifies who we are and where we are going as a people. Our structures, values, habits, and assumptions require basic transformation. But neither politics nor piety as we know them will effect such a change. The crisis of our times cries out for our conversion. At such a time as this, we as a people of faith must remember who we are and to whom we belong.

> It is our common task
> to identify and interpret the signs
> to name the moment
> to make choices for ourselves and our communities
> to challenge the institutions of which we are a part
> to apply the Scriptural Jubilee to every dimension of our
>   lives
> to proclaim the year of God's favor.
> Life and faith depend on it.

For us as Christians conversion begins with awareness of a wrongly chosen, dangerous and destructive path, which requires our turning around and moving in a new direction. We are called to the way of Christ, marked by our biblical faith. While covered by centuries of cultural domestication, it still offers the most fundamental critique and the most compelling alternative vision in a society which is perishing without one.

> We see a crisis,
> we feel a hope,
> we discern a work,
> and we hear a call.
> Let us covenant to walk together. (pp. 3–4)

The document then has a section called "Signs of These Times," which includes social oppression and cultural breakdown, the disintegration of family life, economic injustice, white racism, and "the real possibility of catastrophe at the heart of creation" (p. 9). It includes the following statement of confession and repentance about our churches:

> The crisis is not only in our society. The crisis is in our churches. With notable exceptions, people of faith and churches in our land have failed to recognize and adequately respond to the idolatries that

abound. The very identity of our churches has long been inseparable from the identity of the state. We have readily assimilated the values and priorities of U.S. culture. Thus, too often our churches no longer know who we are and to whom we belong. For the churches, too, this is a kairos moment in which we are called to conversion, our structures, values, habits, and assumptions in need of basic transformation. Instead of challenging the status quo, the church tends to reinforce, if not bless, things as they are, usually under the guise of being "politically neutral." It accomplishes this by spiritualizing, privatizing, and generally undermining God's option for the poor, oppressed, and marginalized. Issues of power, class, gender, and material interests contained in the biblical texts have been too often ignored, even suppressed. (pp. 9–10)

Then there is a section called "Kairos is Opportunity and Hope" with an exposition about that hope and a list of hopeful movements and programs. This is followed by a section on "The Jubilee," which begins with quotations from Leviticus 25 and Luke 4 and continues with an analysis of the meaning of the Jubilee mandates for our time.

The last section of the document is called "The Challenge we Face," and it ends with the following declaration and commitment:

We take the spirit of Jubilee to be a preeminent sign of this kairos time.

We are frightened by the signs of crisis . . .
encouraged by the signs of hope . . .
compelled by the urgency of both.

Thus we commit ourselves to the works of repentance—to reparation, redress, re-valuing.

We commit ourselves to enact the Jubilee concretely
in our communities, our institutions, our lives.

We commit ourselves to a continuing quest—an ongoing journey—a form of faith in itself, a sign of freedom, a mark of serious discipleship. The contours of Jubilee are yet to be defined, but the invitation is clear and the need is great.

In the spirit of community, mindful of truth ever exceeding our knowledge,
let us covenant to live in a manner
explicitly informed by the Gospel we proclaim. Amen. (p. 24)

The Clamor for Land

We want now to take an example from Central America. "*El Clamor por la Tierra*" (The Clamor for Land) is a pastoral letter prepared and published by the Catholic Bishops of Guatemala in February 1988, when the long night of violent repression throughout that country but especially against the large, defenseless Indian population seemed to be coming to an end. This document is divided into three main sections: "The Agrarian Problem in Guatemala," "Theological Reflections," and "Pastoral Conclusions." (It follows the now traditional method of "*see, judge, act*" as we are doing in each chapter of this book.) At the time of its writing, the Guatemalan population numbered about eight million, of which approximately 60% considered themselves to be indigenous Mayans with original rights to all the land and with a millennial culture that prior to the *conquista* surpassed in many ways the European culture. Particularly eloquent are the following introductory paragraphs:

> The clamor for land is, without doubt, the loudest, most dramatic, and most desperate cry heard in Guatemala today. It springs from the hearts of millions of Guatemalans who not only are anxious to possess land, but who also want to be possessed by the land. They are "*Hombres de Maiz*," People of Corn, who feel strongly identified with the furrows, the sowing, and the harvest, yet at the same time they find themselves dispossessed of the land and prevented from uniting themselves with its fertile furrows due to a situation of injustice and sin.
>
> The people are like strangers in the land which has belonged to them for thousands of years, and they are considered second-class citizens in the nation which their heroic ancestors forged.
>
> Perhaps no other theme awakens such inflamed passions and provokes such radical and irreconcilable attitudes as the ownership of the land. Nevertheless, this is a subject which must be faced if we wish to resolve, even partially, the grave problems which confront us. (Episcopado Guatemalteco, 1988, p. 1)

We believe this document resonates with the message of the Old Testament prophets. It identifies the problem of the land as a concern of the Word of God and the exclusion of the Mayan peasants from their land as an act of sin. It denounces this situation of injustice and calls for fundamental change, which we have called repentance, turning around.

> In compliance with our mission as pastors we wish to point out once again the grave conditions in which the vast majority of Guatemalans in the rural areas live. Justly described as inhuman, this poverty is expressed in the high levels of illiteracy and mortality, lack of housing adequate for the dignity of the family, unemployment, underemployment, malnutrition, and other ills which have plagued us for many years.
>
> Once again we clearly state that this painful reality of poverty— and in many cases misery—which we see with the eyes of pastors, causes a deep questioning within ourselves. In essence, we feel questioned because these harmful inequalities between those who enjoy the possession of the fruits of the land, often to excess, and those who

possess nothing or nearly nothing not only daily increase the immense gap between the rich and poor, but because this takes place within a people who confess and consider themselves to be Christians.

This is not the first time that we Bishops of Guatemala condemn this situation as essentially unjust and contrary to God's Plan of Salvation. Nor is this the first time we state that this situation is the greatest challenge in the present historical moment, and that the marginalization which so many human beings suffer challenges us as persons and as Christians. In our previous pastoral letters we have pointed out, in light of the Gospel, that such a deplorable and dramatic situation does not just happen; rather, it is the result of a sinful structure, which impedes a radical solution to the problem. (ibid., p. 2)

This section of the pastoral letter continues with a historical review of the problem of the land in Guatemala from the time of the *conquista* to the present, which has resulted not only in great inequality and poverty but also in inhuman exploitation of the *campesinos*, massive migration to the cities, and growing violence throughout the country. The theological section is made up primarily of references to biblical texts and the early church Fathers. The final pastoral section calls for solidarity, integral development, and a fundamental change of structures without violence but with an adequate legal, legislative framework. The conclusion includes the following:

We have attempted . . . to illuminate this reality with the Word of God and with the Magisterium of the Church, thus demonstrating that this subject is not outside our field of work as pastors of the Church. Neither the sufferings nor the errors of the people who have confided in us could be outside our area of concern. . . .

Our pastoral invitation is directed with urgency to the Government, political parties, productive sector, communications media, and to the private business sector, as well as to the Catholic lay movements, *campesinos*, and indigenous, that they join forces peacefully and fraternally in a project which demands the commitment of all Guatemalans.

We recognize that the most difficult problem is personal conversion. Conversion signifies "turning around," to change radically. As long as one maintains as the only goal increased profit, earnings, enrichment, or the ambition for money or power, it is impossible to understand the truths which we have recognized and to see with a Christian vision the reality which must be transformed. (ibid., pp. 25–26)

Peace accords between the Guatemalan government and the Guatemalan National Revolutionary Unity (URNG) were finally signed on December 29, 1996, almost nine years after this pastoral letter was published. The armed confrontation of thirty-six years is over, the civil patrols have been disbanded, a United Nations mission has published their investigation of past atrocities, and commissions are working out plans for the implementation of specific agreements. But the "war against the poor" continues. Unemployment has reached 70%; only 36% of the population has access to health care; generalized violence, including kidnappings and murders, is worse than ever; police and judicial forces are totally inadequate; and public lynchings are on the rise. There can be no genuine peace in Guatemala until the prophetic voice of the bishops is heeded.

As we were working on this manuscript, we learned of the brutal assassination of Bishop Juan Gerardi, who had served the diocese of Quiché during the height of government and military repression and who had just two days earlier, on April 24, 1998, delivered the report of an archdiocesan commission on human rights violations, over which he had presided. The title of that report—like earlier reports of repression from Argentina, Brazil, and Uruguay—was *Nunca Más* ("Never Again"). According to the exhaustive research of Gerardi's team, which fills four volumes (1,400 pages), 90% of the 150,000 people killed during the thirty-six years of counterinsurgency were defenseless civilians, 75% of them Mayan Indians. The testimonies of horror by families of the disappeared, tortured, and assassinated beggar the imagination. Gerardi's redemptive purpose in pursuing this task was "to break the chains of silence" and "the reign of impunity" as a necessary step toward national reconciliation and genuine peace. His tragic death has once again brought the attention of the world to Guatemala's continuing predicament, and it raises the macabre question whether in fact the martyrdom of innocent peoples and their advocates will happen never again.

The *National Catholic Reporter* of March 12, 1999, cites the Gerardi report and reports extensively on the more recent 3,500-page U.N. report, "Guatemala: Memory of Silence," compiled by the Commission for Historical Clarification. This report documents 42,275 cases of human rights violations out of a total of 200,000 killed or disappeared, 93% committed by "state forces and allied paramilitary groups, 3% by insurgent forces, and the remaining 4% by others." It accuses the U.S. government, the CIA, and U.S. private companies of promoting a Cold War ideology and direct military assistance as the repression against the Mayan population reached genocidal proportions. The report's statistics reveal that there was no real threat of a communist takeover. The "National Security Doctrine" was simply used to deter any and all efforts against Guatemala's autocratic, racist, and oppressive socioeconomic order (Roberts, 1999, pp. 13–16).

4 ✦ ✦ ✦ ✦ ✦ ✦ ✦

Sabbath Economics, Jubilee Spirituality, and Liberty for All

Having focused on the abuse of land, labor, and life, we now want to consider, as we began to do in Chapter 2, the alternatives emerging within or outside today's dominant socioeconomic system, then deepen our understanding of the biblical Sabbath–Jubilee mandates for equality and solidarity, and finally consider our own responsibility for the working out of these mandates in our lives and work. There are in fact many alternatives in today's world, despite the progressive centralization and globalization of the dominant system, so there is no reason for fatalistic inaction, at least at the local level. The Jubilee vision itself, though its roots go back to the early experiences of the tribes of Yahweh, emerged after the destruction of Jerusalem and exile of her leaders, as they considered the possibility of returning and creating the just social order that God had originally intended for God's people. All of this tells us that we too are being called and enabled to live and work for a similar vision. So we ask ourselves:

- ✦ What are those alternative socioeconomic possibilities that can challenge and change the dominant reality of our time?
- ✦ What were the essential components of the Sabbath–Jubilee mandates as the people of Israel entered into a new opportunity to fulfill the divine utopia following the exile?
- ✦ How can we be faithful stewards of our own lives, churches, and societies in the ongoing struggle for fullness of life for all God's people and all God's creation?

Today's World ✦ ✦ ✦ ✦ ✦

Our starting point here, as in the previous chapters, is a recognition that the present socioeconomic order we are living in—locally, nationally, globally—is bringing about increasingly intolerable levels of poverty, exclusion, and death. Furthermore, this order is becoming increasingly totalitarian; it is less and less subject to genuine democratic participation; it is ruled by market dynamics that give full priority to wealth accumulation, not to people nor the environment. We know that millions of people die each year as a result, more than have ever died due to wars, plagues, and other disasters. We know that the future of all living things is being threatened due to the persistence of this market-centered, profit-driven, socioeconomic order. The genius of this system is its ability to gain the support or voluntary submission of such a wide population base, not just the rich but virtually everyone who has money and can accumulate goods, even those with little wealth. We cannot however let it delude us into believing that somehow things will turn out all right. Ulrich Duchrow puts it this way:

> Today we have reached a point where at least two thirds of the world's population are either dying of hunger or living on or below the poverty line. These people are subsequently excluded from the formal economy. From an environmental point of view, our planet and the basic conditions for life will be destroyed if the transformation of nature into commodities-money for the purpose of wealth accumulation continues to accelerate and intensify. It is, therefore, imperative that the focus of the economy be shifted from money accumulation to the people's needs. (Duchrow, 1995, p. 233)

Emerging Alternatives

Whether we choose to work outside the present socioeconomic order or try to modify it, we must consider what alternatives there are, however small they may be, so that we can truly struggle for life and not simply continue to collaborate with the system that is so deadly for others and for ourselves. We must look for alternatives that are life-sustaining rather than profit-producing, that serve real needs rather than ever-increasing desires, that reverse the polarization of rich and poor for the real benefit of all—to enable us to become more human, not more wealthy.

Duchrow provides an extensive list of alternatives that offer the possibility of resisting and even transforming the dominant economic system for the benefit of people and the environment. Following is a brief summary of those alternatives (ibid., pp. 254–277).

◆ Most people believe that business enterprises must grow and increase profits in order to exist and that competition makes concern for labor, the environment, and social benefits difficult or impossible to maintain. These assumptions are not always true. Some companies today make their appeal to investors, employees, and consumers on the basis of these very concerns.

◆ Western technology tends to be capital intensive, expensive, and environmentally damaging, but there are efforts, particularly among Third World countries, to use alternative technologies that encourage local people to organize and take into account their cultural values and resources.

◆ Western agriculture maximizes growth and profit, eliminates small farmers, damages the soil and drinking water, and undercuts Third World farming. In recent years there has been much discussion and promotion of "sustainable agriculture," which gives priority to local communities, small farms, food security, stable income, and renewable resources.

◆ Even banking can offer alternatives to the predominant concern for wealth accumulation. In recent years, some banks have responded to investors' concerns about military industries, the nuclear threat, the destruction of the environment, human rights violations, child labor, and sex tourism. Savers may in future be able not only to direct banks in the use of their money but also choose to receive no interest so that the poor might receive cheaper loans.

◆ At the level of world trade, giant corporations continue to increase their overall domination of markets and production, but there are movements to alert the public about abusive employment practices, deceptive advertising, and unfair competition, on the one hand, and alternative trade networks based on solidarity, fair trade shops, and local credit systems, on the other.

◆ Consumers still play a major role in the dominant economic system, and we have seen the success of consumer boycott campaigns against goods produced under apartheid in South Africa and against Nestlé because of its promotion of infant formula throughout the Third World. Churches and other organizations can do much more to educate their members and the public in general to be more responsible consumers.

◆ Faced with growing income inequality in the world, in our own society, in our businesses and professions, and even in our churches, we can ask about possibilities for alternative income distribution, beginning with our own salaries.

◆ Over against the logic of the dominant economic system, some efforts are being made to open up communication, networks, and alliances for solidarity rather than competition, human concerns rather than profit, ecological wholeness rather than growth. These efforts are mostly small and unimpressive, working primarily at the grassroots level, but they can become seeds for change at other levels.

Toward a Vision of an Economy of Life

The common New Testament and Greek Old Testament word for house or household is *oíkos* or *oíkía*. It refers not just to the physical house but also the home, the family and all its belongings, the household with all its inhabitants. It may even refer to their well-being and their environment. "House of God" can mean the Temple, the family of God, or God's people.

The household, in its basic sense, is intended to gather, cover, sustain, and protect the life of its inhabitants. The inhabitants in turn have the responsibility to take care of their household for the good of all. This concept has become one of the key concerns of the ecumenical movement, most notably the World Council of Churches. The root word *oíkos* appears in three Greek words that represent three major areas of concern for the global human household:

oíkouméne = household, inhabited earth, *ecumenism*
oíkonomía = plan, administration, stewardship, *economy*
oíkología = nature, environment, ecosystem, *ecology*

The modern *ecumenical* movement is concerned with the unity of the church and the unity of humankind; that is, with the building of a household in which all can live in peace, in community, without barriers or prejudices, as God's family. The *economy* is concerned with the planning, administration, and stewardship of the household (family, community, nation, and world) so that all its inhabitants can obtain what they need and live with dignity. *Ecology* is dedicated to the preservation of the environment, nature, and the resources that will secure the future of our ecosystem and our descendents. Thus *oíkos* is centered in the promotion and defense of life.

Much needed today is a debate about the meaning and purpose of property. In his book, *God the Economist*, Douglas Meeks explains that the concept of property has a varied history. It is not a fixed concept but changes according to the ideologies and social and political structures of each time and place. It was not too long ago, after all, that property in the United States could include other human beings. All societies recognize to some degree the right to *exclusive private property*—toothbrush, clothes, bed, and so on. In many societies this right is extended to include a house and all its belongings, one or more vehicles, bank accounts and investments, and the like.

Today's predominant free market ideology expands even more the concept of exclusive private property, absolutizing it to the point at which individuals can do whatever they want with their property without feeling any responsibility for others. The rich and powerful can control the land and use its fruits merely for their own enrichment; they can monopolize the means of production with little concern for the workers; they can manage the economy in such a way that the majority of the population is unemployed and the poor do not have access to the minimum necessities of life. In fact much of what we see in television, films, periodicals, and pulp novels celebrates and glorifies the selfish excesses of the rich.

All societies also have some concept of *inclusive community property*, to which all their members, citizens, or inhabitants should have access. Most aboriginal communities held and used the land in common for pasture, hunting, fishing, and so on. Today almost all countries offer some system of public education, health services, roads, and parks. Socialism has attempted to create equal access to housing, education, health care, recreation, culture, and material goods through centralized planning and state ownership of the means of production. The failure of Soviet socialism leaves us with this question: How might those goals be taken up from a different ideological and political base, so that our national and global economic system might be redirected to serve the common good?

Overcoming the Great Divorce

One of the greatest obstacles to Christian participation in social and economic issues is the divorce that is made between the "material" and "spiritual" dimensions of life. We know that the Hebrew understanding of reality did not make such a radical distinction but rather treated life holistically. God created humankind out of clay by breathing into that clay air/wind/spirit (*ruah*), and it became a living person. When a person died, the air/wind/spirit left. Spirit and living body were one. As noted already, the founding experience of Israel as people of Yahweh was the Exodus, the liberation of the Hebrew slaves from Egypt, which has remained down through history, for Jews and Christians, as faith in a God who continues to liberate from social, economic, political, and military bondage—not just from personal sin.

The whole biblical story stands in marked contrast to the later and modern "spiritualization" of the history of salvation and the continuing divorce of socioeconomic concerns from personal piety and collective worship. It calls us to Sabbath economics and Jubilee spirituality, by means of which we are to struggle for life and liberty for all.

Likewise the Christian Scriptures do not teach the immortality of the soul but rather the resurrection of the body. The incarnation is an affirmation of spirit and body together. Paul tells us in Romans 8 that there is a dichotomy, not between spirit and matter but between spirit and flesh, which is carnality in the sense of sinful, selfish desire. So he speaks of the carnal mind, not carnal matter, and of the struggle within ourselves, mind and body, to serve God or mammon, good or evil, life or death. To be led by the Spirit of God is to struggle for life and peace, *shalom*, integral well-being.

With the rise of Gnosticism in the early church and later with Neoplatonism, this integral understanding of life and reality gave way to a dualism that not only separated spirit and matter but elevated the former over the latter. After the manner of Plato and his successors, the world of the spirit—ideas, the ideal—became the supreme reality, and the world of matter—the body, the physical—became a mere shadow of that other world. So the aim of idealists and Christians alike was to suppress the body and its desires and elevate the importance of intellectual and "spiritual" matters, to depreciate physical labor and exalt music and art, to debase sexuality and elevate worship and prayer. This led to the focus on eternal life in heaven as the ultimate goal of temporal life on Earth and thus to value piety over physical work and pleasure. It became the rationale for tolerating, minimizing, and even justifying the common sufferings of people in this life in favor of seeking and proclaiming the glories of the afterlife.

For almost fifty years of the twentieth century, this dualism of the "spiritual" versus the "material" was used to undergird the Cold War ideology of the "free" world versus the "communist" world, because Marxists denied the existence of God and affirmed the supremacy of matter. In Latin America we discovered that the wars of repression against Marxist-led insurrections and popular movements served principally to maintain the social and economic structures of oppression and exploitation for the benefit of local elites and foreign investors. In Central America, which became a primary battleground for U.S. hegemony in the 1980s, military strategists spoke of "low intensity conflict" and "the battle for the hearts and minds" of the Central American peoples and also of the people of the United States, who had to be indoctrinated to support the terrible massacres perpetrated in their name and paid for with their tax dollars. This explains why close advisors of Presidents Reagan and Bush singled out Latin American Liberation Theology as a primary enemy, why U.S. and Latin American military leaders undertook the study of this theology, and why conservative think tanks in Washington, D.C., generated polemic attacks against it.

The greatest potential for overcoming the great material/spiritual divide probably lies in the growing challenge of gender, arising from the women's movements but equally pertinent for women and men. The perspective of gender includes the biological but goes on to the psycho-social-spiritual dimensions of human self-understanding and cosmovision. Women theologians and others have already made great strides, through sharing at the most elemental levels and analysis at the most theoretical levels, toward a new, holistic vision of life in its day-by-day expressions and in its widest contexts. The long-standing denigration of body and sexuality, of women and their traditional roles, of physical labor and menial chores is changing as women (and some men) recover for all of us the dignity and beauty and pleasure of all God's creation. Gender analysis is leading us to question the rationale of market-centered ideologies that reduce life to production and consumption commodities, to deemphasize hierarchies and promote power sharing, to recover more fundamental values of our humanity, and to discover new ways to understand and struggle for justice and peace and the integrity of creation.

Biblical Faith ◆ ◆ ◆ ◆ ◆

We turn now to the biblical Jubilee, which can help us understand the struggle for life in ancient times and today and also find our place in that struggle. We shall begin with a short summary of the exile experience and the restoration following the Decree of Cyrus in 538 B.C. Clearly both the experience of exile and the return from Babylon offered enormous challenges to the people of Israel to review and renew their self-understanding, their fundamental values, and their worldview as people of Yahweh. This was the context in which the various narrative and legislative traditions of the Pentateuch came together, were reedited and compiled, and took final form. Second, we shall give special attention to the Deuteronomic and Priestly traditions, which played the major roles in this process and in the final formulation of the main Sabbath and Jubilee texts. Third, we shall give some attention to the Isaiah traditions, particularly the reference to "the year of the Lord's favor" in Isaiah 61:1–2, which becomes a key text in Luke's account of Jesus' ministry. Finally, we shall consider the matter of royalty and the royal proclamations of release or liberation that closely parallel the Sabbath–Jubilee mandates. In all four sections we will give some attention to detail, but our main purpose will be to identify and interpret the basic intention of the Sabbath–Jubilee mandates for Israel and later for Jesus and the Christian church.

Exile and Return—The Renewed Search for an Alternative Social Possibility

The destruction of Jerusalem, including the Temple, and the deportation of the leaders of Judah to Babylon had enormous consequences. The exile is usually dated 587 or 586 to 538 B.C., but the history of that period is complex. The first major deportation actually took place in 598 when King Jehoiachin and many officials, warriors, artisans, and elites were taken to Babylon by King Nebuchadnezzar and given certain recognition in his court. The worst destruction took place in 587, but another deportation to Babylon took place in 582. Many Israelites fled to neighboring lands and Egypt. So the majority of the Jews came to live outside of Judah and Jerusalem, leaving behind primarily poor laborers and peasant farmers. "Now that the monarchy had disappeared, the village- and family-based networks of cooperation and support were able to reemerge and strengthen themselves. These systems of organization and identity became an important part of the foundation upon which Jewish life and community would be rebuilt" (Ceresko, 1992, p. 221).

An estimated 20,000 Jews were living in exile in Babylon. They "included the bulk of the ruling classes and important families of Judah and Jerusalem. They may have been settled in isolated or abandoned areas that needed rebuilding and development" (ibid., p. 222). Evidently they were able to maintain their identity by living together in families and communities and by having their deposed king and his family as official representatives before the Babylonian court. This was the prophet Jeremiah's recommendation to the exiles in Babylon:

> *Build houses and live in them; plant gardens and eat what they produce. Take wives and have sons and daughters; take wives for your*

*sons, and give your daughters in marriage, that they may bear sons
and daughters; multiply there, and do not decrease. But seek the welfare of the city where I have sent you into exile, and pray to the Lord
on its behalf, for in its welfare you will find your welfare.*

Jeremiah 29:5–7

Apparently the deported Jews were able to prosper and multiply under
Babylonian and later Persian exile. When they had the opportunity to return
to the Promised Land and rebuild Jerusalem, many stayed behind, but they
provided leadership and financial support for those who returned.

Whereas Babylon imposed its rule over conquered nations by destroy-
ing their power centers and deporting their people, especially the ruling
elites, King Cyrus of Persia, who overthrew Babylon in 539 B.C., offered a
greater degree of self-rule and encouraged local customs and religious practices. It was to his advantage to have voluntary support of local leaders, and
it was to their advantage, given the balance of regional power, to accept limited autonomy in return for Persian recognition and support. Shortly after
his victory over Babylon, Cyrus issued a decree allowing the Jews to return
to Judah, to rebuild the Temple, to support the return through contributions
of gold and silver, to take with them the gold and silver vessels taken from
Jerusalem in 587, and even to receive a contribution from the Persian treas-
ury for the rebuilding of the Temple.

The return to and restoration of Jerusalem took place in stages over at
least the next 100 years. The first group of returning exiles set out from
Babylon in 538 B.C. under Sheshbazzar, who may have been one of King Jehoiachin's sons. The second group, probably much larger, left in 520 B.C.
under Zerubbabel as civil governor and Joshua as high priest with plans for
rebuilding the Temple in Jerusalem. By 515 B.C. the new structure was dedicated, and regular worship and sacrifices were resumed. In 445 B.C. Nehemiah was named governor and sent back with the purpose of rebuilding
the walls of Jerusalem, repopulating the city by gathering people from the
countryside, and reforming the Temple worship. Sometime later the priest
and scribe Ezra returned with the task of establishing the Torah as the official law of the land. Nehemiah 8 describes the assembly at which the Law
was proclaimed by Ezra. What he read that day may have been the then-
completed Pentateuch or the Holiness Code portion in Leviticus 17–26
(Ceresko, 1992, p. 248).

The following notes on the formation of the Pentateuch are based on
Anthony Ceresko's summary. We can assume that the four main strands,
traditionally identified as J-Yahwist, E-Elohist, D-Deuteronomist, and P-
Priestly, all reach back into Israel's mythic heritage from the time of the
tribes of Yahweh following the Exodus and Sinai and settlement in the
Promised Land around 1230 B.C.

The Yahwist material (J) was probably developed by a scribe or advi-
sor of Solomon's court (962–922 B.C.). Stories and traditions were

gathered and knit together as a "kind of national epic for the recently created monarchy" (ibid., p. 52).

Following the death of Solomon, the monarchy broke into the two kingdoms—Israel in the north and Judah in the south—and the Elohist (E) material emerged in the north, probably between 900 and 850 B.C. Its purpose was to provide another national epic that would focus on Israel as a covenant people and give less emphasis to Jerusalem and the institution of monarchy in the south (ibid., p. 63).

With the destruction of the Northern Kingdom by Assyria and the deportation of its people in 722 B.C., the E material was taken to the south and incorporated into the framework of the J epic, especially where it provided different traditions and perspectives (ibid., p. 64). Legal material developed in the north, D, also migrated to the south during that period and came together as the Book of Deuteronomy. The core, Chapters 12–26, has been called the Deuteronomic Code and identified with King Josiah's reform in 622 B.C. (ibid., p. 65).

The Priestly source, P, is a collection of the legal traditions of the Southern Kingdom. It may well incorporate material going back to the tribal period, but it is usually dated in the latter years of the Babylonian exile and the early years of the return under Persian rule (500–450 B.C.). With the loss of national autonomy, Israel's history and identity focused more on the family and the Temple. "It is the latter, the priesthood and the sacrificial ritual of the Temple, which particularly stamped and shaped the traditional materials that had been accumulating and from which the P traditionist would finally create what we know as the Pentateuch" (ibid., p. 65).

With this summary as background, we turn now to the principal Sabbath and Jubilee passages found in Deuteronomy and Leviticus, respectively. These passages clearly represent central concerns of the D and P traditions at critical moments in the history of the people of Yahweh: at the close of the monarchy, both north and south, and at the time of the exile and return. At such momentous times the people of Israel had to renew their identity and their commitment to the God who had both intervened on their behalf, freeing them from Egypt and giving them the Promised Land, and sent terrible judgment upon them for their betrayal of the covenant.

The Deuteronomic and Priestly Traditions—The Sabbath Year and the Jubilee Year

The Deuteronomic Tradition. The Deuteronomic history was originally a collection of books running from the Book of Deuteronomy through 2 Kings, but later the Book of Deuteronomy was separated from that collection and added to Genesis through Numbers to form the Pentateuch. Jeffries M. Hamilton, whose thesis, *Social Justice and Deuteronomy: The Case of Deuteronomy 15*, we will use in this section, states that

Deuteronomy displays a particular concern for those who have none of the built-in supports which Israelite society normally provided—specifically those supports provided by one's tribe and family. This concern is expressed through the oft-repeated refrain which points to the widow, the orphan, and the sojourner as objects of particular concern. This humanitarian tendency is present in Deuteronomy 15 as well, which, though it holds out the ideal of a land without poverty (15:4), recognizes that it is the ongoing existence of the poor which causes the law to be given (15:7,11). (Hamilton, 1992, pp. 2–3)

This peculiar concern for social justice is evident throughout the following books of the Deuteronomic history, the Prophets, especially Jeremiah and Isaiah, and on into the New Testament, especially the Gospels. The beginning and ending of Deuteronomy, Chapters 1–3 and 31–34,

create a book which self-consciously places the portrait of the ideal society imparted in the legal corpus in a specific historical moment: the gathering of the people of YHWH on the plains of Moab, just on the brink of the Promised Land. This literary artifice serves to place the Torah before the people at a moment of decision. Deuteronomy asks what will be the appearance of the nation of God's people which is about to come into being. The History which follows tells the story of what happens after God's people have their land. (ibid., p. 3)

Deuteronomy 15 contains the Sabbath Year laws of release: the remission of debts and the freeing of slaves every seven years.

Every seventh year you shall grant a remission of debts.
Deuteronomy 15:1

If a member of your community, whether a Hebrew man or a Hebrew woman, is sold to you and works for you for six years, in the seventh year you shall set that person free.   Deuteronomy 15:12

Hamilton makes several detailed observations about the entire passage to show that it is not simply a rehearsal of laws but a powerful rhetoric to bring out the reason and importance of these laws, to show how Israelite society should operate and why it should operate that way, to state the laws with their consequences, and to persuade hearers/readers to fulfill these covenant responsibilities. The foundation for these mandates is, as we have noted previously, God's liberation of the Hebrew slaves from Egypt. This is stated explicitly in relation to the second mandate, concerning slavery, in verse 15: "Remember that you were a slave in the land of Egypt, and the Lord your God redeemed you; for this reason I lay this command upon you today." It is stated indirectly, but no less powerfully, in relation to the first mandate, concerning debts, in verse 9: "Your neighbor might cry to the Lord against you, and you would incur guilt"—just as they themselves had cried out against their taskmasters in Egypt and the Lord heard their cry, delivered them, and punished their taskmasters.

The conditions and purpose for the law regarding remission of debts in the Sabbath Year, Deuteronomy 15:1–11, are expressed in the ideal society set forth in verses 4–6:

> *There will, however, be no one in need among you, because the Lord is sure to bless you in the land that the Lord your God is giving you as a possession to occupy, if only you will obey the Lord your God by diligently observing this entire commandment that I command you today. When the Lord your God has blessed you, as he promised you, you will lend to many nations, but you will not borrow; you will rule over many nations, but they will not rule over you.*

The purpose is that there be no poor; all will have their needs met. For that to happen, God's blessing is crucial, and for God to bless, Israel must keep this commandment. As we have noted many times, failure to fulfill covenant obligations led to God's judgment and resulted in destruction and exile.

The following paragraph, verses 7–11, explains the purpose of this mandate, the expected attitude for its fulfillment, and the positive and negative consequences. The concern is to build a socioeconomic order in which the needs of the poor are met. At the beginning of this passage this concern is expressed with the conditional clause, "If there is among you anyone in need. . . ." It ends with the clause, "Since there will never cease to be some in need on the earth. . . ." The mandate to remit debts at the time of the Sabbath Year is precisely to resolve this situation. It is a commandment from the Lord who gave them the land (v. 7), who responded to their cry in Egypt (v. 9). Obedience to this mandate must come from the heart, as noted in the following expressions:

> *do not be hard-hearted or tight-fisted toward your needy neighbor*
> (v. 7)

> *open your hand, willingly lending enough to meet the need* (v. 8)

> *be careful that you do not entertain a mean thought* (v. 9)

> *give liberally and be ungrudging* (v. 10)

> *open your hand to the poor and needy neighbor in your land* (v. 11)

The positive consequence is this: "On this account the Lord your God will bless you in all your work and in all that you undertake" (v. 10). The consequence of disobedience is insinuated by the reminder of Israel's original experience of deliverance: "Your neighbor might cry to the Lord against you, and you would incur guilt" (v. 9).

The mandate to release slaves at the Sabbath Year, Deuteronomy 15:12–18, is founded, as we have noted, on the deliverance of the slaves from Egypt:

> *Remember that you were a slave in the land of Egypt, and the Lord your God redeemed you; for this reason I lay this command upon you today.* (v. 15)

Insofar as the people of Israel owe their own freedom, indeed their very existence, to God's intervention, they must obey God's mandates. Insofar as they were liberated from slavery, they must likewise free the slaves among them, and if they do so "the Lord your God will bless you in all that you do" (v. 18). The implied intention is that there will be no slaves and no poor in Hebrew society. Thus the slaves set free in the Sabbath Year are not to be sent away empty-handed, which might well result in a return to slavery, but rather they are to be given liberally of the flocks, grains, and wine that they helped to produce, so that they might be self-sufficient.

However advanced the release laws of Deuteronomy 15 must have been among the peoples of the ancient Near East, they present a serious problem for modern readers, because they do not apply to aliens, and they do not eliminate entirely the practice of slavery even among Hebrews. Jeffries Hamilton explores this matter at some length and proposes the following elements for consideration. He notes that Deuteronomy 23:15–16 presents the case of escaped slaves in basic tension with the manumission law of Deuteronomy 15:12–18, for here no distinction is made between Hebrews and aliens; all slaves shall be free and not be returned to their owners; thus the institution of slavery is itself undermined. Moreover this text indicates that they may choose to live "wherever they please," which is language that "Deuteronomy normally reserves for God's choosing of the divine dwelling-place" (Hamilton, 1991, p. 118).

The release laws of the Sabbath Year point to an ideology of social justice in which *inclusion* of the poor, the indebted, the slave is central. The remission of debts and the liberation of slaves are essential means to overcome the usual tendencies toward *exclusion*. Peasant farmers lived under the perpetual risk of losing their crops, falling into debt, losing their land, and ending in slavery. Wealthy and powerful elites tended to look for opportunities to extend their land holdings and accumulate more wealth by exploiting the plight of these poor farmers, offering loans at high interest, taking their land as failed mortgages, and enslaving them as bond servants. This predicament could to a large extent be resolved if Israel would obey the Lord God who saved them from slavery in Egypt.

In Deuteronomy the concern for aliens, orphans, and widows is ultimately a concern for the fidelity of all God's people in the creation of that new, alternative social possibility going back to the Exodus and the giving of the Promised Land. A key to that alternative socioeconomic order is the inclusion, restoration, and reinstatement of the poor to fullness of life in the community. The disadvantaged and vulnerable members of God's people are not to be marginalized and forgotten, as usually has happened throughout history. They are to be drawn back into full participation in concrete fulfillment of Yahweh's demand for justice. This is one of the central concerns of Deuteronomic Law or spirituality.

The Priestly Tradition. The Priestly Tradition, with sources going back to premonarchic Israel, brought the Pentateuch to final form during the critical periods of the exile and restoration, ending by 400 B.C. In his book, *Land Tenure and the Biblical Jubilee: Uncovering Hebrew Ethics through the Sociology of Knowledge*, Jeffrey Fager comments on the social function of the priestly writings:

> The purpose of P is basically threefold: (1) to preserve the ancient traditions now endangered by the Babylonian conquest, (2) to explain that conquest in terms of divine punishment, and (3) to provide a foundation for proper living in the future (as is especially seen in P's use of the Holiness Code). The Jubilee land laws were used by P to perform this threefold function in the social milieu of the exile for the sake of the community and in order to promote some of their own interests. (Fager, 1993, p. 52)

As we have seen, it is very likely that the roots of Sabbath and Jubilee legislation go back to the early experience of the tribes of Yahweh and their decentralized political economy based on the family, clan, and tribe and centered in the Liberator-God who required them to reject the surrounding models of wealth accumulation and slavery and to institute practices that would protect the life and well-being of the large peasant population. These ideals were reformulated at critical moments in Israel's history, and the Priestly Tradition played an important role in maintaining these mandates as sacred, not just civil, obligations. The destruction of Jerusalem and the Babylonian exile produced an unprecedented disruption of every dimension of Israel's life and worldview. When the possibility of a return to the Promised Land under Persian rule became a reality, the priests played a major role in the recreation of Israel's identity, cult, and socioeconomic practice.

The principal Jubilee passage is Leviticus 25, a key text from the Holiness Code. This passage includes portions concerning the Sabbath Year (vv. 1–7 and 18–22), but the rest concerns the Jubilee Year. It may of course be that Jubilee originally referred to seven-year cycles and later to forty-nine- or fifty-year cycles. In any case the remarkable addition in Leviticus 25 is the mandate that would permit every Israelite to return to his or her land and home at the time of Jubilee. This mandate completes the socioeconomic intention of the Sabbath release laws of Deuteronomy 15, that is, the reversal of the mechanisms of wealth accumulation and marginalization. Not only should debts be remitted and slaves freed but the land itself, the fundamental basis for agrarian life, should be returned to all the families of Israel. Every fifty years the good news of Jubilee was to be proclaimed on the Day of Atonement as "liberty throughout the land to all its inhabitants" (Leviticus 25:10).

> Even if those peasants who lost their land were able to sell their labor to the large landowners, landless agricultural workers typically earn smaller incomes than landowning peasants. In addition, the landless are much more vulnerable to destitution in periods of crisis than those who farm their own land. With all of this, it appears certain that the peasant farmers were severely hurt under the Canaanite economic system that viewed land as a commodity rather than a birthright. Thus, the Jubilee did not present a merely ideological alternative to one particular system; it was a countermeasure to a system that provided wealth for a few at the expense of many. It attempted to restrict the latifundism [large land holding] which was prevalent in the ancient Near East in order to keep the means of production evenly distributed among independent families. Possibly because of that prevalence, the Jubilee recognized the constant threat of the loss of land, so it established a means of regaining the proper balance. (Fager, 1993, p. 88)

With the return from exile and the rebuilding of Jerusalem, the Jews had to deal with conflicting interests even among their own people. The poor families that had remained on the land following the Babylonian invasions had no doubt occupied many properties other than their own. Some of those returning from exile deportations represented the former elites and officialdom of Jerusalem with corresponding expectations. The priests themselves played a central role in the reestablishment of Temple worship as the central focus of Israel's life and may have played a central role also in the distribution of the land. Their literary work in formulating the P material and integrating the other strands served to reinforce the sacred nature of the Sabbath and Jubilee mandates.

> The provisions of the Jubilee are not merely civil regulations carried out in the normal process of human government, but they are carried out within the confines of sacred time as an act of religious righteousness before God. The cultic nature of the Jubilee expresses the notion that proper ownership by God entails acts which benefit the poor. The implementation of the belief in an equitable distribution of the land is a sacred act defined by proper rituals and times that express its holiness. The fact that the priests turned the Jubilee into cultic law reinforced by the motive clause "I am the Lord your God" removed the issue of land tenure from the realm of economic expediency and introduced it into that of divine interest. The priests intended to make the issue of land tenure one of cosmic importance, the neglect of which would court a return to chaos. (ibid., p. 107)

The spiritual–theological foundations of the Sabbath and Jubilee mandates in Leviticus 25 are definitive. They are divine mandates, as the text declares repeatedly:

v. 1   *The Lord spoke to Moses on Mount Sinai . . .*

v. 2   *the land that I am giving you . . .*

v. 2   *the land shall observe a Sabbath for the Lord . . .*

v. 4   *in the seventh year there shall be a Sabbath of complete rest for the land, a Sabbath for the Lord . . .*

v. 9   *on the Day of Atonement . . .*

v. 10   *you shall hallow the fiftieth year . . .*

v. 12   *it shall be holy to you . . .*

v. 17   *you shall fear your God; for I am the Lord your God.*

v. 18   *You shall observe my statutes and faithfully keep my ordinances . . .*

v. 21   *I will order my blessing for you in the sixth year . . .*

v. 23   *the land is mine; with me you are but aliens and tenants.*

v. 36   *fear your God . . .*

v. 38   *I am the Lord your God, who brought you out of the land of Egypt, to give you the land of Canaan, to be your God.*

v. 42   *For they are my servants, whom I brought out of the land of Egypt; they shall not be sold as slaves are sold.*

v. 43   *You shall not rule over them with harshness, but shall fear your God.*

v. 55   *For to me the people of Israel are servants; they are my servants whom I brought out from the land of Egypt: I am the Lord your God.*

These mandates form what we might today call a Jubilee spirituality. They establish how the people of God are to live in relation to each other, in community, in an alternative socioeconomic–spiritual order. They reject the dualistic separation of religion from the economics of real life and the complicity of religion in economic exploitation.

> The Jubilee repudiates the human tendency to divide sacred and profane realms within life so that parts of a person's or society's existence are matters of indifference to the deity. While economic systems are often legitimated by a community's religion, in practice the economy is allowed to progress independently from religious considerations. The Jubilee declares that what some consider "private" transactions do fall under the rule of God. In particular, persons' access to the means of survival—land—is watched over by God, and the maintenance of proper access for everyone is a religious obligation, not a matter of social choice or even economic expediency. (Fager, 1993, p. 114)

Like the Sabbath mandates, the Jubilee is concerned for the life of the poor and marginalized, but it is also concerned for the life of the entire community. The practice of social justice is a matter of the physical and spiritual well-being of all.

> Ultimately, an unequal distribution of land among the people is not only a matter of injustice, it threatens the survival of the whole community by bringing about the destruction of the framework upon which life itself can continue to exist. (ibid., p. 115)

This understanding is a rejection of the commodification of the land, of labor, and of life, which takes place in socioeconomic systems that prioritize the accumulation of wealth. With the equal distribution of the land among all the families of Judah, the Jubilee provides for their ongoing economic and social security. The Sabbath fallow year provides for the renewal of the earth and for those who work the land. The Jubilee mandate to return to the land provides for each family's identification with and respect for the land.

Following is a resume of Leviticus 25 based on Christopher Wright's article on the Jubilee in *The Anchor Bible Dictionary* (Wright, 1992, pp. 1025–1030). Verses 1–7 and 18–22 refer, as we have noted, to the Sabbath Year, an expansion of the fallow year of Exodus 23:10–11. Verses 8–12 announce the Jubilee Year and focus on the return of each Israelite to his or her property and family in the fiftieth year. Verses 13–17 are concerned with financial implications of the Jubilee Year, with the sale of land being calculated according to the number of harvests leading up to the fiftieth year. Verses 23–24 contain the heading and theological foundations for the remaining paragraphs, which provide practical details of redemption of the land and the Jubilee. Verses 25–55 focus on "three descending stages of poverty with required responses, interrupted by parenthetic sections dealing with homes in cities and Levite properties [29–34] and non-Israelite slaves [44–46]. The stages are marked off by the introductory phrase, 'If your brother becomes poor' " [vv. 25, 35, 39, 47] (ibid., p. 1026). To sort out the final part of the chapter, we have summarized Wright's outline.

> *vv. 25–28, Stage 1*—Hardship forces sale of land but nearest kinsman may preempt sale or redeem it; seller may redeem it; reverts to original owner at Jubilee
>
> *vv. 29–31, Exception (i)*—Not applicable to homes in walled cities because were not part of that productive economic base, but applicable to village dwellings
>
> *vv. 32–34, Exception (ii)*—Levites may benefit from redemption and Jubilee provisions
>
> *vv. 35–38, Stage 2*—Poverty deepens, kinsmen should maintain poor relation as dependent laborer with interest-free loans
>
> *vv. 39–43, Stage 3a*—Total economic collapse, must sell self and family as bonded servants to wealthier kinsman, should be treated as resi-

dent employee, at Jubilee freed with right to return to patrimony, make fresh start

vv. 44–46, Exception (iii)—Foreign slaves and resident aliens not included (not land holders)

vv. 47–55, Stage 3b—If debt bondage outside of clan, whole clan should redeem; non-Israelite creditor should keep same rules toward Israelite debtor; Jubilee applies. (ibid., pp. 1026–1027)

We believe that the social and theological and spiritual significance of the Sabbath and Jubilee mandates reaches far beyond the question about their historical application. Nevertheless that question does arise. There is no general record of systematic Sabbath Year and Jubilee practice in Israel, but there are many possible references. Some cite King Zedekiah's release of slaves in Jeremiah 34, which is tied to the seventh year mandate, but it was shortlived, and the slaves were returned to their masters. Ezekiel refers to the Year of Liberty or release in 46:16–18. Nehemiah 5 tells of a reform and restoration of land and houses and interest taken from the poor, but it makes no reference to the Sabbath Year or Jubilee. The Book of Jubilees (135–105 B.C.) uses a cycle of Sabbatical and Jubilee Years for the celebration of festivals but does not develop the corresponding mandates. Josephus makes several references to the fallow year and refers to the Jubilee in terms of land purchases.

It may be tempting to disqualify the Jubilee as utopian in the negative sense, because we cannot prove that it was ever practiced faithfully. It can, however, be affirmed as utopian in the positive sense, as a continuing challenge and vision for life according to God's clear intention for our lives. The principal Jubilee heritage is of course found in Isaiah 61:1–2a and its use by Jesus in Luke 4:18–19, which we shall consider further on.

The Isaiah Traditions

The Book of Isaiah is generally understood to be composed of three or four large blocks of material out of different periods with some common themes or concerns:

First Isaiah—Chapters 1–39
The Little Apocalypse—Chapters 24–29
Second Isaiah—Chapters 40–55
Third Isaiah—Chapters 56–66

In her landmark study, *Jesus, Liberation, and the Biblical Jubilee: Images for Ethics and Christology*, Sharon Ringe notes that the key reference to the Jubilee in Third Isaiah, 61:1–2, "gives evidence that Jubilee imagery was as much at home in the poetry of the visionaries as in the legislation of their rivals" (1985, p. 29). Third Isaiah deals with "the end of the exile and the need to restructure life in the community that had returned" (ibid., p. 28).

The key oracle concerning Jubilee is found in Isaiah 61:1–2, which is eschatological but not other-worldly:

> *The spirit of the Lord God is upon me,*
> *because the Lord has anointed me;*
> *he has sent me to bring good news to the oppressed,*
> *to bind up the brokenhearted,*
> *to proclaim liberty to the captives,*
> *and release to the prisoners,*
> *to proclaim the year of the Lord's favor,*
> *and the day of vengeance of our God,*
> *to comfort all who mourn.*

As is true of Third Isaiah in general, this text gathers themes and concerns rooted in Second Isaiah and also in Psalm 146, "where God is depicted as creator and as the sovereign who carries out the royal obligation of doing justice among the people, as well as in the Jubilee traditions found in Leviticus 25" (Ringe, 1985, pp. 29–30). The phrase, "to bring good news to the oppressed," can also be translated, "to bring good news to the poor," or even better, "to bring good news to the oppressed-poor." The phrase, "release to the prisoners," is an obscure construction in Hebrew and may be translated, "open the eyes of the blind," which is how it appears in Luke 4:18. The reference to the Jubilee is clear in the phrase, "to proclaim the year of the Lord's favor," though the Isaiah passage does not contain the specific Jubilee mandates concerning the remission of debts, return to the land of one's family, and the fallow year. The emphasis is clearly on liberation of the oppressed-poor, which, as we have seen, is the central concern of the Sabbath Year and Jubilee texts, Deuteronomy 15 and Leviticus 25.

> The blending of images in the fourth purpose clause, and their combination with those in the first three, leads to the conclusion that the beginning of God's eschatological reign is to be marked by the "proclamation of a release" from all the experiences of enslavement or imprisonment that characterize human life. (ibid., p. 30)

In his book, *God So Loved the Third World: The Bible, the Reformation, and Liberation Theologies*, Thomas Hanks notes that the Isaiah 61:1–2 passage as cited by Jesus in Luke 4:18–19 contains an additional phrase from Isaiah 58:6: "to let the oppressed go free" or "to send the oppressed away liberated." This could of course be a later scribal gloss, but Hanks insists that this was most likely the work of Jesus himself.

> The hypothesis I propose to defend here is that the insertion of Isaiah 58:6 in Isaiah 61:1–2 is best explained by recognizing that both of them reflect the teaching of Leviticus 25 concerning the Year of Jubilee, and that the originality and boldness exemplified in relating the two texts is best accounted for as reflecting Jesus' own exegetical insight and passion for *liberation*. (Hanks, 1983, p. 99)

It is interesting that Isaiah 58:1–12 is a Sabbath text—framed by references to the Sabbath in 58:13 and 56:2—and that the central concern of this passage is true fasting. "Although four other fasts began to be observed in the post-exilic period (Zechariah 7:3, 8:19), the only fast *commanded* in the Law is that of the Day of Atonement (Leviticus 26:29–31). The Year of Jubilee began precisely on that day (Leviticus 25:9), the day of fasting *par excellence*" (ibid., p. 99). The message of Isaiah 58:3–7 drives home the central Sabbath–Jubilee message and declares, as we found earlier, that religion without justice is rejected by the God who liberates.

> *Look, you serve your own interest on your fast day,*
> *and oppress all your workers.*
> *Look, you fast only to quarrel and to fight*
> *and to strike with a wicked fist.*
> *Such fasting as you do today*
> *will not make your voice heard on high.*
> *Is such the fast that I choose,*
> *a day to humble oneself?*
> *Is it to bow down the head like a bulrush,*
> *and to lie in sackcloth and ashes?*
> *Will you call this a fast,*
> *a day acceptable to the Lord?*
>
> *Is not this the fast that I choose:*
> *to loose the bonds of injustice,*
> *to undo the thongs of the yoke,*
> *to let the oppressed go free,*
> *and to break every yoke?*
> *Is it not to share your bread with the hungry,*
> *and bring the homeless poor into your house;*
> *when you see the naked, to cover them,*
> *and not to hide yourself from your own kin?*

The vision of that alternative socioeconomic order mandated in Sabbath–Jubilee legislation is also portrayed poetically by Third Isaiah in the utopian "new heavens and a new earth," 65:17–25:

> *For I am about to create new heavens*
> *and a new earth;*
> *the former things shall not be remembered*
> *or come to mind.*
> *But be glad and rejoice forever*
> *in what I am creating;*
> *for I am about to create Jerusalem as a joy,*
> *and its people as a delight.*
> *I will rejoice in Jerusalem,*
> *and delight in my people;*

no more shall the sound of weeping be heard in it,
 or the cry of distress.
No more shall there be in it
 an infant that lives but a few days,
 or an old person who does not live out a lifetime;
for one who dies at a hundred years will be considered a youth,
 and one who falls short of a hundred will be considered accursed.
They shall build houses and inhabit them;
 they shall plant vineyards and eat their fruit.
They shall not build and another inhabit;
 they shall not plant and another eat;
for like the days of a tree shall the days of my people be,
 and my chosen shall long enjoy the work of their hands.
They shall not labor in vain,
 or bear children for calamity;
for they shall be offspring blessed by the Lord—
 and their descendants as well.
Before they call I will answer,
 while they are yet speaking I will hear.
The wolf and the lamb shall feed together,
 the lion shall eat straw like the ox;
 but the serpent—its food shall be dust!
They shall not hurt or destroy
 on all my holy mountain, says the Lord.

With this vision, the Sabbath and Jubilee mandates are radicalized. The concern of Yahweh is the creation of a socioeconomic–spiritual reality in which all human injustice and ailments are overcome, and genuine peace (*shalom*) is achieved. The Sabbath and Jubilee cycles and mandates are broadened to a permanent provision of healing and wholeness for all God's people.

Royal Decrees

In Chapter 3 we found that Israel's demand for a king led to a fundamental denial of Israel's covenant with Yahweh, a tragic rejection of Sabbath economics and Jubilee spirituality, an application of the logic of centralization practiced by the surrounding nations. Within the royal traditions of Israel and the ancient Near East there was, however, a positive element not unlike the Sabbath–Jubilee mandates. It was not uncommon for kings to begin their rule with "good news for the poor" through royal decrees declaring release from debts and/or slavery, which would be an effective way to gain popular support and perhaps undercut the power of rivals. This may in fact be the origin of King Zedekiah's decree freeing the slaves in Jeremiah 34:8–22 and Nehemiah's decree canceling debts in Nehemiah 5:10–13. It provides an interesting parallel to the Sabbath–Jubilee mandates in Exodus, Deuteronomy, Leviticus, and Isaiah that we have considered, for in these mandates Yahweh is the true ruler of God's people, the liberator who frees and requires the practice of freedom.

Antonio Tovar, in his thesis concerning the agrarian laws in Leviticus, points out that the Hebrew word *deror* appears seven times in the Old Testament with the meaning "release" or "liberation": once in Leviticus 25:10 (the proclamation of Jubilee), four times in Jeremiah 34 (concerning the release of slaves), once in Ezekiel 46:17 ("the year of liberty" when land was to be returned), and once in Isaiah 61:1 ("liberty to the captives" at "the year of the Lord's favor" (Tovar, 1983, p. 92).

The convergence of Sabbath–Jubilee mandates and royal decrees of release may be extended even further by taking into account the Enthronement Psalms. In his book, *Israel's Praise: Doxology against Idolatry and Ideology*, Walter Brueggemann explores the meaning of Israel's worship as "constructing a world in which Israel can viably, joyously, and obediently live" (1988, p. 6). Liturgy, rightly practiced, is "world-making," "the creation and maintenance of a life-world and a socioeconomic–political order that makes public life possible and sustainable" (ibid., p. 8). In the early days of the Jerusalem Temple, the king sponsored and supervised an annual festival in which Yahweh was re-enthroned for the coming year and the incumbent king was re-enthroned on behalf of Yahweh, pronouncing or enacting Yahweh's message of health, justice, peace, *shalom*. In this celebration, the people participated not only in the affirmation but in the creation of a world in accordance with God's character. To praise Yahweh was to enact God's will. It was to celebrate the life that God creates and liberates. This was good news.

> *Give the king your justice, O God,*
> *and your righteousness to a king's son.*
> *May he judge your people with righteousness,*
> *and your poor with justice.*
> *May the mountains yield prosperity for the people,*
> *and the hills, in righteousness.*
> *May he defend the cause of the poor of the people,*
> *give deliverance to the needy,*
> *and crush the oppressor.* Psalm 72:1–4

The new social possibility born through the Exodus, nurtured among the tribes of Yahweh, and articulated in the Sabbath–Jubilee mandates, was not entirely lost under the monarchy, nor was it destroyed with the Babylonian conquest and exile. Israel continued to believe that Yahweh was really their King, and Jesus centered his message and ministry on the coming of God's rule, that is, the enthronement of Yahweh.

Responsible Discipleship ◆ ◆ ◆ ◆ ◆

As we conclude this chapter, we also conclude the first half of the book, which has been based on the Sabbath and Jubilee teachings of the Hebrew

Scriptures. So we would like to conclude this chapter with questions for readers rather than suggestions and examples we might provide. Up to now each chapter has concluded with challenges of "Responsible Discipleship" deriving from an opening discussion of some aspects of "Today's World" and basic explorations into our "Biblical Faith." Having worked through four chapters with the same sequence, we will simply pose here some questions so that readers and study groups will themselves articulate the challenges they perceive for their own lives and faith communities out of our study to this point.

The next two chapters will focus on Jesus' understanding of the Sabbath and Jubilee mandates. Then Chapter 7 will consider Jubilee practices in the early church, and the final chapter is entitled "Jubilee—Celebrating Life Together." These final four chapters are based primarily on the Christian Scriptures, which of course are based on the Hebrew Scriptures. As we saw in Chapter 1, the Jubilee and Sabbath motif runs right through the Bible and provides a fascinating key to the entire biblical message, one that is vitally important for our human predicament at the close of the twentieth century. It is an invaluable key to the struggle for life for all God's people today as in biblical times.

The Stewardship of Our Lives

We have suggested that Jubilee spirituality, the challenge of the biblical Jubilee, is concerned with personal transformation, whatever else it may be also concerned with. We have considered very serious global problems in today's world, above all the polarization of rich and poor with the result of accelerating rates of poverty and unnecessary mortality, and we have looked for alternatives to the dominant economic system. All of us are involved in numerous ways with this system, and all of us have some room to respond—in terms of our own lifestyle, use of resources, employment, solidarity, and so on. We have examined at some length Hebrew Scripture texts that deal with similar tendencies through critical periods of Israel's history, and we have found in these texts very direct mandates for God's people. So now we ask ourselves:

What will our response, my response, be?
1. How do I view our global, national, and local economic order, and what is my responsibility to do something about it?
2. What has the Sabbath–Jubilee material taught me about my responsibility as a member of God's household and heir to these mandates?
3. What examples of people and organizations working for change can I identify with and perhaps relate to or become involved with?

The Stewardship of God's Household

We have also suggested that the biblical Jubilee is concerned about ecclesial transformation. We have all experienced the church in many different ways, some of which may have been very discouraging. We have considered here the concept of the church as a household (*oíkos*) within the larger household of the whole human family. In both dimensions, God's concern is for an economy (*oíkonomía*) that cares for the well-being of all its inhabitants (*oíkouméne*) and its environment (*oíkología*). Yet we know that, as members of the church and of the whole human family, we reach beyond ourselves only rarely and in very limited ways. In the Sabbath and Jubilee mandates, we have seen that the God who liberated the slaves from Egypt required very fundamental commitments and concrete actions to resist and overcome the human tendencies to accumulate wealth at the expense of others. In a hungry, poor, increasingly marginalized world, we need to ask ourselves and our faith communities:

How can our churches be more faithful to the Jubilee and promote Sabbath economics so that all God's people have enough—in our communities, in our country, in the world?

1. How can I work with my church or synagogue in terms of its understanding of the current drive toward the globalization of our market-oriented economic system?
2. How can I begin to foster within my church or synagogue the Sabbath and Jubilee mandates for us as biblical people?
3. What efforts of my own and other churches or synagogues can help us understand and fulfill more effectively our vocation as God's people?

The Stewardship of Creation

We have seen that the Sabbath and Jubilee mandates are concerned about social and global transformation. We have all heard repeatedly that the global economy is driving the world over the limits of ecological survival. Yet we continue to hear repeatedly that the economy must continue to grow. In fact success is still measured largely in terms of GNP; the super-rich are still admired for their excesses; and we are all pressed constantly to consume more. Sabbath–Jubilee economics calls for all creation and all God's people to break the cycle of production and consumption in order to rest and renew our possibilities to survive and to leave to future generations the great but diminishing resources of our planet. So we ask ourselves, in the face of doomsday prognoses and simple common sense:

How can we contribute more to the renewal of life on this planet?

1. What possibilities do I have to set limits to my own consumption and expectations, so that others might have enough and the environment might be relieved?
2. How can I encourage myself and others to consider the basic insights of the biblical mandates and take steps in our lives toward greater economic and ecological responsibility?

3. What movements and programs and organizations dedicated to these ends should we support?

From the outset of this study we have chosen as our subtitle, "An Invitation to Personal, Ecclesial, and Social Transformation." The questions we have raised here are just that, an invitation. We have tried to capture and share the extraordinary vision of Jubilee, which comes to us ultimately not as condemnation or burden but as challenge and freedom. We are invited, as members of God's family, to bring rest and restoration to all of creation and to build a social possibility in which all people can enjoy fullness of life. This is a grand and joyful responsibility. It is given to us by God's grace.

5 ◆ ◆ ◆ ◆ ◆ ◆ ◆

Jesus' Proclamation of God's Reign as Jubilee

With this chapter we move quite naturally to the Gospels, especially the synoptic Gospels, to see how Jesus used the Sabbath and Jubilee perspectives and mandates in his message and ministry. This will open up for most of us, as we suggested in Chapter 1, new and surprising insights into God's will for God's people. As Martin Luther wrote, Jesus Christ is the Bible within the Bible, the most important key to the whole biblical message. So we need to examine how Jesus and his immediate followers and interpreters took up the socioeconomic–spiritual challenges of the Sabbath Day, the Sabbath Year, and the Jubilee set forth in the Hebrew Scriptures. But first we will examine certain dimensions of today's world, for which we need biblical guidance of this kind, especially in terms of the structures and prejudices that marginalize and exclude so many people, not just socioeconomically but also politically, ideologically, and spiritually. At the end of this chapter we will consider some avenues for personal, ecclesial, and social transformation in keeping with Jesus' proclamation of Jubilee in response to our human predicament today. These concerns are summarized with the following questions:

◆ In our world today—locally, nationally, and globally—in what ways are so many people marginalized and excluded, and how are we responsible?

◆ How did Jesus use the Sabbath and Jubilee teachings of the Old Testament to confront the structures and prejudices that marginalized and excluded so many in first-century Palestine?

◆ How are followers of Jesus confronting and overcoming the structures and prejudices of marginalization and exclusion today, and what are we called to do in our own lives, in our churches, and in our local, national, and global communities?

Today's World ◆ ◆ ◆ ◆ ◆

Socioeconomic Structures and Prejudices That Marginalize and Exclude

In earlier chapters we made some analysis of the factors at work in our world, above all economic factors, to maintain and accelerate the accumulation of wealth on the one hand and poverty on the other. These factors may or may not be intentional with regard to either beneficiaries or victims. In fact many people at both ends of the spectrum may be unconscious collaborators in the dominant system that is so dramatically portrayed in the champagne glass analogy. Following is an example of this kind of confusion that we ourselves may harbor.

Several years ago, in Torreón, Mexico, we came across an unpublished paper on research into the potential benefits of the then-imminent North American Free Trade Agreement (NAFTA) between the United States, Canada, and Mexico. No doubt many of us hoped that NAFTA would open up an enormous market and bring prosperity to many more poor people in Mexico and perhaps later be extended to Central America and even South America. It seemed only reasonable that Mexican peasant farmers would have a significant advantage because their wage levels are so low. We assumed that many companies would move their operations from north to south to take advantage of cheap labor. But this paper revealed that low wages do not necessarily mean lower production costs or greater competitiveness. It indicated that in 1988 annual agricultural production per Mexican farmer came to $1,799; per U.S. farmer it came to $45,052. In Mexico a ton of corn required 17.8 working days; in the United States, 1.2 hours. U.S. farmers were producing 100 times as much rice and beans per person or per hour. Why? In Mexico there was one tractor for 50 workers, in the U.S. 1.6 tractors per farm worker. In Mexico they were applying 191.9 kilos of fertilizer per farmer; in the United States, 5,812 tons. Thus the production cost of a ton of corn in Mexico was $258.62, even though salaries were very low; in the United States, where farmers' income was 25 times higher, the cost was only $92.74 per ton of corn. So the establishment of a "free" market between the United States, Canada, and Mexico, instead of opening up new possibilities for Mexican farmers, would endanger their very subsistence.

To take this example one step further, we might go on to suggest, following the logic of "free" market economics, that Mexican farmers need to adopt U.S. means of capital intensive agribusiness so as to compete in NAFTA and the world market. The eventual effect of such a policy would be to push most Mexican farmers off the land into the already enormous pool of rural and urban unemployed and underemployed. Increasing numbers would no doubt join the economic refugee trail to the United States, where they would probably find higher seasonal pay but also would face legal threats, economic uncertainty, social prejudice, and family disruption.

On January 1, 1994, the day the North American Free Trade Agreement went into effect, the Zapatista movement, made up primarily of Mayan Indians, the poorest of Mexico's poor, which had been hiding in Chiapas, rose up in armed protest. This was a complete surprise, because it had been assumed that guerrilla insurgencies for radical social change had ended with the peace accords in Central America. If the long and terribly costly struggles in El Salvador and Guatemala were able to achieve only very minimal goals due to U.S. opposition, and if the Sandinista Revolution and its subsequent socioeconomic and cultural achievements were later undermined and overthrown by the U.S.-sponsored *contra* war, then there would be no hope for systemic change in the region. Such was our assumption. But the Zapatistas declared otherwise, and the response throughout Mexico, among virtually all social sectors, was overwhelmingly positive. There were huge demonstrations in major cities and declarations by churches and organizations of all kinds in support of their demands. Interestingly, the Zapatistas were careful not to identify themselves with any ideology or political movement. They refused to form any political movement of their own. Their cry, which awakened support and hope around the world, was simply, "*un mundo donde quepan todos*" ("a world where there is room for all"). Their struggle is for the indigenous peoples of Chiapas to have access to their land; to be free of the market forces of exploitation; to be recognized as having histories, cultural identities, and languages of their own; to have a right to decent health care, education, and housing. In fact they voiced the very needs felt by people throughout Mexico and around the world. And they knew that the launching of NAFTA on New Year's Day 1994 marked a tragic intensification of their struggle to survive in this world, let alone to have a place and a future for their children.

Political–Ideological Structures and Prejudices That Marginalize and Exclude

The economic dimension of life is certainly a critical, basic dimension of the marginalization and exclusion of persons, peoples, nations, and now whole continents. But it is by no means the only important dimension. Pablo Richard, a colleague at the Latin American Biblical University and currently director of the Departamento Ecuménico de Investigaciones in Costa Rica, has pointed out that other dimensions of the political–ideological structures and prejudices were evident from the early years of the conquest of Latin America. He reminds us of the theological debates going on in sixteenth-century Spain, Portugal, and the Vatican and cites the now incredible arguments of Juan Inés de Sepúlveda:

> with perfect right the Spaniards rule over the barbarians of the New World and adjacent islands, who in terms of prudence, ingenuity, vir-

tue and humanity are as inferior to the Spaniards as are children to adults and women to men, having among them such difference as that which is found between wild and cruel people and very clement people . . . and I might say monkeys and humans.

. . . being by nature servants, the barbarians, uncultured and inhuman, fail to admit the domination of those who are more prudent, powerful and perfect than they, domination that would bring them most wonderful utilities, being furthermore a just thing, by natural right, that matter obey form, body the soul, appetite reason, brutes humans, women their husbands, children their parents, imperfection perfection, worse better, for the universal good of all things. (Richard, 1996, p. 5)

This mentality has of course been contested for over 500 years, and progressive changes have taken place over the centuries. Women have made great strides, especially during the past 100 years, but still today the United States has failed to approve an Equal Rights amendment to the Constitution for the full equality of women and men in the workplace, and women continue to face violence and abuse of many kinds in the home, at work, and on our streets. Native peoples have obtained certain status as nations with their own histories, cultures, and some of their traditional lands, but in general they continue to be marginalized by alien structures and prejudices, and they suffer from inordinately high levels of unemployment, addictions, poverty, and social alienation. Many African Americans have been successful in every branch of our socioeconomic, scientific, and professional life, but the general statistics regarding life expectancy, incarceration, unemployment, poverty, addictions, and family instability among African Americans bear tragic witness to institutional racism. We say we recognize the importance and vulnerability of children, but one third of all U.S. children live below the poverty line. Few would dare to speak or write in the manner of Juan Inés de Sepúlveda today, but we still have a long way to go to overcome the realities that have been spawned by the prejudices and structures that such attitudes in our own history have built.

Religious–Spiritual Structures and Prejudices That Marginalize and Exclude

All too often, religious and spiritual movements and institutions emulate and strengthen the structures and prejudices that marginalize and exclude the poor and unemployed, women and children, indigenous and African Americans, and others. Some local churches, denominations, ecumenical and interfaith bodies, and numerous coalitions deal seriously with human rights, justice, and peace concerns, but in general the "established" churches have great difficulty confronting their own people with the evident injustices that are so much a part of their lives individually and corporately. Through their relative silence they become accomplices in the oppression and exploitation of the domination system.

During the 1980s many U.S. denominations engaged in major studies on the crisis in Central America and took a very strong stand against our government's policies that supported military regimes in this region, especially El Salvador and Guatemala, and rejected political asylum for refugees from El Salvador and Guatemala. During some of those years we lived in Los Angeles, worked with refugee organizations, and were often invited to speak in the churches about the biblical call to provide sanctuary for oppressed aliens. Those were difficult times, and most congregations were not able to declare themselves sanctuaries or take a public stand regarding the wars in Central America, but many people did at least consider their Christian responsibility and the church's mission in a new light.

Now when we visit the United States we present a different analysis of the situation in Central America, one that reflects on the global situation we have been discussing in this book. We have to tell our colleagues and friends that there is *more* poverty, malnutrition, hunger, suffering, and unnecessary death than before or during the wars of the 1980s and that this is largely due to economic policies imposed by the United States and its allies in the IMF, World Bank, and Inter-American Development Bank. In a wider sense the increased inequity is the direct result of global economics and the ideology of the "free market." How are we to interpret the mission of the U.S. churches in terms of this new reality? We find that the biblical Jubilee provides a necessary key to our understanding of God's purpose for all God's people not only in ancient times but also in today's world.

Biblical Faith ◆ ◆ ◆ ◆ ◆

Our task now is to examine the New Testament Gospels to see how they deal with this fundamental human problem. We shall begin with Mark's Gospel, because it is considered to be the oldest Gospel, though traditionally it has been studied with little or no reference to the Jubilee. Then we shall look for Jubilee material in the Gospel of Matthew, and finally we shall take up Luke's Gospel, which in its opening story of Jesus' ministry refers to the key Jubilee passage in Isaiah 61:1–2a. This must be a limited, selective approach, but it will offer important perspectives on the central message and mission of Jesus in the synoptic Gospels, perspectives that may change significantly our understanding of the whole biblical message and provide invaluable grounding for our own ministries in today's world.

Sabbath–Jubilee Texts in Mark

Mark's Gospel provides only a very brief introduction with clues as to the meaning and purpose of Jesus' ministry. Commentaries have traditionally pointed out the apparent reference to the anointing of a king (Psalm 2:7) and the suffering servant (Isaiah 42:1) in the voice from heaven at Jesus' baptism (Mark 1:11). The story of Jesus' ministry begins with mention of John the Baptist's arrest and Jesus' coming to Galilee proclaiming "the good news of God" and saying:

> *The time is fulfilled, and the kingdom of God has come near; repent, and believe in the good news.*   Mark 1:15

Clearly Jesus' mission is directly related to the realization of God's reign. We shall now examine some important passages to find out just what the coming of God's reign meant to the writer and readers of Mark's Gospel.

Healing and Liberation. The healing of a paralytic man in Mark 2:1–12 is a complex passage. The text appears to be made up from two stories, a healing miracle and a controversy about forgiving sins. It takes place in a context of poverty, as is indicated by the nature of the house, the crowd (*óchlos* often means the common people or the lower classes), and the mattress lowered down through the roof. The surprising element is Jesus' announcement, "Son, your sins are forgiven" (v. 5). In fact this expression is repeated four times in this one passage. Why did Jesus say this? Did he want to free the paralytic not only from his impediment but also from the common stigma so often attached to this kind of condition, as though the paralysis were the result of his or his parents' sin? What is the meaning of the verb used here: *àphíemi*?

Sharon Ringe, whose book *Jesus, Liberation, and the Biblical Jubilee* we referred to in the last chapter, points out that the verb *àphíemi* and the noun *àphesis* are used to express the release of slaves and the cancellation of debts in the Septuagint Greek version of key Old Testament Sabbath–Jubilee texts: Deuteronomy 15, Leviticus 25, and Isaiah 58:6 and 61:1. "Such usage is consistent with the secular, legal significance that these words had in classical Greek where they referred to one's release from bonds, debts, or other legal requirements" (1985, p. 65). This language is also used in the Septuagint to refer to the forgiveness or release from sin and guilt in a cultic, religious, or ethical sense. In the New Testament, *àphíemi* refers to the release from or forgiveness of monetary debts (Matthew 18:27, 32), prisoners (Luke 4:18), and sin (Matthew 6:14–15), thus including both the cultic and the legal dimensions of human bondage.

> Indeed, ethical and cultic concerns in general can be distinguished but not separated in Gospel usage. Both are means of talking about the effect of the advent of God's Reign in breaking the tyranny of evil in all of its forms. In that context, "release" is more than a metaphor for God's work of redemption and reconciliation, and the economic image of the cancellation of debts is not simply another way to speak of God's forgiveness of humankind. Rather, "forgiveness" or "release" in all arenas of human life is portrayed as one of the principal characteristics of humankind's encounter with God's Reign. Building on the

background of that term in the Jubilee traditions, one can see that it is in social, political, and economic arenas that the sovereignty of God finds its primary expressions, breaking the stranglehold of the old order on those we have come to recognize as "the poor." (ibid., p. 66)

Building on a broad understanding of the Sabbath–Jubilee mandates, we can now see that in Mark 2:1–12 Jesus is most likely responding to the multiple bonds under which the paralytic man is suffering (along with his family and friends): the paralysis, resultant poverty, social exclusion, presumption of sin, and inevitable indebtedness from a life of dependence. Release for this "oppressed-poor" man had to be more than simple healing, however wonderful that was in itself. It had to be more than simple forgiveness of sin, however necessary that too was. Full Jubilee liberation had to include freedom from accumulated debts so that this healed, forgiven man could be completely restored to his family and community. In his pivotal commentary on Mark, *Binding the Strong Man,* Ched Myers puts it this way:

> In choosing to introduce the language of the debt code, Jesus is elaborating the symbolics of hierarchy. The man's lack of bodily wholeness would have been attributed to either his own sin, or, if a birth defect, inherited sin; he was thus denied full status in the body politic of Israel. Jesus summarily releases him from all debt—hence restoring his social wholeness and thus his personhood, which is equated with the restoration of physical wholeness. (Myers, 1988, p. 155)

Predictably, the scribes, guardians of the status quo, were furious, and they accused Jesus of blasphemy, which in those days was worthy of death, thus pointing toward the intensification of Jesus' conflict with the religious–ideological domination system that would end at the cross. In this context, Mark introduces the apocalyptic figure, the Son of Man, the Human One, who has authority to forgive that transcends the authority of the scribes.

Conflicts over the Sabbath Practice.   Mark 2:23–28 is one of several Sabbath controversy stories in Mark's Gospel. The disciples plucked grain as they went through the grainfields on a Sabbath Day, thus violating one of the most important observances of Pharisaic Judaism. Jesus defends this behavior by referring to a similar incident when David and his men were hungry and took holy bread of the Presence (1 Samuel 21:1–6). He then declares, "The Sabbath was made for humankind, and not humankind for the Sabbath; so the Son of Man is lord even of the Sabbath" (Mark 2:27–28). Here as in many of the Gospel stories the commentaries tend most often to focus on the christological significance of the text, as indeed the early church tended to do, that is, to see in this incident another indication of Jesus' superior authority over the Sabbath. On the basis of our earlier studies of the Sabbath and Jubilee mandates, however, we find here a manifest concern for the poor who are hungry and for the ritual limitations of the Sabbath regarding access to basic grains.

> The disciples' commandeering grain against Sabbath regulations must from this perspective be seen as a protest of "civil disobedience" over the politics of food in Palestine. Jesus is not only defending discipleship practice against the alternative holiness code of Pharisaism, he is going on the offensive, challenging the ideological control and the manipulation of the redistributive economy by a minority whose elite status is only aggrandized. Mark consistently argues that solidarity with the poor also means addressing oppressive structures. This may well mean breaking the law, but such action is legitimated by the Human One. (Myers, 1988, p. 161)

Sabbath observance was a primary concern of the Pharisees and their followers. Sabbath economics was a primary concern of Jesus and his followers. The Pharisees' spirituality served to further burden the poor, many of whom were debtors, some were debt prisoners, and many were landless day laborers and bond servants. The Sabbath–Jubilee mandates promised good news to the oppressed-poor in terms of debt relief, freedom for prisoners, healing of the sick, redistribution of land to the landless, and liberation of slaves. This confrontation was to have very serious consequences for Jesus and his followers.

Mark's grainfield episode is followed immediately by another conflict story, Mark 3:1–6, and once again Jesus engages in civil disobedience. Here again the context is the Sabbath Day, but now the setting is public and official—the synagogue—and Jesus is now being watched to see whether he will overtly break the Sabbath rule by healing a man with a withered hand.

> As in the modern practice of civil disobedience, which might break the law in order to raise deeper issues of its morality and purpose, so Jesus, just before "crossing the line," issues a challenge to his audience. Pitting his mission of compassion and justice to the poor against the imperatives of the dominant order, Jesus calls the entire ideological edifice of the law to account. He paraphrases the watershed question of Deuteronomic faith (Deuteronomy 30:15ff): "Is it lawful on the Sabbath to do good or to do evil?" (Myers, 1988, p. 162)

Having shifted the focus from legalistic tradition to the struggle for life and dignity for the marginalized, Jesus puts his enemies on the defensive. Faced then with the healing of the man with the withered hand, they can only withdraw and conspire to destroy Jesus. We find here that for Jesus the central meaning of the Sabbath is not only in securing access to food but also in healing every infirmity—in the struggle for fullness of life for all God's people, especially the vulnerable and excluded ones.

The Meaning of Sabbath Economics.   We shall turn now briefly to Mark's first extended teaching section, 4:1–34, the seed parables, which we will relate to Jesus' encounter with a rich man and subsequent teaching about wealth, Mark 10:17–31. Mark 4:1–34 has provided much material for preachers and missiologists who have used them primarily to promote evangelism and church growth. We do not intend here to examine the text closely but rather to point out what should be obvious: Jesus uses the agricultural idiom to talk about the abundance of God's creation. In the so-called parable of the sower, some of the seeds fall on the path, rocky ground, or among thorns, but that which falls into good soil yields thirty- and sixty- and a hundredfold. In the parable of the growing seed, the earth itself produces the sprout, the stalk, and the head full of grain. And in the parable of the mustard seed, that tiny seed grows up into a great shrub, and the birds make their nests in its shade. These little stories lend themselves to allegorization and spiritualization. In fact the text itself provides a full-blown allegorical exegesis for the first parable. But what do the parables look like through the eyes of Sabbath economics and Jubilee spirituality?

The expression "a hundredfold" links this text to another passage in Mark that uses the same expression. We shall turn quickly to that passage, because it provides important insight into this one, and then return. It is the story of Jesus' encounter with the rich man, who asks what to do to inherit eternal life, Mark 10:17–22, and Jesus' subsequent teaching to his disciples about wealth, Mark 10:23–31. This is the only time in Mark's Gospel that this question about eternal life is raised. Jesus' response refers to the Ten Commandments, but he adds rather remarkably the phrase, "You shall not defraud," which may well be a challenge to the landed class, who tended to withhold wages and take advantage of mortgages that the poor could not repay. In any case Jesus goes on to state that traditional fidelity to the Law is meaningless without a fundamental commitment to the poor and action for socioeconomic justice. As we have seen, the purpose of the Law was in fact to create and maintain a socioeconomic order in which all would have enough and none would have too much. So Jesus, even as he loves this pious man, has to challenge him to enter God's reign through Sabbath economics, Jubilee spirituality:

> *You lack one thing; go, sell what you own, and give the money to the poor, and you will have treasure in heaven; then come, follow me.*
>
> Mark 10:21

In the subsequent exchange between Jesus and his disciples he states that it is impossible for the rich to enter God's reign. Wealth must not be used to accumulate more wealth, as the dominant, market-oriented system dictates. Wealth must be distributed so that the poor might have enough, as Jesus dictates. Pious, religious discipline in keeping with a superficial reading of the Ten Commandments is not at all adequate. Religion without justice is, as the prophets of the Old Testament made very clear, false religion.

Solidarity with the poor is not a minor addendum to faith; it is its essence. So Jesus said to them:

> *How hard it will be for those who have wealth to enter the kingdom of God!* Mark 10:23

> *Children, how hard it is to enter the kingdom of God! It is easier for a camel to go through the eye of a needle than for someone who is rich to enter the kingdom of God.* Mark 10:24–25

The nature of God's rule is such that rich people exclude themselves by their riches. Yet, with God as ruler the impossible becomes possible. The disciples were beginning to experience the new reality of God's reign, sharing everything to follow Jesus (Mark 10:28). They were discovering that right now in this present life (in community) they were receiving a hundredfold. So Jesus said:

> *Truly I tell you, there is no one who has left house or brothers or sisters or mother or father or children or fields, for my sake and for the sake of the good news, who will not receive a hundredfold now in this age—houses, brothers and sisters, mothers and children, and fields, with persecutions—and in the age to come eternal life.*
> Mark 10:29–30

These are not casual references but fundamental dimensions of socioeconomic life that were being transformed through Jubilee spirituality. Family members provided the labor force; the household was the focus of consumption; and the fields were the primary base for the production of the necessary means for life. Through sharing, the Jesus movement was to be a community in which all would have enough and none would have too much.

The disciples had already seen this reality in the feeding of the multitudes. They were to experience it again at Pentecost. It became the central liturgical experience of the early church through the celebration of the Lord's Supper (see Chapter 7).

Turning back now to the seed parables of Mark 4:1–34, we can see that they too have an economic intention. Over against the predominant economy of scarcity and polarization, God's reign brings economic abundance, not through human effort but through the gift of God's prodigious creation. There are enemies, to be sure, that eat up, scorch, and choke the seeds and the seedlings, just as wealthy landholders take away the land of the poor, governing elites tax and consume their meager resources, and scribes and Pharisees impose additional burdens. But Sabbath economics provides enough for all when all share what they have.

This good news is dramatically revealed in the feeding of the multitudes in the desert, Mark 6:30–44 and 8:1–10. In the first passage, the disciples urge Jesus to send the people into the surrounding countryside and villages to buy food, in keeping with market economics; they calculate that it would take 200 denarii or 200 days' wages to feed the crowd. In both passages they assume that the crowd (*óchlos*) is poor and lacking in supplies. But Jesus asks them to find what they can, tells them to have the people sit down on the ground, blesses what little they bring him, and then breaks it into pieces and distributes them. What has traditionally been interpreted as a miracle from heaven turns out to be an experience of Sabbath sharing! When all share what they have, all have enough, and there is more than enough. Exodus 16 becomes, at least momentarily, a reality.

Sabbath–Jubilee Texts in Matthew

Compared with Mark, Matthew has a long introduction, which offers important clues to that Gospel's understanding of Jesus' mission and message. We note, in particular, Jesus' temptation in the wilderness. His forty days of fasting parallel the forty years of Israel's wandering in the wilderness, and the first temptation makes direct reference to Sabbath economics. The tempter tells Jesus to make stones into loaves of bread, but Jesus quotes Deuteronomy 8:3: "One does not live by bread alone, but by every word that comes from the mouth of God" (Matthew 4:4). He does not disregard the need for bread or spiritualize the text. The larger Deuteronomy passage (8:2–3) shows that Jesus was recalling the lesson of the manna in wilderness.

> *Remember the long way that the Lord your God has led you these forty years in the wilderness, in order to humble you, testing you to know what was in your heart, whether or not you would keep his commandments. He humbled you by letting you hunger, then by feeding you with manna . . . in order to make you understand that one does not live by bread alone, but by every word that comes from the mouth of the Lord.*

We know from Exodus 16 that God was teaching Israel to create a new socioeconomic order in which all would have enough and none more than enough. This too is what Jesus came to do, according to Matthew's Gospel.

Following Mark, Matthew begins the story of Jesus' ministry with his proclamation, "Repent, for the kingdom of heaven has come near" (Matthew 4:17). We shall turn now to Matthew's record of that ministry to see how he develops the meaning of the coming of the kingdom of heaven, which is his equivalent to God's reign.

The Beatitudes and the Jubilee Vision. We shall give our attention to the first of Matthew's long discourses, Matthew 5–7, which is usually called the Sermon on the Mount, for here we find the first and perhaps the clearest exposition of Jesus' understanding of his message and mission. The sermon is introduced briefly by a reference to the crowds (*óchlos*) and the mountain (evocative of Sinai), to Jesus' sitting down and his disciples coming to him. Then his teaching begins with the Beatitudes. We can assume that Matthew located the Beatitudes at this place in his Gospel because he considered that this passage would be a key to the meaning of the coming of God's reign.

We note first that God's reign or kingdom comes as "blessing," which of course parallels the "good news," as affirmed at the outset of Mark's narration of Jesus' ministry, Mark 1:14–15, and also in Luke's opening story of Jesus' ministry, Luke 4:18. In Matthew's telling, Jesus not only affirms the good news or blessing of God's reign for the poor but provides a whole litany of blessing, good fortune, or happiness.

> Blessed are the poor in spirit,
>   for theirs is the kingdom of heaven.
> Blessed are those who mourn,
>   for they will be comforted.
> Blessed are the meek,
>   for they will inherit the earth.
> Blessed are those who hunger and thirst for righteousness,
>   for they will be filled.
> Blessed are the merciful,
>   for they will receive mercy.
> Blessed are the pure in heart,
>   for they will see God.
> Blessed are the peacemakers,
>   for they will be called children of God.
> Blessed are those who are persecuted for righteousness' sake,
>   for theirs is the kingdom of heaven.   (5:3–10)

Earlier, we suggested that Isaiah 61:1–2 not only refers to "the year of the Lord's favor," the Jubilee, but radicalizes it in response to a wide range of oppressions experienced by God's people. So here Jesus declares God's gracious blessing upon a whole range of needs.

Concerning the first and last Beatitudes, the poor in spirit and those who are persecuted for righteousness' sake, Jesus says explicitly, "theirs is the kingdom of heaven," which is to say that they have God as their king. The others may be considered not as different categories of people but rather additional characteristics of those who are responding to God's reign, who make God their only ruler. When God's reign comes, as it does with Jesus and his movement, it looks like this: In general those who respond are those who are excluded by the dominant socioeconomic–religious–political system. They are the poor in spirit, the oppressed-poor, for whom a new socioeconomic–spiritual order is required. They mourn now, but they will be comforted. They are the meek, most likely those who have been pushed off the land, not the rich and powerful and self-righteous ones, but they will inherit the land, as promised by the Jubilee year. They hunger and thirst for righteousness, which simply means justice according to Yahweh's dictates, a justice that is not blindly objective but looks out especially for orphans, widows, and aliens and seeks to reorder unjust structures. This justice reverses the propensity of the powerful to accumulate wealth and marginalize the rest. They will see God, for they are pure in heart, which is another way to say that God is their ruler. They are peacemakers, working for the integral well-being of others, and they will be called God's children. Finally, they are persecuted, because they work for justice, which brings them into confrontation with the established order.

Throughout this eloquent passage we hear echoes of Sabbath economics, Jubilee spirituality, liberation, and fullness of life for all God's people. Much has been written about the apparent "spiritualization" of the Beatitudes in Matthew as compared with Luke, but this may be a misreading of Matthew. Matthew's Beatitudes take on concrete, socioeconomic–spiritual meaning when they are read in the light of the Sabbath–Jubilee mandates of the Hebrew Scriptures, which were Jesus' and Matthew's most important point of reference. It is precisely by practicing Jubilee solidarity, Sabbath economics, that these blessings become a reality.

The Beatitudes thus provide basic understanding for the subsequent portions of the Sermon on the Mount, which in turn provide further insight into the Beatitudes. How are Jesus' followers to be salt and light? By "good works" that demonstrate God's reign as defined above (Matthew 5:13–16). How does Jesus fulfill the Law and the Prophets? By calling his followers to carry out the commandments of God's rule, which is to practice justice exceeding that of the scribes and Pharisees (Matthew 5:17–20). So if the Beatitudes reflect the Sabbath–Jubilee vision of God's reign, then these texts also should be interpreted in that same light.

The Lord's Prayer as Sabbath Mandate.   We next find clear allusions to that vision in the Lord's Prayer, Matthew 6:9–13.

> *Our Father in heaven,*
>   *hallowed be your name.*
> *Your kingdom come.*
> *Your will be done,*
>   *on earth as it is in heaven.*
> *Give us this day our daily bread.*
> *And forgive us our debts,*
>   *as we also have forgiven our debtors.*
> *And do not bring us to the time of trial,*
>   *but rescue us from the evil one.*

"Your kingdom come" is a reiteration of the coming of God's reign, the central, overarching theme of Jesus' message and mission (Matthew 4:17). What does the coming of God's reign mean? It means, first, to ask that God's will be done here on Earth and not just in heaven, as revealed in the Law and the Prophets. It means, second, to ask for "our daily bread," no more and no less, which is, as we learned from Exodus 16, a Sabbath Day mandate. It means, third, to be forgiven of debts and to forgive debts, which is, as we saw in Deuteronomy 15, a Sabbath Year mandate. Finally, it means to resist the evil one, who tempts God's people, as he tempted Jesus, to disobey and break their covenant with Yahweh. The Lord's Prayer is a call to Sabbath–Jubilee spirituality as envisioned for the tribes of Yahweh in the Promised Land, a socioeconomic possibility that Israel abandoned under the monarchy so that some could become rich and powerful and others would become poor and marginalized.

Immediately following the Lord's Prayer, Matthew refers to Jesus' mandate to forgive "trespasses" or "sins." Luke includes forgiveness of both "sins" and "debts" in his version of the Lord's Prayer (11:2–4). Some English versions of the New Testament—and many readers—leave out the reference to debts, probably because it has lost its meaning as a Jubilee mandate.

God's Reign and Sabbath Economics. Later, in Matthew 6:19–21, Jesus speaks about treasures on Earth and in heaven.

> Do not store up for yourselves treasures on earth, where moth and rust consume and where thieves break in and steal; but store up for yourselves treasures in heaven, where neither moth nor rust consumes and where thieves do not break in and steal. For where your treasure is, there your heart will be also.

This passage has been read as a life insurance policy for eternity, but in the context of the Beatitudes and our understanding of Sabbath economics and Jubilee spiritually it takes on a different meaning. It is a call to practice justice here in this life rather than to accumulate wealth in this life. In fact the reference to moth and rust sounds very much like the experience in Exodus 16 of those who in disobedience to God's clear instruction tried to hoard the manna—to accumulate wealth—"and it bred worms and became foul" (v. 20). So here, too, Jesus is teaching Sabbath economics.

The following verses, Matthew 6:22–24, carry a similar message.

> The eye is the lamp of the body. So, if your eye is healthy, your whole body will be full of light; but if your eye is unhealthy, your whole body will be full of darkness. If then the light in you is darkness, how great is the darkness!
>
> No one can serve two masters; for a slave will either hate the one and love the other, or be devoted to the one and despise the other. You cannot serve God and wealth.

The eye is the light of the body. If, as Jesus has explained from the beginning of the Sermon on the Mount, one's eye sees and seeks justice, it is healthy and the whole body will be full of the light of God's reign. If, however, one's eye sees and seeks personal gain and unjust wealth accumulation, it is unhealthy and the whole body will be full of darkness. This is not a question of being religious in the traditional sense. It is a matter of letting God rule our lives in terms of Jubilee spirituality, which brings fullness of life for all God's people.

We see still another exposition of the Sabbath–Jubilee vision in the following portion, Matthew 6:25–34. This passage deals with the human tendency to worry about the future, which becomes the rationale for hoarding and the accumulation of wealth. The birds of the air and the lilies of the field are examples of God's reign and God's justice.

> *Look at the birds of the air; they neither sow nor reap nor gather into barns, and yet your heavenly Father feeds them. . . . Consider the lilies of the field, how they grow; they neither toil nor spin, yet I tell you, even Solomon in all his glory was not clothed like one of these. . . . But strive first for the kingdom [reign] of God and, his righteousness [justice], and all these things will be given to you as well.*

The Sabbath–Jubilee vision is founded ultimately on God's grace. It is based on the memory of slaves who were liberated from Pharaoh's Egypt and given the Promised Land. It is not sheer romantic idealism. By practicing Sabbath economics, all can be assured of having enough, and no one needs to hoard at the expense of others. The Jubilee is the year of God's grace, in which the basic forces of injustice are reversed so that all God's people can return to their land and live in freedom. God's people can learn to live each day without worry for the next, even as Jesus has taught us to pray for our daily bread. As we saw in Chapter 3, God's people need not and must not strive to accumulate wealth as did Solomon at the expense of the poor but rather share what we have so that all will have enough. Jesus himself lived without concern for the morrow, like the birds of the air and the lilies of the field. He taught and he showed by his life what God's reign really is.

The Parable of the Talents. We cannot leave Matthew without some reference to the parable of the talents, Matthew 25:14–30, which in contrast to Matthew 6:25–34 seems to teach hoarding and wealth accumulation. It should be very relevant to our concern, for it focuses on basic socioeconomic matters. In this story, a wealthy man entrusts varying sums to his slaves with the expectation that they will produce significant profit during his absence. When he returns, he finds that the one who had received five talents had gained five more, the one who had received two had gained two, and the slave who had received one had just buried it for safety. The wealthy man then takes away that one talent, gives it to the slave who already had ten, and condemns the poor slave.

This story seems to be a golden text for market economics and wealth accumulation. Apparently it affirms investment of money to gain more money, that is, usury. It appears to be a direct contradiction of all that we have found concerning Sabbath economics and the sharing or redistribution of wealth. It seems to idealize the rich slave owner's actions with a concluding aphorism, which is the reverse of Exodus 16:

*For to all those who have, more will be given, and they will have an
abundance; but from those who have nothing, even what they have
will be taken away.*   Matthew 25:29

There is, of course, another way to read this parable, not as a repre-
sentation of the kingdom or reign of God but as its antithesis. As William
Herzog suggests, its intention may be to unmask the world of oppression it
so aptly describes. This is what the anti-reign was like in first-century Palestine. This is what Jesus came to resist, confront, and transform. If such a
reading is possible, then the rich man of the story does not represent God
but the wealthy elites, and the poor slave is not a failure but the "whistle
blower" who exposes his owner as "a harsh man, reaping where you did
not sow and gathering where you did not scatter seed" (Matthew 25:24).
Rather than participate in the owner's economics of exploitation, this slave
simply buries his one talent and returns it without interest. And he suffers
the consequences—just as Jesus and his followers later were persecuted and
killed (Herzog, 1994, pp. 150–168).

Sabbath–Jubilee Texts in Luke

Like Matthew, Luke's introduction is long, and it contains many indications
concerning the meaning and purpose of Jesus' ministry. Mary's song, for example, affirms with eloquent poetry parallel to 1 Samuel 2:1–10 God's intention for Jesus and his movement.

He has shown strength with his arm;
*   he has scattered the proud in the thoughts of their hearts.*
He has brought down the powerful from their thrones,
*   and lifted up the lowly;*
He has filled the hungry with good things,
*   and sent the rich away empty.*   Luke 1:51–53

The narrative concerning John the Baptist demonstrates that the coming of Jesus required repentance, baptism, and actions consonant with Sabbath economics. As John presented it,

*Whoever has two coats must share with anyone who has none; and
whoever has food must do likewise.*   Luke 3:11

John had more specific instructions for tax collectors and soldiers concerning money and the abuse of the poor.

Luke's introduction contains many more clues to the meaning of Jesus'
mission and message, but these will suffice to confirm that we must look for
Sabbath–Jubilee teaching in the rest of Luke's Gospel.

Jesus' Mission as Jubilee. Luke's narration of Jesus' ministry begins at
Luke 4:14–15, which is a summary statement parallel to but different from
Mark and Matthew at this point.

> *Then Jesus, filled with the power of the Spirit, returned to Galilee,*
> *and a report about him spread through all the surrounding country.*
> *He began to teach in their synagogues and was praised by everyone.*

This summary statement gives no indication of the content or theme of Jesus' message and mission, as do Mark (1:15) with his reference to "the kingdom of God" and Matthew (4:17) with his reference to "the kingdom of heaven." Rather Luke has chosen to identify the central theme of Jesus' message and ministry in the following paragraph, 4:16–30, which is the story of Jesus' appearance at the Nazareth synagogue and his reading of the key Jubilee text from the Old Testament, Isaiah 61:1–2a. This paragraph does not use the expression, "kingdom [or reign] of God." In fact that key phrase first appears in Luke's Gospel at 4:42–44, which is the next summary statement, closing the first group of paragraphs concerning Jesus' ministry. So Luke provides in his opening story about Jesus' appearance at the Nazareth synagogue a clear indication that Jesus proclaimed God's reign as Jubilee. This then is the critical key to the reading of Luke's Gospel.

Here is Jesus' reading of Isaiah 61:1–2a according to Luke 4:18–19.

> *The Spirit of the Lord is upon me,*
> *because he has anointed me*
>   *to bring good news to the poor.*
> *He has sent me to proclaim release to the captives*
>   *and recovery of sight to the blind,*
>   *to let the oppressed go free,*
> *to proclaim the year of the Lord's favor.*

"The year of the Lord's favor" is generally understood to be a direct reference to the Jubilee Year, though it could include the Sabbath Year as well, as we found in Leviticus 25. The whole text of Luke 4:18–19 expresses the central thrust of the Sabbath–Jubilee mandates. "To bring good news to the poor" does not mean to provide a heavenly home after death. It means to change the basic socioeconomic and spiritual realities of indebted peasant farmers, landless people, and unemployed or enslaved laborers in this world. "To proclaim release to the captives" originally referred to the exiles in Babylon, but in Jesus' day it probably referred to debtors who were in prison with no means to repay their debts. "Recovery of sight to the blind" had long been one of the eschatological expectations, and it may be understood to refer both to the widespread need of the poor for healing of every kind and to the moral and spiritual blindness of the people and especially of their leaders. "To let the oppressed go free" should be interpreted not only in terms of the specific Sabbath–Jubilee mandate to free the Israelite slaves but also in the larger sense of developing a social reality within which the conditions leading to slavery through debts and loss of land would be reversed. Similarly, we may suggest that "the acceptable year of the Lord" or "the year of the Lord's favor" that Jesus proclaimed as the coming of God's reign was no longer strictly one year in seven or one year in fifty but a new age of perpetual liberty for all God's people from every kind of oppression.

There are many important questions and many important studies concerning Luke 4:16–30. We cannot say definitively whether the Isaiah reading was chosen for or by Jesus. We should note that Luke does not include the following phrases found in Isaiah 61:1–2: "to bind up the broken-hearted," "the day of vengeance of our God," and "to comfort all who mourn." We mentioned in Chapter 4 that Luke adds a powerful phrase from Isaiah 58:6, "to let the oppressed go free." There are various opinions regarding the initial and subsequent reactions of the people to Jesus in Luke's story, which concludes with a threat to his life, no doubt as foreshadowing of his crucifixion. There are various opinions regarding the relationship between Luke's story here and Mark's and Matthew's story of Jesus at the Nazareth synagogue later in their narratives. For a full discussion of these and other questions, we recommend Michael Prior's book, *Jesus the Liberator: Nazareth Liberation Theology (Luke 4:16–30)*. Our concern is simply to affirm Luke's presentation of Jesus' ministry in terms of "the year of the Lord's favor," which closely matches the Sabbath–Jubilee vision. Prior concludes his review of Jesus' message at Nazareth this way:

> Insofar as the brief Lukan account reflects what actually happened, it could do no more than summarize the lively debate which ensued. The core of Jesus' message is that the good news of Isaiah 61, originally directed at the consolation of the returned exiles from Babylon, is transposed into good news for all who are oppressed. . . . The introduction of Isaiah 58:6 into the Isaiah 61 text intensifies the social implications of Jesus' message of freedom. Moreover, Jesus declares the moment of liberation to be Today. (Prior, 1995, p. 141)

Of particular interest for our study is Jesus' use of two examples to illustrate God's intervention on behalf of those in need. The first is the provision of meal and oil for a widow in Sidon and her son through Elijah (Luke 4:25–26); the second is the healing of a Syrian man through Elisha (4:27). The first is a woman, a widow, and a foreigner; the second is a sick and impure foreigner. After hearing these extraordinary examples, the Nazarenes were enraged and tried to kill Jesus. So here we find that Jesus' primary concern was not only for the poor and oppressed in general but specifically for widows and orphans and aliens, a recurring theme of Deuteronomy closely related to the Sabbath mandates.

The other Lucan text in which Jesus declares most clearly his mission is Luke 7:18–23. John the Baptist sends two of his disciples to inquire whether Jesus is the Messiah, "the one who is to come." Jesus responds:

> *Go and tell John what you have seen and heard: the blind receive*
> *their sight, the lame walk, the lepers are cleansed, the deaf hear, the*

dead are raised, the poor have good news brought to them. And blessed is anyone who takes no offense at me. Luke 7:22–23

There is no mention of "the year of the Lord's favor," but the references to the blind and the poor are closely parallel to Luke 4:18 and Isaiah 61:1. The references to the lame, lepers, deaf, and dead are further amplifications. The references to leprosy and offense echo Luke 4:27 and 28.

The importance of this passage is that Jesus is being asked to identify himself as the Messiah, and he responds by defining his mission in terms very similar to his declaration at the Nazareth synagogue. He thus stands in the prophetic tradition, as does John the Baptist, the contemporaneous Elijah, who is also mentioned in the Nazareth synagogue story. Thus we find Jesus' mission identified with the Jubilee vision in the two passages in Luke's Gospel in which Jesus reveals most directly and clearly his mission.

The Parables as Sabbath–Jubilee Message. In his book, *Parables as Subversive Speech: Jesus as Pedagogue of the Oppressed*, William Herzog examines afresh the parables of Jesus using insights from Paulo Freire's pedagogy of the oppressed. He finds that

> the parables were not earthly stories with heavenly meanings but earthy stories with heavy meanings. . . . Instead of reiterating the promise of God's intervention in human affairs, they explored how human beings could respond to break the spiral of violence and the cycle of poverty created by exploitation and oppression. (Herzog, 1994, p. 3)

We will consider briefly here just a few of Luke's parables from this perspective.

The parable of the rich fool, Luke 12:13–21, is set in the context of a squabble over a family inheritance. Jesus begins by warning against the dangers of greed, "for one's life does not consist of the abundance of possessions." Then he tells a story about a rich man who produces abundant crops and decides to build larger barns in order to store them—to hoard and accumulate more wealth. His expectation is to enjoy a luxurious lifestyle and be happy for many years, but alas he dies. "So it is with those who store up treasures for themselves but are not rich toward God." Here we find a negation of Sabbath economics, an expression of the predominant economics of accumulation, which must have been common in Jesus' time as it has been down through history. The reference to the building of larger barns may have brought to Jesus' listeners' minds the experience of the Hebrew slaves in Egypt, when they had the task of building the great storage or supply cities to benefit Pharaoh's empire. The death of this rich man is simply one way of expressing the divine judgment upon that socioeconomic ethic and lifestyle, which proposes overabundance for some at the expense of many but ultimately leads to death.

Luke 14:7–14 provides another glimpse into a common occurrence in Jesus' day and down through history. The parable of the wedding banquet describes how the invited guests scramble for the seats of honor and recommends prudently that one should rather take the lowest place and wait to be moved up by the host. Seating was traditionally arranged in terms of power and prestige with corresponding economic and social benefits for the host and his family. In the latter part of the story, Jesus takes a radical turn with these words, "When you give a luncheon or a dinner, do not invite your friends or your brothers or your relatives or rich neighbors, in case they may invite you in return, and you would be repaid. But when you give a banquet, invite *the poor, the crippled, the lame, and the blind*" (14:12–14, emphasis added). This is the Jubilee option for the poor and oppressed, the sick and excluded, the debtors and imprisoned, for whom God's reign as Jubilee brings good news, healing, and liberation. These are the ones who cannot repay the invitation of God's coming reign and so they are precisely the ones who are to be invited.

The same option is repeated in the following parable of the great dinner, Luke 14:15–24. In this story the invited "proper" guests make excuses and send their regrets. Then the master of the household sends his slave into the streets and lanes to "bring in *the poor, the crippled, the blind, and the lame*" (emphasis added). Finally the master sends the slave to "compel people to come in," taking into account those so humble that they would be too fearful to respond on their own. Those who would traditionally be the honored guests exclude themselves, because they are too busy building their own fortunes or because they disdain the invitation being offered to them. The poor-oppressed-disabled come instead, not because of their virtues but precisely because they do not presume to have any virtues. They receive God's reign; they are the ones who can participate in Sabbath economics, Jubilee spirituality, liberty for all God's people.

Throughout Jesus' ministry his Sabbath–Jubilee message invited the poor and oppressed and those whom the religiously correct considered to be impure sinners. This led to increasing rejection by the authorities and eventually to his death. As we shall see more clearly in Chapter 6, Jesus was confronting the domination system of his time, beginning at the bottom of the socioeconomic–religious order and ending at the power center, the Temple-state in Jerusalem in league with the Roman Empire.

Responsible Discipleship ◆ ◆ ◆ ◆ ◆

We want now to offer experiences that reflect the Sabbath–Jubilee perspectives that we have found in the synoptic Gospels. In some of the following cases, those most directly involved did not consciously or explicitly use the Sabbath and Jubilee mandates as the foundation for their commitment and actions, but we believe that these mandates help us to interpret their contributions, and they may help us to make our own commitment and take action in faithfulness to our calling as followers of Jesus.

Encountering the Holy among the Most Vulnerable

Throughout our study of the Sabbath and Jubilee mandates we have tried to integrate socioeconomic and spiritual concerns, to overcome the artificial divorce that has so long prevailed in Western religion and culture. In this chapter we have considered some of the structures and prejudices that marginalize and exclude minority and even majority populations—the poor, women and children, certain racial–ethnic populations, the sick, and many others. We have found in Jesus' message and mission a fundamental concern for the economically, socially, physically, and religiously marginalized, which echoes the Sabbath–Jubilee mandates. We believe that this concern is also fundamentally a concern for the spiritual well-being of the rich and powerful, the privileged ones, who so often fail to discover God's reign because they refuse to practice solidarity with the excluded ones.

During the 1980s many North Americans were deeply moved by the struggles of the peoples of Central America and by the testimonies of Central American refugees who arrived on their doorsteps. The sanctuary movement opened up opportunities for churches and synagogues and other organizations to hear the refugees' stories and to respond personally and even politically to their cause. Many groups and individuals traveled to Central America to see for themselves what was happening there and to make their own judgment about U.S. government policy and media reports. In September 1986 Jesuit theologian Jon Sobrino of El Salvador made a special presentation at the National Sanctuary Conference in Washington, D.C. His words capture the extraordinary, spiritual impact of the sanctuary and solidarity movements concerned with Central America. His point of departure was Isaiah 57:15:

> For thus says the high and lofty one
> who inhabits eternity, whose name is Holy:
> I dwell in the high and holy place,
> and also with those who are contrite and humble in spirit,
> to revive the spirit of the humble,
> and to revive the heart of the contrite.

Following is a selection from Sobrino's unpublished presentation adapted for liturgical reading. The people's response, also based on Isaiah 57:15, has been added.

The Oppressed-Poor, A Call to Conversion and Life

"The holy" has appeared in history. The "holy" that has appeared in history is the threatened life of the poor.

The Holy One lives among the oppressed-poor.

This life—not only threatened but negated and annihilated so many times—is what makes us tremble by its own tragic and cruel reality, and by being in itself a terrifying question for us about our responsibility for its existence.

The Holy One lives among the oppressed-poor.

We call this life of the poor "holy" because it appears as the ultimate question of God: "What have you done with your brother, your sister?"

The Holy One lives among the oppressed-poor.

We also find ourselves in touch with hope, with creativity, and with the struggle for life, with that which teaches and converts us and shows us a way to be human beings.

The Holy One lives among the oppressed-poor.

In the threatened lives of the poor, we find our brothers and sisters; we find God; and we find ourselves. Once this triple encounter has taken place, living can only mean living in solidarity.

The Holy One lives among the oppressed-poor.

Let us remember that this has arisen, and will continue to arise, in the encounter with the poor, with the crucified peoples, where God and reality are revealed to us with the force of a demand and a call for unity.

The Holy One lives among the oppressed-poor.

Sobrino had no intention of idealizing the poor. He knew very well that they too are so often caught up in the very same machinations that seduce, dehumanize, and destroy. But he and his Jesuit colleagues, who were so brutally murdered by state security forces in November, 1989, had been enabled by the poor to see the institutional, structural nature of sin and were empowered by them to give their lives for the sake of God's reign and God's justice.

Finding God's Word through Openness to Others

In the first part of this chapter, we referred to an article by Pablo Richard in which he cites the prejudices of sixteenth-century Spaniard Juan Inés de Sepúlveda against indigenous peoples, women, children, and the physical body. In that article, Richard goes on to consider the challenge that this mentality represents today in terms of our increasingly globalized reality. He is concerned about the indigenous peoples of Latin America, who continue to suffer the effects of this mentality. He is concerned about women, children, youth, African Americans, and others who are likewise affected by these prejudices. He is also concerned about the dominant peoples of Latin America, whose understanding of reality and whose humanity is distorted by this kind of thinking. As a Bible scholar he is determined to clarify the real meaning of the biblical message among all peoples and social sectors.

> An interpretation of the Bible from the perspective of Indians, women, and the body is therefore a spiritual interpretation carried out with the Spirit with whom it was originally written. The Occidental and colonial reading of the Bible, carried out against Indians, women, and the body is an interpretation that perverts the spiritual sense of the Bible. The Bible was not written with a colonial, patriarchal, and anti-corporal spirit but with the Spirit of the poor and oppressed. Therefore only a hermeneutic of liberation can be a hermeneutic of the Spirit, which is the hermeneutic with which the Bible was written. (Richard, 1996, p. 9)

Richard insists that indigenous peoples and other racial and cultural sectors, women, and popular movements have not only the right but the necessity to resist the impositions of Christendom and to affirm their own spiritual roots. Only in this way will they be able to discover the true message of the Bible and to help us all to construct a true spirituality. Indigenous people, African Americans, women, and other marginalized and excluded sectors must play an essential role in the recovery of the Bible as foundation for faith and ministry for both the excluded and the dominant, for the poor and the rich.

> The Bible is read and interpreted in the bosom of movements of indigenous and African American peoples, workers and peasants, women, ecologists, and youth. The Word of God is read with the Spirit that becomes visible and active in these movements in relation to the body, culture, women, nature, youth. The experience of the Spirit is not found in the soul over against the body but in the affirmation of life over against death. Life is affirmed clearly as fullness of life of the body, the life of the poor, the Indian, the Black, the woman, the youth, and nature. The space of the Spirit is the world defined as the relation body-culture-gender-work-nature. An interpretation of the Bible from the body, culture, women, work, nature is a requirement of the Spirit. In the popular reading of the Bible the experience of the Spirit occupies a new social place in history. (ibid., p. 9)

We have noted at several points that the perspectives of the poor, indigenous peoples, women, and other marginalized people enable us to understand the Jubilee vision and mandate.

Discovering Our Own Humanity by Affirming the Full Humanity of Others

Since the 1960s, Latin American Liberation Theology has made an enormous impact on the churches, cultures, and peoples of the region, and it has been a point of reference in many other regions. Its fundamental insight into the struggles of the Latin American peoples, into the biblical message, and into the church's mission has been socioeconomic. Social analysis has become essential for theology and ministry and for the critique of society and of the church itself. The depth and breadth of the task of reworking theology and ministry from this perspective is evident in the outpouring of formal publications and popular literature, primarily in Spanish and Portuguese, both Catholic and Protestant. It is precisely this new socioeconomic perspective that has driven us back to the biblical vision of Jubilee.

Now we see that this is only a beginning. Since the 1980s, Latin American women and men have been pressing for similar efforts in terms of gender, which is now increasingly recognized to be as important as socioeconomic analysis, because it forces us to deal with the most intimate and pervasive dimensions of oppression and liberation. Furthermore, it deals with the most basic processes of formation, nurture, and identity, beginning with the birth of every human being. Surrounding the 500th anniversary of the European invasion of the New World, efforts to rethink and rewrite history and theology from the perspective of the indigenous and African peoples of Latin America have multiplied. Important work has begun from the perspective of children, people with various limitations, seniors, and others. We believe that these efforts all correspond to the Sabbath–Jubilee vision of alternative socioeconomic–spiritual possibilities in which all God's people enjoy fullness of life, where all are subjects and participate in the formation of that life, where all find dignity and pursue their dreams for themselves and for their children.

As the human frontiers multiply, the biblical, theological, and pastoral possibilities and demands multiply as well. As we engage in and cross those frontiers, we deepen and broaden our own humanity. The palette of our personal and collective humanity is becoming wonderfully varied; it is being enriched far beyond anything we could have imagined, even as the suffering of humanity is ever more deeply disturbing. This is how we now see the message and ministry of Jesus in keeping with the Sabbath and Jubilee mandates. We shall carry forward these concerns in the next chapter, which will consider Jesus' confrontation with the domination systems of his time.

6

Jesus and the Domination System

The history of our world, especially of our Western world and particularly of the United States, is to a remarkable extent a history of domination—domination of White Europeans over native and African peoples, men over women, rich and powerful elites over poor and disenfranchised majorities, various ethnic and social groups over others, owners and employers over skilled and unskilled workers, citizens over immigrants, military-economic-political empires over variously subjugated nations. The Bible likewise is the story of domination by successive empires and regimes, by men over women, by ruling political, economic, social, and religious elites, but its message is largely a message from the perspective of the oppressed and on behalf of their liberation. So we shall now consider how Jesus dealt with the domination system of his own people and his world, using the Sabbath–Jubilee materials as a key to this investigation. We come to this task with the following questions:

- How are we to understand our world today in light of the now more than 500 years of oppression, patriarchy, and racism in our North American culture?
- How did Jesus and his followers deal with the domination system in first-century Palestine?
- How can we confront, resist, and overcome the more than 500 years of accumulated entitlements that rule our lives?

These questions will take us through our now accustomed process of analysis of "Today's World," "Biblical Faith," and "Responsible Discipleship."

Today's World ◆ ◆ ◆ ◆ ◆

500 Years of Conquest

No record of the conquest of the New World is more powerful and disturbing than Eduardo Galeano's book, *Open Veins of Latin America: Five Cen-*

112

turies of the Pillage of a Continent, which was first published in Spanish in 1971 and has gone through scores of printings in Latin America. He portrays the morbid consequences of the fanatic lust for gold and silver, lands, and power among the Spanish and Portuguese *conquistadores* and also among the English and the emerging rulers of the U.S. empire to the north. No period of civilization has seen more devastation and genocide over so many by so few, and the legacy of that conquest is very much with us today. We can now see that not only the aboriginal peoples of Latin America and North America but also the African continent and the rest of the entire world have borne the impact of that conquest that began at the end of the fifteenth century. For it was the wealth extracted from the mines and fields and labor of conquered America that financed the Iberian empires, the Industrial Revolution, the British and Dutch empires, and eventually the U.S. empire, so that they could impose their political and economic rule all around the planet in order to reap a disproportionate and expanding share of the world's wealth and accelerate consumption of the world's natural resources. This has been the primary force behind the twin tragedies of our time: the massive growth of poverty and the progressive contamination and destruction of the Earth's ecosystem.

Fearful lessons are to be learned from that conquest:

◆ Wealth and technology give enormous power to some over others.
◆ That power advantage has been used to spawn unlimited exploitation of the disadvantaged.
◆ Greed has pushed that exploitation to impose unconscionable oppression.
◆ That oppression has taken the form of inhuman privation, torture, massacres, and even genocide.
◆ Such inhuman treatment has been reinforced by patriarchy, racism, and religious bigotry.

We can hardly imagine the thinking and behavior unleashed by the enormous military advantage of the "Christian" European conquerors. Hernán Cortés landed at Veracruz, Mexico, with 100 sailors and 508 soldiers, and he conquered resplendent Tenochtitlan, the Aztec capital, now Mexico City, which then had 300,000 inhabitants, five times as many as Madrid. Francisco Pizarro, "an illiterate pig-breeder," entered Cuzco, the capital of the great Inca empire, with 180 soldiers and 37 horses (Galeano, 1973, pp. 26–29). The inordinate power of the European weapons combined with limitless greed led to unheard of exploitation, oppression, and slaughter. As Galeano tells it,

> Between 1503 and 1660, 185,000 kilograms of gold and 16,000,000 of silver arrived at the Spanish port of Sanlucar de Barrameda. Silver shipped to Spain in little more than a century and a half exceeded three times the total European reserves—and it must be remembered that these official figures are not complete. (ibid., p. 33)

The great silver mines of Potosí in what is now Bolivia are credited with the death of 8 million indigenous human beings over a period of 300 years through forced labor, cold, malnutrition, and disease. Overall, the pre-Columbian population of the Americas is estimated to have totaled 70 million; 150 years later it numbered perhaps 3.5 million (ibid., p. 50). With incredible arrogance the European conquerors assumed the right to expropriate, rape, enslave, torture, and kill with impunity. Gradually advocates of indigenous rights were able to formulate laws in their defense, but by then so few remained that massive kidnapping and importing of African slaves was underway to replace them.

However remote these events must seem to the average North American today, we must take notice of the fact that Latin American analysts are saying that the abuses and violence, exploitation and privation of the last twenty-five years are in many ways comparable to that earlier conquest. To be sure, the reign of terror by military regimes of the 1970s and 1980s (Guatemala, El Salvador, Brazil, Uruguay, Argentina, Chile, etc.) was largely executed by local officials, supported by the United States, and those regimes have now been replaced by more benign economic elites. Nevertheless the logic of wealth accumulation and poverty intensification is producing more suffering and death than ever before in Latin America and throughout the world. We must ask ourselves how such inhumanity is possible today and what is the role of North Americans and Europeans in this current conquest.

500 Years of Economic Oppression, Patriarchy, and Racism

Another invaluable resource for North Americans is Howard Zinn's book, *A People's History of the United States, 1492–Present*. Zinn recognizes that history is usually written by the winners and as such is inevitably distorted. So he has given us, not unlike Galeano, a "rereading" of U.S. history "from the underside," that is, from the perspective of Native Americans, poor white serfs, African Americans, women, workers, and worldwide victims of U.S. "manifest destiny." The result of Zinn's approach is devastating, especially for those of us who were history majors in college and never saw this side of our own history. It should be required reading, if not in schools and universities, certainly in our churches, as a necessary part of our education and preparation for life in this terribly unjust world. It is especially important for those of us who belong to the privileged sectors of our society and our world—if we are to escape from the structures and prejudices that benefit us at the expense of others and if we intend to recover our own humanity in solidarity with others whose humanity is threatened by our privileges.

From the beginning of our North American history there have been, of course, various mechanisms by which powerful and wealthy elites have gained, maintained, and augmented their privileges at the expense of those at the bottom of the social and economic pyramids. White craftsmen and poor Whites were invited to make common use of their racial "superiority" in exploitation and abuse of Blacks and natives. White men exploited and abused both White and non-White women because of their gender "superiority." Periodically, the dominant White elite made concessions and compromises with middle class and other "inferiors" so that the rebellious sectors could be quelled and the basic socioeconomic pyramids could be kept relatively stable.

Zinn analyzes the peculiar nature of the exploitation and oppression of women, who have been largely absent from earlier histories of our country. He refers to women as "the intimately oppressed" because of the way they have been kept in the background and treated as inferiors. Among African and Native Americans and among the poor, women have been doubly oppressed. Among all groups they were for so long given tasks as "a convenience for men, who could use, exploit, and cherish someone who was at the same time servant, sex mate, companion, and bearer-teacher-warden of his children" (Zinn, 1995, p. 102). In the early sixteenth century, "women were imported [to the Americas] as sex slaves, child-bearers, companions" (ibid., p. 103). Many came as indentured servants. Servant and slave girls were commonly abused sexually. Black slave women were often separated from their husbands and even from their children. According to the dominant cultural and religious ideology, White women were expected to be subject to their husbands, to be occupied in the home and not in public affairs, to turn over their property to their husbands, and to be sexually pure. The vicissitudes of life in the colonies and on the frontier, however, often required them to assume responsibilities on a par with men.

The progress of women and of men toward full participation and full humanity from those beginnings, through many struggles, is one of the great unfolding mysteries coming to light finally in our own generation. Even now resistance is evident in many sectors and dimensions of our personal and collective life. The failure to adopt an Equal Rights amendment to the U.S. Constitution, something that Costa Rica achieved years ago, is symbolic of the difficult road that we walk still.

The struggle of Native North Americans is perhaps the most tragic of all, and it continues. From the time of the original colonies, through the White migrations across the Appalachian Mountains, on to the Rockies, and finally to the West Coast, the great native nations have had their lands taken, their villages burned, their women raped, their cultures and religions vilified, their right to life denied. Their story is replete with official deceit and betrayal, massacres and forced removals, and endless treaties leading to genocide. It can be argued that the wars and skirmishes against the native peoples played a decisive role in the formation of the heroic, military, chauvinistic American mind, which in the twentieth century has wreaked havoc on Third World peoples around the world through military intervention, secret operations, and economic warfare.

The human cost of the slave system will forever be incomprehensible to nonslaves, especially to Whites. The legacy of slavery in the U.S. psyche, for both Blacks and Whites, may never be fully exorcised. Toni Morrison's novel *Beloved* plumbs the depths of that suffering in almost mystical terms through the story of a mother who kills her own daughter rather than submit her to a life of slavery. Howard Zinn entitles his chapter on this subject, "Slavery without Submission," in his effort to capture the struggle of African Americans for survival, dignity, and freedom through 200 years of slavery in the United States (Zinn, 1995, pp. 177–205). By 1860 there were four million slaves in the south, producing enormous profits for their White owners, and there were 200,000 free Blacks in the north. The fruits of this iniquitous system are still borne by the women, children, and men of Harlem, South Chicago, and South Central Los Angeles. They are also borne among the still largely White suburbs of all our cities. The humanity of rich and poor of both races will be fundamentally deformed as long as this racism persists.

500 *Years of Entitlement as Addiction*

It is easy to see that the prevailing patterns of domination in our culture have been tremendously profitable, though dehumanizing, for those who are at the top. We have seen how devastating they have been and continue to be for those at the bottom. We are now beginning to see that they are "addictive," so much so that it is difficult to see how they can be overcome.

Ann Wilson Schaef is a feminist who has had professional experience with substance addictions (alcohol, drugs, nicotine, caffeine, food) and process addictions (money, gambling, work, religion, worry). Her book, *When Society Becomes an Addict*, applies her understanding of these addictions to the addictive force of social entitlements: She provides the following definitions and applies them to U.S. society.

- ◆ An addiction is any process over which we are powerless. It takes control of us, causing us to do and think things that are inconsistent with our personal values and leading us to become progressively more compulsive and possessive. A sure sign of an addiction is the sudden need to deceive ourselves and others—to lie, deny, and cover up. (Schaef, 1988, p. 18)
- ◆ An addiction keeps us unaware of what is going on inside us. We do not have to deal with our anger, pain, depression, confusion, or even our joy and love. (ibid., p. 18)
- ◆ As we lose contact with ourselves, we also lose contact with other people and the world around us. (ibid., p. 19)
- ◆ We are aware that something is very wrong, but the addictive thinking tells us that it could not possibly be our fault. (ibid., p. 19)

◆ The longer we wait to be rescued, the worse our addiction becomes. Regardless of what we are addicted to, it takes more and more to create the desired effect, and no amount is ever enough. (ibid. 19)

◆ Like any serious disease, an addiction is progressive, and it will lead to death unless we actively recover from it. (ibid., p. 18)

The concept of codependence helps to establish the relationship between personal and collective addictions. Alcoholics Anonymous has given much attention to the patterns that family members and friends develop in order to cope with their addicted loved ones. Rather than provide solutions, these behavior patterns tend to "enable" addicts to continue their downward spiral and also to trap their concerned relatives and friends in emotional and even physical self-destruction along with them. Our culture approves and encourages codependence—above all with the patterns of economic, gender, and racial domination.

Schaef goes on to describe the characteristics and processes of our addictive culture. She affirms unequivocally that "The White Male System is the Addictive System; the Addictive System is the White Male System. They are one and the same, signifying that the system in which we live has set our society on the path toward non-living" (ibid., p. 37). All of us who live within this system are addicted to it unless we resist, are recovering from it, and pursue an alternative system that is life-affirming. Schaef lists the characteristics of the addictive system, which are the same as the characteristics of specific substance addictions: self-centeredness, the illusion of control, crisis orientation, depression, stress, dishonesty, abnormal thinking processes, negativism, defensiveness, tunnel vision, frozen feelings, ethical deterioration, fear, illusion (ibid., pp. 37–95). She then analyzes the processes by which the addictive system holds sway over our society. Virtually no one is free from these characteristics and processes, which is why we must all resist, recover, and pursue an alternative system. If we do not, we shall continue down the path to nonliving and contribute to the death of colleagues, friends, and loved ones and also of multitudes around the world. Further, the organizations of which we are a part, even our churches, will continue to be addictive, fostering both substance and social addictions, if we do not, individually and collectively, resist and recover from our own addictions.

Sooner or later, relatively rich First World Christians have to face the agonizing reality of economic, gender, and racial–ethnic injustice. We need to ask ourselves again and again why we have so much, not just material goods but privileges and opportunities of all kinds, when so many have so little. As injustice deepens and the results of inequality intensify, threatening the very survival of our sisters and brothers around the world, we must deepen our analysis of these socioeconomic and cultural realities, our search for biblical–theological guidance, and our commitment to fundamental change and effective involvement in the struggle for life for all God's people.

We can readily see, however, that most First World people, including most Christians, avoid and deny these realities with increasing intensity even as they become more evident and more urgent. In the United States the super-rich press for major tax breaks; the middle class complains about loss of buying power; and the poor face reduction of employment opportunities, salaries, welfare, and even education, health care, and housing. We all assume that we are entitled to whatever we receive and want more, especially those of us who are most privileged and most powerful. Almost all of us adjust our lifestyle—and our indebtedness—upward as quickly as we can. Fed by the media and the advertising industry, our wants become needs, and needs become entitlements. Any reversal of this tendency is unacceptable, perhaps unthinkable. We are addicted to our self-made entitlements. When we hear about devastating poverty in Africa or India, when we see homelessness in our own cities, and even when members of our own churches, neighborhoods, and professions face serious economic crises, we hold onto our material resources ever more tightly as our right, our private business. Certainly we may be moved to contribute marginally from our disposable income, but we would never consider giving up our own capital, whether hard-earned or inherited.

The matrix of entitlements that we now face is very complex and very seductive. No matter where we find ourselves in the socioeconomic, professional, educational, racial–ethnic, gender, and age pyramids, we can always point to others who have more advantages than we do. Simplistic critiques of class, race, and gender polarization are totally inadequate. They can even foster and justify more polarization. There is nothing romantic or pure about being poor, female, Black, or whatever. The struggle is not just between rich and poor, men and women, Whites and Blacks. The dominant system of domination is far more sophisticated. Each pyramid, especially the socioeconomic pyramid, functions rather as a continuum all the way from the poorest of the poor to the super-rich, and all of us, however poor or however rich, contribute to the stability of this pyramid by striving to climb higher, usually at the expense of others. This is the genius and the perversion of the current market-centered socioeconomic system, which is driven by competition and ideologies of success. In order to overcome the addiction of these entitlements, we must find new biblical–theological foundations and new spiritual–pastoral models.

Biblical Faith ◆ ◆ ◆ ◆ ◆

We turn once again to the Gospels. We shall build on our work in the previous chapter, which demonstrated that Jesus proclaimed the coming of God's reign as Jubilee. We shall also continue to base our understanding of the Sabbath–Jubilee vision on our earlier exploration of its Old Testament roots, according to which Yahweh requires God's people to resist mechanisms and structures of oppression and build a liberating socioeconomic–spiritual order in which all might enjoy fullness of life. We will now approach the four Gospels and try to see how Jesus' ministry, with its Jubilee orientation, led inevitably to a confrontation with the current system of domination, which led in turn to his death on the cross. Our first step will be to consider Jesus' teaching and action as subversive of the current socioeconomic and religious–political culture of first-century Palestine. Our second step will be to examine the nature of the Jesus movement as an alternative community with an alternative style of leadership. And our third step will be to trace Jesus' confrontation with the domination system from the beginning of his ministry in Galilee to his final condemnation and crucifixion at Jerusalem.

Subversive Teaching and Action

Jesus' Call to the Tax Collectors. The calling of Levi the tax collector is found in Mark 2:13–17, Matthew 9:9–13, and Luke 5:27–32. In those days tax collectors were despised as collaborators and extortionists, for they were authorized to collect fees and taxes for the Jerusalem authorities and for Rome, and they were expected to make a profit for themselves. They enriched the social and religious elites and also themselves by extracting whatever they could from peasant farmers, artisans, and small businesses. Apparently Levi left behind this lucrative business (Luke affirms he "left everything") to follow Jesus. Nevertheless, when Levi invited Jesus and his disciples to dinner at his house, he also invited "many tax collectors"—his associates and friends. The surprise element in this story is that Levi also invited "many sinners" and that they accepted his invitation. We must assume, on the basis of earlier observations, that these sinners were poor, oppressed debtors of the underclass: "the scribes of the Pharisees saw that [Jesus] was eating with sinners and tax collectors" (Mark 2:16). These are the makings of a real conflict.

This is not, however, simply a conflict between self-righteous Pharisees and humble sinners. It is also a meal shared by creditors (tax collectors) and debtors (sinners). Table fellowship had deep social, even sacred, meaning in those days. The Pharisees refused to eat with sinners, because the latter could not live up to the rigorous ritual cleansings of the former, and to sit or recline at table together would imply inclusion in the same group as equals. So it was to be expected that the scribes of the Pharisees would criticize Jesus for eating with outcast sinners. But in this case Jesus was eating with sinners *and* tax collectors, which must have suggested a political threat to the Pharisees, for now those natural enemies were coming together around Jesus. This Jesus, who was undermining the authority of priests and scribes by casting out unclean spirits (Mark 1:21–28), healing lepers (Mark 1:40–45), and forgiving sins/debts (Mark 2:1–12), was apparently developing a movement among outcast sinners and disaffected tax collectors! Crowds of poor, unclean, disenfranchised people (*óchlos*) were gathering about him (Mark 2:13). And he was proclaiming to them the coming of God's reign!

So they criticized Jesus, and he replied:

> *Those who are well have no need of a physician, but those who are sick; I have come to call not the righteous but sinners.*   Mark 2:17

It is tempting to see this as a rejection by Jesus of the self-righteous Pharisees, but it may in fact be one of his many attempts to call them too to repentance and faith. He saw clearly that they were excluding themselves from God's reign by their exclusion of the poor and oppressed, of sinners and debtors. He was proclaiming God's reign as a free, gracious offer of liberation from poverty and oppression, sin and debt. Those who knew that they were sick were welcoming the Great Physician, but tragically those who thought they were well refused God's healing reign in their lives. They considered themselves to be the "righteous" ones, and they did not recognize that they were accomplices in a powerful system of injustice. They failed to see in Jesus' teachings and actions the coming of Jubilee.

In Luke's Gospel the story of the calling of Levi near the beginning of Jesus' ministry is complemented by the story of the calling of Zacchaeus, another tax collector, at the end of his ministry, Luke 19:1–10. Zacchaeus was "a chief tax collector and was rich," but he was eager to see Jesus, "so he ran ahead and climbed a sycamore tree to see him." Jesus sees him and invites himself to Zacchaeus' house, which causes grumbling. Zacchaeus is converted, announcing, "Look, half of my possessions, Lord, I will give to the poor; and if I have defrauded anyone of anything, I will pay back four times as much" (v. 8) This reminds us of Jesus' recitation of the Ten Commandments to the rich man with the additional phrase, "Do not defraud." It further reminds us of the Sabbath–Jubilee mandates to redistribute wealth, forgive debts, and free slaves. Jesus says to Zacchaeus, "Today salvation has come to this house" (v. 9).

Jesus' identification with tax collectors and sinners/debtors, the transformation of Levi and Zacchaeus, and their subsequent actions were all subversive of the dominant customs and structures of oppression. They were manifestations of Sabbath economics, Jubilee spirituality, and liberty for all God's people.

Jesus' Call to the Pharisees.   Stories about the anointing of Jesus appear in all four Gospels, though they are given very different contexts and meanings in each. We shall look at Luke 7:36–50. In this case Jesus is invited to the house of Simon, a Pharisee, and while they are at table a woman, "who was a sinner," comes to Jesus and bathes his feet with her tears, dries them with her hair, and anoints them with ointment. It is in many ways an extraordinary occurrence. This was a dinner for men only, and they were Pharisees, concerned always for ritual purity and social correctness. This woman should not even appear in their company. A woman should not let down her hair except in the privacy of her bedroom. And she should not touch another man, at least not in public in this intimate fashion. So Simon and his friends are scandalized, and because Jesus is not, Simon questions whether Jesus really is a prophet.

Jesus proceeds to tell Simon a parable about two debtors, which brings to mind the Sabbath–Jubilee theme of debt forgiveness. Simon interprets the parable well, indicating that greater debt forgiven will bring greater love. So Jesus compares this woman's outpouring of love with Simon's failure to provide even the required foot washing for his invited guest. He concludes by saying to him, "her sins, which were many, have been forgiven; hence she has shown great love. But the one to whom little is forgiven, loves little" (v. 47). To the woman Jesus says, "Your sins are forgiven. . . . Your faith has saved you; go in peace" (vv. 48, 49).

We find in this story that Jesus is challenging and overturning the domination system at a very basic, personal level. The woman is liberated by Jesus from the social stigma of her sinful/debtor/impure status. She accepts the coming of God's reign as sheer grace, and she pours out her love freely on Jesus. The Pharisees, however, remain aloof, critical, condemning, and excluding "sinners." They are unable to accept the coming of God's reign as grace, for they are bound by their own prejudices, self-justification, and selfishness. Clearly Jesus' action toward the woman and his parable are directed toward them and their system of religious–ideological domination. In effect, he invites them to enter God's reign as this sinful woman has, to receive and to give freely. That would enable them to practice Sabbath economics, Jubilee spirituality, freedom and well-being for all God's people.

Jesus' Call for Socioeconomic Justice. The parable of the rich man and Lazarus, Luke 16:19–31, relates clearly to the Sabbath–Jubilee mandates. The rich man, "who was dressed in purple and fine linen and who feasted sumptuously every day," represents the small urban elite who acquired their wealth by taking advantage of unpaid mortgages of peasant farmers, accumulating large landholdings, exploiting landless laborers and bond slaves, and engaging in profitable trade arrangements with the Temple and itinerant merchants. His mansion had a gate to guard him from the poor. The poor man, Lazarus, "covered with sores, who longed to satisfy his hunger with what fell from the rich man's table," represents the other side of the same socioeconomic coin, the urban poor. They probably came from peasant families that lost their land or no longer had sufficient land to feed all their children. So all but the eldest had to try a trade, work as farm laborers, or migrate to the city. As urban workers, their fate varied with seasonal and long-term conditions. Lazarus lost out and was cast out by the system, falling into extreme poverty, hunger, malnutrition, disease, and death.

The parable then makes a dramatic turn when both men die. The poor man, whose life manifested total rejection, "was carried away by the angels to be with Abraham." The rich man, whose life appeared to manifest God's blessing, was tormented in Hades. He called out to Father Abraham to send Lazarus to cool his burning tongue, but Abraham responded that the separation they had experienced in life was now translated into an unbridgeable chasm. The rich man then begged Abraham to send Lazarus to warn his five brothers, but Abraham replied, "They have Moses and the prophets; they should listen to them." And when the rich man insisted that someone from the dead would bring them to repentance, Abraham replied, "If they do not listen to Moses and the prophets, neither will they be convinced even if someone rises from the dead."

Many interpretations have been made of this parable, but none makes more sense than a simple application of the Sabbath–Jubilee perspective. Jesus calls his audience to listen to Moses (the Law) and the Prophets, which forbade the accumulation of wealth and the exclusion or marginalization of the poor. In those days the Temple-state with its sacrifices and the Pharisees with their rigorous legalism and purity rites presumed they were applying the Law, but they were violating the fundamental call to socioeconomic justice, which was at the heart of the Law and the Prophets. They had adopted the ways of other nations, so that there were a few very rich, like the character of the parable, and there were many very poor, like Lazarus. As William Herzog sees it,

> The parable is not a story about abstract social types but a story about representatives of two social classes, the urban elites and the desperate expendables, those who had nearly everything and those who had almost nothing. In this case, wealth may indeed lead to Hades, for such wealth could be obtained only by the systemic exploitation of the poor, and it could be maintained only by their continual oppression. The urban elites who lived at the expense of the poor twisted Torah and Temple to serve their ends. They read the Prophets for their comfort and Moses to study the purities lest they should become unclean. Their wealth and its use in conspicuous consumption, their rapacious greed and its extraction of any surplus from the poor, their pursuit of power and privilege with its accompanying suppression of the people of the land, all these characteristics of the rich man's class reveal that its wealth is no sign of blessing but a curse on the land. The rich man is not overtly condemned for his wealth, and the parable probably assumes that he is pious and Torah-observant because those were characteristics of the ruling elites in Jerusalem and other urban areas. But his fate after death and his subsequent refusal to perceive Lazarus as kin describe the nearly insurmountable barriers erected by his class and its privilege. Conversely, aside from his name, Lazarus is nowhere portrayed as patient, pious, or trusting Yahweh. (Herzog, 1994, p. 128)

This parable was subversive teaching! It undermined the prevailing assumption that prosperity was a sign of God's blessing. It reversed the common belief that "good people," those who do well in this life, go to be with Abraham and "sinners/debtors" go to Hades and suffer punishment. It brought into the open the socioeconomic realities of life in first-century Palestine and challenged them with the Sabbath–Jubilee vision. It reveals why Jesus was attacked so violently by the domination system of his day. It may also be read as an ironic reference to those who continued to ignore Jesus' message even after his rising from the dead.

Creating Alternative Community

At the center of Mark's Gospel we find a concentration of events and sayings in which Jesus clarifies the meaning of discipleship. The first part of Mark (1:14–8:26) takes place in Galilee. The last part (11:1–16:8) takes place in and around Jerusalem. The middle section (8:27–10:52) covers Jesus' journey from Caesarea Philippi, north of Galilee, to Jericho, on his way south to Jerusalem. This geographical progression is symbolic of the impending, decisive confrontation between Jesus and the religious, economic, social, and political leaders of the domination system of that time. Jesus is on his way to his death on a cross. Mark makes this very clear with three passages in which Jesus declares his intention to go to Jerusalem (8:31–33, 9:30–31, l0:32–34). In relation to each of these three announcements of his coming judgment and sentencing at the hands of the authorities in Jerusalem, Jesus calls his followers to an alternative kind of leadership in an alternative kind of community. This whole middle section of Mark's Gospel begins with the incident at Caesarea Philippi, when Jesus asks his disciples, "Who do people say that I am?" and "Who do you say that I am?" and Peter makes his declaration, "You are the Messiah" (8:27–30). It is precisely from this critical point that Jesus begins to declare that he must go up to Jerusalem.

The response of the disciples to these three announcements is truly remarkable. From the perspective of the early church and the Gospel writers, the Twelve Disciples were revered. They were the ones closest to Jesus throughout his ministry. Yet in the first passage (8:31–33), Peter, whatever his good intentions, is presented as a satanic obstacle for Jesus. Immediately following the second passage (9:30–31), we find the Twelve arguing among themselves about who is the greatest. And following the third passage (10:32–34), James and John ask for the foremost places in Jesus' kingdom, and when the other ten disciples hear about it they are angry, because they too want to be foremost. In all three cases, Jesus is declaring his intention to go up to Jerusalem, not to assume greatness, power, or privilege but to give himself up for the sake of God's reign.

The words of Jesus in Mark 10:42–45 sum up Jesus' intention for himself and for his followers:

You know that among the Gentiles those whom they recognize as their rulers lord it over them, and their great ones are tyrants over them. But it is not so among you; but whoever wishes to become great among you must be your servant, and whoever wishes to be first among you must be slave of all. For the Son of Man came not to be served but to serve, and to give his life as a ransom for many.

Jesus clarifies for his disciples the fundamental difference between his movement and the dominant socioeconomic order. He refers to "the Gentiles" or "the nations," but he might just as well have included his own people, the Jews, for they had conformed themselves to the rule of Rome as had other nations under the Roman Empire. We are in fact reminded here of the time when the tribes of Israel demanded a king as the neighboring peoples had. They wanted the security of a central power structure to defend them from their enemies and to create privileges and power for some over others. Similarly, being so close to the Messiah, the Twelve could not escape the temptation to grasp for privileges and power. They did not yet comprehend the revolutionary nature of Jesus' movement, whose privilege was to be servants/slaves, whose power was to be found in self-denial and self-giving.

Far too little attention has been given to the often repeated, pithy aphorisms concerning discipleship found here in these three passages and elsewhere in the Gospels. The fact that they appear so many times indicates that they were important for Jesus' ministry and also for the early church. They must be important for Jesus' followers today. Following is a partial list from Mark 8:27–10:52:

If any want to become my followers, let them deny themselves and take up their cross and follow me.

Mark 8:34

For those who want to save their life will lose it, and those who lose their life for my sake, and for the sake of the gospel, will save it.

Mark 8:35

For what will it profit them to gain the whole world and forfeit their life? Indeed, what can they give in return for their life?

Mark 8:36

Whoever wants to be first must be last of all and servant of all.

Mark 9:35

Truly I tell you, whoever does not receive the kingdom of God as a little child will never enter it.

Mark 10:15

It is easier for a camel to go through the eye of a needle than for someone who is rich to enter the kingdom of God.

Mark 10:25

Many who are first will be last, and the last will be first.

Mark 10:31

*Whoever wishes to become great among you must be your servant,
and whoever wishes to be first among you must be slave of all.*

Mark 10:43–44

The Sabbath and Jubilee mandates have taught us that God's intention is for God's people to resist and reverse the human propensity toward self-aggrandizement in terms of wealth and power. These mandates are grounded in God's intervention on behalf of an enslaved, exploited, oppressed people. Jesus evidently assumed these same mandates when he proclaimed God's reign as Jubilee and gave himself in the struggle for fullness of life for the poor, the marginalized, the oppressed, the sick and impure, the little ones, the outcast. He called his disciples to renounce privilege, wealth, and power—that was the meaning of discipleship. He expected this mandate to lead to the cross—for himself and for his followers.

Confronting Structural Sin

That Jesus was confronting the domination system of first-century Palestine is evident throughout the Gospels, particularly in the conflict stories, some of which we have already considered. We have intimated also that this confrontation and these conflicts were inevitable consequences of Jesus' proclamation of God's reign as Jubilee. The Sabbath–Jubilee mandates were a direct challenge to the way power and wealth and even religion were organized. So we need to consider how the domination system worked and how Jesus carried out his struggle for the fullness of life of his people in confrontation with the domination system.

The Temple in Jerusalem was one of the richest, most powerful institutions in the world at that time. Under the authority of the Roman Empire, backed by the Roman army that occupied Palestine, the chief high priest exercised political power like that of a king. The high priests were selected from a tiny circle of privileged families of the Jerusalem oligarchy, which included owners of major businesses and large landholders. The high priests maintained close ties with Rome, were responsible for collecting Rome's taxes and tributes as well as the Temple taxes and fees, and they controlled shipments of basic grains and the transfer of capital. They were in fact administrators for the Roman Empire in Palestine. They presided over the Sanhedrin, which served as the national legislature, and provided religious–ideological justification for Roman rule. The Temple monopoly included the trade in animals, birds, oil, and grains for sacrifices. This explains Jesus' burst of anger at the money changers, which was evidently directed at the whole Temple apparatus of exploitation and oppression. It also explains the close tie between the high priests and the landed oligarchy, for the latter needed to do business above all with the Temple.

The scribes and Pharisees, who are so prominent in the Gospels, played an essential role in the stabilization of the religious and socioeconomic pyramid. The scribes in Jerusalem included members and close friends of the Sanhedrin; the scribes of Galilee were closely related to the synagogues. As interpreters of the Law, their function was to support the local and national religious structures, notably the debt code and tributary system. The Pharisees maintained the religious purity code, with rigorous rites and rules, in tacit support of the status quo. The Herodians and Sadducees were even more closely allied with the high priests and Rome; they were the wealthy elite, the Jewish ruling class. All these sectors ultimately collaborated in the exploitation of the people for their own benefit, and they all collaborated ultimately in the conspiracy to do away with Jesus and his movement.

There was also an intermediate class made up of independent artisans, small farmers, and some 18,000 minor Temple functionaries. But most people were poor, constituting a significant underclass. They provided the labor that produced the income that was funneled upward to the ruling class and Rome. They were largely passive and obedient to those above them for obvious economic and religious reasons. Only through the authoritative channels could they sell their produce, pay their taxes and fees, and provide for their families at a minimal, subsistence level. Below the poor farmers and workers were the impure (tanners, garbage handlers, shepherds, prostitutes, Samaritans) and last of all the expendables (lepers, demon-possessed, beggars, slaves). The danger of falling into these lowest classes—which inevitably led to extreme poverty, hunger, disease, and death—was a permanent threat to the population as a whole, a constant prod to work hard, obey the authorities, and avoid reprisals. This explains why Jesus' ministry among the poor, the impure, and the expendables caused such outrage. It explains why any hint of the Jubilee in his message would have provoked massive opposition among those who were tied into the status quo.

In all four Gospels Jesus' ministry concludes with the story of his confrontation with the Jerusalem authorities, his death, and his resurrection. The setting is the Passover Festival, which commemorates the deliverance from Egypt, itself the foundation for the Sabbath–Jubilee vision. We will not examine those long passion narratives, but we would like to mention Walter Wink's research into the biblical "principalities and powers." His volume, *Engaging the Powers: Discernment and Resistance in a World of Domination*, provides a helpful understanding of the structural dimension of oppression. On the basis of extensive lexical and exegetical studies of the New Testament Greek word for "world" (*cosmos*), Wink concludes that in many places that word, which seems to indicate that Jesus belongs to some other world, should be retranslated or reinterpreted not as "world" but as "domination system," which Wink defines as "the human sociological realm that exists in estrangement from God" (Wink, 1992, p. 51).

Thus in John 7, Jesus tells his brothers to go the Festival of Booths without him because "the [domination system] cannot hate you, but it hates me because I testify against it that its works are evil" (v. 7). Similarly, in John 8:23, Jesus says to the scribes and the Pharisees, "You are from below, I am from above; you are of this [domination system], I am not of this [domination system]." At the end of his ministry, when Jesus is on trial for his life, he responds to the high priest, the supreme representative of the system of religious, social, economic, and political domination, "I have spoken openly to the [domination system]; I have always taught in synagogues and in the Temple" (John 18:20). Then he stands before the Roman governor, Pilate, and testifies, "My kingdom is not from this [domination system]" (John 18:36). Thus Jesus' disciples are likewise to reject the domination system, for "those who hate their life in this [domination system] will keep it for eternal life" (John 12:25, cp. Mark 8:37).

This very simple but very basic correction in our reading of the Gospels and also of other parts of the New Testament can help us overcome the latent dualism so widespread and so damaging among sincere Christians. It helps us to see that Jesus' intention was not to lead his followers into otherworldly communities but rather to create alternative, this-worldly communities that would resist and challenge the systems of domination as he himself did at such great cost.

The reign of God that Jesus proclaimed throughout the Gospels was precisely that alternative socioeconomic–spiritual order inculcated in the Law and the Prophets, epitomized in the Sabbath–Jubilee vision. As Richard Horsley and Neil Asher Silberman explain so effectively in *The Message and the Kingdom*, Jesus renewed the subversive memory of the tribes of Yahweh and the expectation of God's reign among the villages of Galilee. Then he carried that expectation to Jerusalem. After Pentecost his followers were to proclaim good news to the poor and liberation to the oppressed by recreating simple, village-like communities throughout the urban centers of the Roman Empire.

Responsible Discipleship ◆ ◆ ◆ ◆ ◆

The more we examine our Western heritage and our biblical foundations, the greater is our challenge as followers of Jesus. We began this chapter with a cursory analysis of the legacy of 500 years of conquest, oppression, patriarchy, and racism, which have taken the form of social entitlements as difficult to overcome as are any of the substance addictions. We went on to consider the domination system that Jesus faced in first-century Palestine and the way he confronted that domination system. Now we must draw upon our heritage as descendents of the Jesus movement and take up the challenge he left for his disciples. We must look at the possibilities for personal recovery from the addiction of entitlements, ecclesial renewal in today's world, and social transformation in the face of economic oppression, patriarchy, and racism.

Possibilities for Personal Recovery

Within the dominant paradigm of Western Christianity, both conservative and liberal, discipleship is largely concerned with one's personal, private relationship with God through God's Son, Jesus Christ. Christians are to repent and believe, to worship and serve God, and to build God's reign by bringing other individuals to faith in Christ. This kind of piety is concerned with overcoming the common sins of personal behavior, but it has little to do with the primary human predicaments that have been examined in this book. It is generally ineffective in the struggle to overcome economic polarization, social marginalization, racial and ethnic discrimination, and gender oppression. So we would like to explore another model of discipleship more in tune with our reading of Jesus' message and ministry and more responsive to the major oppressions of our time.

We have already suggested that Europeans and North Americans are weighted down with privileges or entitlements that we and our predecessors have accumulated over centuries. We are bound up in socioeconomic structures and dynamics that benefit us and marginalize others. We have seen in the Hebrew Scriptures and in the Gospels that these structures and dynamics are sin; they are contrary to the Sabbath and Jubilee mandates, a betrayal of God's covenant with God's people. But when we try to face those structures and dynamics in our own lives, we find that we are addicted to them in such a way that it is almost impossible to escape from them. What, then, should it mean for us to repent, believe, and follow Jesus?

Some Christians are exploring the Twelve Step model of recovery as one way to rethink and reorient discipleship in terms of the social addictions that we are called to overcome. Alcoholics Anonymous is well known for its success in confronting alcohol abuse, and its methods have been adapted successfully to combat a growing variety of substance and relational addictions. What would the Twelve Step model of recovery look like if it were adapted for a new understanding of discipleship as recovery from the dominant social addictions of our time, as resistance to the domination systems of our time, and as Jubilee struggle for life for all God's people?

As we have noted elsewhere, to repent is to turn our life around, to change direction, to call into question the direction our lives have followed and take a new direction, to resist and overcome the evils we face. In terms of addiction, it means to make a radical decision to stop the abuse and undertake a permanent process of recovery. It means to live each day and each situation as a challenge to resist the temptations that lead back to slavery and death, to continue on in freedom into life. This struggle may have to deal with substance and relational abuses, but it will primarily be concerned with social addictions such as consumerism and economic privilege, patriarchalism and sexism, racism and other kinds of prejudice. The foundation for this struggle is not our own strength or resolve but our faith in the gracious intervention of God in history and in our own lives. In the history of Israel and in the life and teachings of Jesus, we have seen that God has freed us so that we might live in freedom and build a new socioeconomic–spiritual possibility. This is what "repent and believe" now mean. It is a conversion that takes place once and for all *and* on a daily basis. It is a new direction for our lives led by God's Spirit, and accompanied by others who are committed to this same struggle.

The content of this struggle must be worked out in our personal lives as we deal with the various oppressions that we have mentioned. In terms of the ubiquitous culture of consumption and wealth accumulation, we need to learn to resist and reject the constant demand to buy and to have; decide what to do with our wealth and income; consider ways to change the structures and dynamics that are skewed to benefit some, probably including ourselves, at the expense of others; right the injustices that we see around us and around the world.

In terms of the equally prevalent culture of patriarchalism and sexism, we need to examine our own personal lives within marriage and family relationships and across the gender divide in every context; examine critically the images of women projected in the media and the constant abuse of and violence toward women in our society; use whatever influence we have to advocate equality, dignity, and justice for women; and work for the recuperation of men's full humanity in relation to themselves and to women.

In terms of racism and ethnocentrism, we will want to reread our own history and analyze our present local and global reality from the perspective of disadvantaged and depressed social sectors; examine our own relationships within our communities, churches, work situations, and wider social contexts to uncover and correct latent and overt elements of prejudice; and join the struggle for full dignity and equal opportunity and full participation of all people. With our emerging understanding of and commitment to the gospel, these concerns are no longer secondary or marginal but central to our discipleship as followers of Jesus Christ.

Possibilities for Ecclesial Renewal

Alcoholics Anonymous (AA) presents a powerful challenge to the addict, who is told in no uncertain terms that he or she must choose the road to recovery and life or continue on the road to dissolution and death. This is only realistic. No one is likely to "make it" alone on the road to recovery and life. So AA provides regular meeting places and encourages each alcoholic to maintain that road to recovery and life through constant reaffirmation of that decision at meetings with like-minded recovering addicts. Each recovering addict is encouraged to be available to at least one other companion, day or night, to help overcome special temptations and moments of depression as needed. This model is certainly a challenge to our understanding of church. In general we Christians gather together in our churches not as forgiven and recovering sinners but as good people, upright citizens; we confess our sins routinely but have little sense that we are confronting, personally and collectively, the devastating oppressions of our time; we rarely recognize that we ourselves and our families and institutions are part of the domination system; and we fail to take decisive steps to resist and overcome the prevailing culture of consumerism and economic oppression, patriarchalism and sexism, racism and prejudice.

How might our churches be renewed if we began to take seriously the perspectives arising out of our understanding of Sabbath economics, Jubilee spirituality, and the struggle for fullness of life for all God's people? Our gatherings and our communities may organize themselves very differently from AA groups, but they can have the same sense of urgency and commitment. Every one of us faces now the constant threat of unemployment for ourselves or for some member of our family or for other colleagues. We need solidarity to resist the drive for wealth accumulation in the face of this insecurity. Every couple has to work hard to build their marriage with infinite love in the face of innumerable pressures and daily vicissitudes that drive us apart. Our families need understanding and support in caring for aging parents and raising children with values that supersede the greed, sexism, and prejudices of the dominant culture. We all need to sharpen our analysis of the structures and dynamics of domination in order to equip ourselves for the work place and even for reading the daily paper and watching the daily news. For all of these reasons we may need to renew our understanding of church and redesign our times of worship, communion, and nurture.

Local church and synagogue groups can engage in discussion of Jubilee issues and practice in concrete terms. Will O'Brien, a contributing editor of *The Other Side*, sent us the following list (selected and adapted) from a local interfaith "brainstorm" discussion of personal, communal, and political possibilities in response to four questions arising from the biblical mandates:

How do we practice Sabbath rhythms of work/rest?
Observe religious traditions of no work, no consumption or production, no technological transport.
Special celebrations.
Practice hospitality, enjoy leisure, teach the value of rest.
Thirty-hour work week. Job sharing.
Voluntary and paid community service.
New ethos in the workplace.
Slower work, less stress, retreats, getting workers outside, physical activity, building relationships.
Contemplative prayer groups.

Living wage campaign.

Shorten store hours. Change shopping habits.

Resist culture of instant gratification.

Reroot ourselves in communities.

How do we let the land lie fallow?

Support urban gardening, organic farms, crop rotation, timber rotation.

Practice green consuming. Avoid environmentally harmful products and overpackaged products.

Learn food preparation, use whole foods.

Create economic incentives to reduce car use, regulate car traffic, expand funding for public transportation, support bicycle use.

Support policies for whole days of neighborhood cleanups.

Campaign for a week without TV.

How do we practice release of debt/bondage?

Support Jubilee 2000 campaign versus debt of poorest countries.

Develop community programs to cancel student loans.

Regulate credit card marketing, especially for young people.

Limit one credit card per person. Host a credit card burning event.

Release ourselves from debt, resist the debt economy.

Create alternative community trust funds, credit unions, loan funds.

Require banks to reinvest in communities.

Explore restorative justice models for criminal justice system.

Practice personal forgiveness.

How do we redistribute the land/capital?

Encourage community reinvestment.

Broaden health coverage.

Seek free university education.

Study personal decisions about investment, inheritance, charity.

Strengthen the labor movement, environmental concerns, fair wages, enhanced working conditions locally and internationally.

Critique World Bank and IMF policies toward Third World countries.

Promote minimal salary differentials, a maximum wage, progressive tax policies, designated taxes.

Revive the public sphere.

Possibilities for Social Transformation

Concerned persons can easily gain access to and participate in programs, projects, and movements dealing with the various kinds of oppression and domination in their society. Many churches and ecumenical bodies offer avenues of service and witness for integral human transformation. We conclude this chapter with a declaration prepared by the *Unión Evangélica Pentecostal Venezolana* at a national gathering in 1996. It is the fruit of their reflection on the biblical Jubilee and the needs of the Venezuelan people and it has had a significant impact on the members of that church and other churches of Latin America. As "Che" Guevara said many years ago, if the Christians of Latin America would live out what they preach, there would be no need for social revolution in that region. What might be the impact if the churches of North America were to declare and to live out the Sabbath–Jubilee vision?

Letter from Guanare

We have been called together under the theme: JUBILEE: FESTIVAL OF THE SPIRIT, a theme that we consider to be of great relevance for the present reality of Venezuela and Latin America. The Jubilee refers to the festivity celebrated by the Hebrew people and designed to value the land as a community possession, to proclaim the freedom of the slaves, to restore mortgaged lands, to forgive unpayable debts and reduce to a minimum the economic and social differences accumulated among the people (Leviticus 25).

Recognizing the distance of time, space, and historic development, we affirm that the ethical principles that gave origin to these norms remain in force and constitute a biblical paradigm capable of calling us to the commitment to build a form of social relation founded on justice, solidarity, and peace.

As a church close to the sufferings of the people, we are concerned about the deepening poverty that is occurring as a result of the economic measures that are being applied to our people and that, among other things, manifest our dependence with respect to the centers of world power. We have reflected on the weight that the external debt has on the process of impoverishment of our people. Precisely, the biblical paradigm of the Jubilee calls us to pray and work so that the unpayable debts are not transformed into perverse mechanisms that enslave and sacrifice our people on the altars of the creditors.

◆ ◆ ◆

We join the voices of the churches and sectors of good will that call for the realization of an ecumenical Jubilee that will lead to a profound revision of the debt and the remission of the same for the countries that are not able to pay, taking into account that this debt is immoral because it was contracted illegally and behind the backs of the people, who are ultimately the ones who suffer the consequences. So that this may become a reality, we exhort the peoples and governments of Latin America to work together in the search for a more just international economic order.

Likewise, we also call upon the churches and Christians in general to understand that the clamor for justice for the weak has reached the ears of God. It is necessary that we announce before the world the proclamation of the Year of Grace that Jesus inaugurated at the beginning of his messianic ministry (Luke 4:18–21). That together we bring hope to the people and commit ourselves to pray, work, and orient our people so that we become aware of the challenge that we all have in the face of this great crisis and that we become involved in concrete actions, that they not reduce the Jubilee proposal to mere celebrations and declarations, but that they become effective in the establishment of a greater degree of justice for our people, at the door to the Third Millennium.

The Comisión Evangélica Pentecostal Latinoamericana (CEPLA) took up this call for Jubilee at its September 1998 gathering in Havana, Cuba, with delegates from most of the Latin American countries. The report of that regional meeting is entitled, *Jubileo, la Fiesta del Espíritu.*

7 ◆ ◆ ◆ ◆ ◆ ◆ ◆

Jubilee Practices
in the Early Church

In this chapter we shall build on reflections of the previous chapters as we consider the possibility of a new paradigm, a new way of viewing our world, our faith, and our vocation as disciples of Jesus Christ. We need to focus our thinking coherently in order to establish a base for further reflection and action. As we have seen, Sabbath–Jubilee perspectives appear right through the Bible, and they relate to a wide spectrum of concerns that are very pertinent today. As we turn now to Jubilee practices in the early church, we shall consider passages from the Book of the Acts of the Apostles and from Paul's Epistles that will help us to shape this new theological–spiritual paradigm and apply it in our daily thinking and acting. The following questions indicate the immediate task before us in this chapter.

◆ Because wealth accumulation through free market competition is so harmful to humanity as a whole and to our individual humanity, where can we find an alternative socioeconomic paradigm to guide our understanding and our lifestyle?
◆ Because privatistic views of sin and salvation and spirituality are inadequate for responsible living in today's world, what can we learn from the New Testament church's experience of basic problems similar to our own?
◆ Because traditional church programs do not seem to challenge and prepare us for today's struggle for life for all God's people, how can we begin to reshape our personal, ecclesial, and social life?

Today's World ◆ ◆ ◆ ◆ ◆

The Free Market Economy—Is It Humane?

However confusing and futile it may seem, we all must begin to think seriously about the economic system under which we live, some with enormous advantages, others with enormous disadvantages, locally and globally. As

Gandhi put it years ago, "The earth provides enough for everyone's need, but not for everyone's greed." With the growth of the world's population we are approaching the outer limits of sustainability, and with the growth of free market economics, which is not sustainable, global poverty is escalating dramatically, pushing hundreds of millions of people beyond the limits of survivability. As we have emphasized again and again, this reality is, for us, not just an economic problem but a spiritual problem. It is undermining our humanity, wherever we find ourselves in the pyramids of domination. This problem is particularly disturbing for relatively rich Christians living in North America and Europe. We must find alternatives.

This challenge is stated at a very basic level in the cookbook we referred to in Chapter 1:

> Time was—and not long ago—if you wanted to live in such a way as to be warmly connected with other people, the world supported your efforts. Today that really is not true. If you want community in any form, or family, or home, you just about have to invent it. Your version will be unique with you. But the first and all-important step is to dig in where you are and make a place. . . . We are on a frontier, surrounded by wilderness, and the job at hand is to make a clearing—to clear a space and determine that what goes on within that circle will be a prototype of the world as you would like it to be. The thrilling thing is to see those small circles begin to touch upon one another here and there, and overlap—sturdy outposts, ground for hope. (Robertson et al., 1986, p. 31)

This concern for the rehumanization of life will have to deal not only with our personal and family struggles for human community. Among the social dimensions of our collective life, we will have to struggle for the decommodification and redignification of labor. Clearly labor is one of the most important activities of life, but in the current evolution of global production, industrial labor, including agribusiness, has been reduced largely to meaningless, repetitive performance that is rapidly being replaced by machines and robots. The most blatant form of this kind of labor is now evident in most Third World factories and in First World urban sweatshops, primarily among immigrants who are forced to take any kind of work. The international roll call of these factories, known now by the Spanish name *maquiladoras*, is to be found on the labels of most clothing sold in the United States. We know that they are merely the logical result of a global system that presses the profit motive to its ultimate consequences. This logic takes the following shape:

◆ Local governments compete to attract foreign companies with offers of "free trade zones" that do not charge the usual import–export taxes and services for infrastructure.

◆ In some cases local governments actually set up buildings and contract cheap labor for foreign companies at a flat rate.

◆ These companies normally maintain a tacit or declared policy prohibiting unions, so they can impose their own standards of discipline, and they hold the threat of leaving the country overnight if they wish.

◆ In some cases this means that workers are allowed two three-minute bathroom stops per day, that they may have to work ten or twelve hours with no extra pay to meet order deadlines, that they are not allowed to talk with neighbors during working hours, and that they must endure any abuse inflicted by bosses and administrators.

◆ Women are often subjected to sexual abuse, and pregnancies are discouraged by monthly inspection of sanitary napkins or other methods (to avoid medical costs).

◆ Workers may be routinely laid off prior to the deadline for formal contracts with benefits, then rehired.

◆ Salaries are kept at a minimum in order to ensure competitiveness and to maximize profit, which are considered to be laws of the marketplace.

◆ Some types of work require young, dexterous hands, between sixteen and thirty years of age, after which permanent layoff is automatic.

In the United States, since the beginning of the Reagan administration, there seems to have been a campaign against organized labor with relatively little public outcry. Organized labor has long been vilified as corrupt and autocratic so little political or social support remains. Interestingly, Samuel Gompers, the founder and first president of the American Federation of Labor, had this to say about the fundamental concerns of labor:

> What does labor want?
> We want more schoolhouses and less jails,
> More books and less guns,
> More learning and less vice,
> More leisure and less greed,
> More justice and less revenge.
> We want more opportunities
> To cultivate our better nature. (Deats, 1997, p. 3)

In recent years big business has invested increasingly in its top management and reduced salaries for workers. In the United States it is reported that twenty years ago the average CEO of a major U.S. corporation made forty times as much as the average worker in his company. Today, it is 180 times as much. At some point, sooner rather than later, people of concern will have to decide whether we can continue to abide by or collaborate with such free market economics. If not, we must find ways to modify or replace it.

Free Market Ideology—Does It Have a Conscience?

Since the collapse of the socialist regimes in Europe most people seem to accept without question that the only possible economic order is free market capitalism. In fact for some the great achievement of the twentieth century has been the triumph of capitalism over socialism. The stable growth of the U.S. economy in recent years is seen by many as proof of the superiority of our economic system. Certainly the accumulation of wealth, which is the primary goal of this system, is impressive, as reflected in these phenomena:

◆ The soaring of stock values reported daily on Wall Street
◆ The massive building of luxury homes across the country
◆ Enormous shopping centers loaded with seemingly unlimited goods
◆ The abundant offerings of supermarkets and megastores
◆ The flow of new cars on our freeways and crowded air travel to almost everywhere
◆ Constant offerings through advertisements and promotion of sales
◆ The geometric proliferation of information and communication possibilities
◆ The growth of entertainment and recreation possibilities

But what is happening to the soul and heart of the people who have access to so much? Clearly we must look for alternatives both for the sake of those who have so much and for the sake of those who are increasingly being excluded.

With the collapse of Soviet socialism at the end of the 1980s, socialist movements and political parties throughout Latin America and elsewhere have lost credibility. It can be argued, however, that those Soviet regimes were in fact examples of state-run capitalism, that they were victims of Russian imperialism, and that they were simply overwhelmed by the dominant capitalist paradigm. Furthermore, it can be noted that within a very few years Eastern Europeans have become so disillusioned with Western capitalism that they are voting again for socialist parties and a return to the social benefits that they had previously enjoyed.

We may be drawn therefore to a reconsideration of at least some of the principles of socialism as a necessary antidote to capitalism as we know it today in North America and around the world. In the face of recent moves to dismantle social welfare in the United States, we must affirm that governments are instituted precisely to protect the general welfare from the very powerful drive of those who can to accumulate personal wealth at the expense of those who cannot. In the face of growing investment in police forces and prisons and weaponry, we must insist on more fundamental responses to the true needs of all social sectors, especially those sectors that have historically been abused and marginalized. In the face of the opposition of the rich to taxation, we must recover the essential validity of taxes as an indispensable tool to adjust and in part to rectify the enormous disparities of our societies. In the face of efforts to undermine public education and access to adequate health care, we must insist that these are inalienable human rights for all, which determine the quality of life for everybody. In the face of growing xenophobia and legislative efforts to close our borders and eliminate social and economic benefits for legal as well as undocumented immigrants, we must remember that all of us, other than Native Americans, are aliens or descendents of aliens with no legitimate reason to exclude others from the wealth that this country continues to accumulate from the natural and human resources of the entire world.

People often ask why Costa Rica is so different from the rest of Central America. There is no simple answer, of course, but there are interesting pointers. In the first place, the Spaniards who occupied what is now Costa Rica in the sixteenth century did not find a large Native population upon which to build large plantations as they had in other Central American countries. It is not clear whether the original population was very small, whether they were decimated by the *conquistadores*, or whether they fled. In any case, the colonizers could only manage relatively small farms, for they had to do the work themselves. Second, Costa Rica was far from the center of power and wealth in Central America; it could not impose its will on others to extract wealth and build its own power base. The region was conquered and directed at first from Guatemala; each country subsequently sought its own independence. Third, as land and wealth were distributed relatively evenly throughout Costa Rica, democracy was far more welcome and meaningful there than in the neighboring countries, which were built by competing fiefdoms and parties and dictatorships. Costa Ricans say that their democracy goes back 150 years, and their national monument depicts the defeat of William Walker, an unprincipled U.S. southern adventurer bent on creating a slave state in Central America as the United States moved toward the Civil War and the elimination of slavery.

Finally, Costa Rica experienced its social revolution in the 1940s, at a time when the United States was fully occupied with World War II and Russia was an ally. A government coalition that included the local communist party and the Catholic Church enacted legislation providing health care and education for all, progressive labor laws including the right to strike, the nationalization of the entire banking system, so that priority could be given to national development rather than private gain, and the creation of semi-autonomous entities for basic infrastructure, such as electricity, communications, fuel, housing, to serve the whole country. The most dramatic alternative for which Costa Rica is famous came in 1948, when a political dispute led to a military conflict, and the winner, José "Pepe" Figueres, himself a wealthy farmer and military man, abolished the army. From that point on Costa Rica was able to invest its resources and its energy in basic human development for all its people.

Today Costa Rica continues to enjoy a relatively high standard of living, education, health care, and life expectancy—far higher than its neighbors. However, we now see a growing gap between rich and poor, migration of small farmers to the cities, growing slum areas, deterioration of education and health care, and rapidly increasing delinquency, prostitution, domestic violence, and alcohol and drug abuse. We now speak of the "Centralamericanization" of Costa Rica, and the chief cause of this tragic development is the imposition of economic policies by the IMF and World Bank, led by U.S. ideologues and supported by Costa Rican elites. These policies are forcing Costa Rica and other debtor nations around the world to reduce government participation in economic and social concerns, to privatize government entities and services, to reduce tariffs and allow transnational corporations to take over local businesses—that is, to follow the ideology and laws of free market economics. As Costa Rica continues to carry a high per-capita debt, it must adhere to these dictates, whatever party may take its turn in power.

Privatistic Spirituality—Is It Adequate?

At the beginning of each previous chapter we have tried to focus not only on socioeconomic and political–ideological but also religious-spiritual dimensions of "Today's World." Here we believe it is important to consider Western Christianity's long-standing divorce between personal faith and social responsibility, between Sunday worship and daily life, between theology and economics. We fear that one of the main deterrents to social justice and ecological integrity is precisely this divorce, which continues to determine how many in our churches perceive and respond to the issues we have just raised and to the basic challenge of the biblical Jubilee.

Genuine spirituality is concerned essentially not with sentiment as such but with the guidance of God's Spirit, that is, with the reign of God "on earth as it is in heaven." We have observed with great interest the growth of New Age spirituality in the United States and the growth of neo-Pentecostalism throughout Latin America. Not long ago there was talk of the demise of religion and the growth of secularism. What we have seen is an almost spectacular growth of religion along with the growth of secularism. But when we look closely, we suspect that neither this new religiosity nor this secularism is guided by God's Spirit. Rather, these religious and spiritual expressions have become, at least to some extent, a cover for the domination system of economic oppression, patriarchalism, and even racism or ethnocentrism. Why? Because they are privatistic and self-centered—with important exceptions.

Many of us have wondered, perhaps since childhood, about the morality of traditional Christian pietism that appeals fundamentally to each individual to secure a place in heaven by accepting Christ as personal savior. We have all seen that supposedly Christian nations have invoked God's blessing for their pursuit of empire at immeasurable cost and suffering to the victims. Christian theological traditions have been used to provide ideological and spiritual justification of slavery in the United States and apartheid in South Africa. Millions of North American Christians attend congregational worship faithfully Sunday after Sunday with little or no consideration of their participation in the present national and global economic order that is wreaking havoc in the lives of billions and in the biosphere.

We cannot deny that personal, privatistic religion or spirituality can offer great benefits to individuals and to church communities and to society as a whole. The churches have always played an important role in saving lives from meaninglessness 'and alienation, in providing opportunities for worship and nurture, in serving urgent and ongoing needs of people for health care, education, and development. But there is something essentially inadequate about any spirituality that is fundamentally selfish and private, concerned first and foremost for one's own eternal salvation. We cannot forget the lesson of the parable of the sheep and the goats in Matthew 25:31–46, which is one of the few cases in which Jesus refers to eternal life and final judgment. The most remarkable thing about this long passage is that eternal life is granted not to those peoples or nations (*éthne*) who seek it or accept Christ or even believe in God but simply to those who feed the hungry, clothe the naked, care for the sick, and visit those in prison—without any regard for personal gain on earth or in heaven. Eternal punishment is not just for the devil and his angels but also for those who fail to do these very things. Also, as we find in Matthew 7:21, "Not everyone who says to me, 'Lord, Lord,' will enter the kingdom of heaven, but only the one who does the will of my Father in heaven." In any case these passages are not concerned about heaven so much as they are concerned about the presence of God's reign and God's Spirit here and now.

At the end of this chapter and in Chapter 8 we will consider some ways to create a spirituality that will incarnate these biblical perspectives and motifs and sustain us for the costly, ongoing struggle for life for all God's people. We need to forge personal and communal life in faithfulness to God's Spirit. This personal and communal life must enable integral human transformation to take place, including the social and economic dimensions of our reality. Toward that end we turn now to important indications of Jubilee practices in the early church that will inform and undergird this emerging spirituality.

Biblical Faith ◆ ◆ ◆ ◆ ◆

The biblical passages we look at here have been selected with the following rationale. We have chosen first the experience of Pentecost as reported in the Book of Acts, for it deals with the founding of the early church and its mission. We want to review the impact of the outpouring of the Holy Spirit as that relates to the Sabbath–Jubilee mandates and perspectives. Second, we shall consider the experience of the Lord's Supper as reported in 1 Corinthians 11:17–34, for this has been the most sacred expression of Christian worship from the very beginning. We will see how Paul relates that liturgical act with the Sabbath–Jubilee mandates and perspectives. Third, we shall examine Paul's efforts to gather offerings from the emerging congregations for the poor Christians in Judea as an extension of Sabbath economics to the early missionary movement. We cannot begin to offer here a full accounting of Sabbath–Jubilee elements in the early church or in Paul's letters to the churches. But we do hope to open up avenues for further study in these areas as we take up the challenge of Sabbath economics and Jubilee spirituality.

Pentecost as Jubilee

Ched Myers points out that Pentecost, the Jews' Feast of Weeks, was set fifty days after Passover, just as Jubilee was to be celebrated every fifty years, beginning on the Day of Atonement. Falling between Passover and the Feast of Tabernacles, it was a thanksgiving celebration for the harvest of the first fruits. As an agricultural event for an agrarian society, it was "unavoidably social and economic" (Myers, 1996, p. 5). Much has been written about the experience of the Holy Spirit on the first Christian Pentecost and about subsequent experiences of the Holy Spirit, which we call spirituality. When we read this passage in light of the Jubilee, however, we find, as Myers affirms, "The Acts narrative of Pentecost is not about ecstatic individual spiritual experience, but a challenge to the entire order of things, personal and political" (ibid., p. 7).

> *When the day of Pentecost had come, they were all together in one place. And suddenly from heaven there came a sound like the rush of a violent wind, and it filled the entire house where they were sitting. Divided tongues, as of fire, appeared among them, and a tongue rested on each of them. All of them were filled with the Holy Spirit and began to speak in other languages, as the Spirit gave them ability.*
> Acts 2:1–4

No doubt it was an extraordinary experience that transformed that small band of Jesus' followers from fearful fugitives hiding in an upper room into fearless witnesses to God's power in the streets of Jerusalem. The infilling of the Holy Spirit took two forms, tongues of fire distributed to each of them and the ability to speak in other languages so as to communicate their message to the crowd of devout Jews and proselytes who had gathered from around the Roman Empire for the Feast of Pentecost. Peter preached to the crowd, explaining that this was not drunkenness but the fulfillment of prophecy and proclaiming that the man whom they had crucified, Jesus of Nazareth, had been raised up and was exalted at the right hand of God. Then Peter exhorted them to repent and be baptized in the name of Jesus Christ so that their sins (debts) might be forgiven (*áphesin*) and they might receive the gift of the Holy Spirit.

The following paragraph goes on to report:

> *All who believed were together and had all things in common; they would sell their possessions and goods and distribute the proceeds to all, as any had need. Day by day, as they spent much time together in the Temple, they broke bread at home and ate their food with glad*

and generous hearts, praising God and having the goodwill of all the
people. And day by day the Lord added to their number those who
were being saved. Acts 2:44–47

Here we find another extraordinary dimension of the experience of Pentecost, and it is not unrelated to the others. Commentators point out that the
word "distributed" appears just two times in the Book of Acts: once for the
distribution of the tongues of fire in 2:3 and again for the distribution of
possessions in 2:45. The coming of the Holy Spirit led directly to the practice of what we have called Sabbath economics and Jubilee spirituality. The
phrase "day by day" in 2:46 and 48 suggests an allusion to Exodus 16 and
the daily gathering of food for each day's need and also to the Lord's Prayer
and the petition for "our daily bread." The root word for community, *koi-*
nonía, appears in 2:42 to refer to the communion among the growing body
of believers and in 2:44 to refer to the community of goods, "all things in
common."

This is Luke's version of the founding of the church at Pentecost. Having seen the centrality of Sabbath economics–Jubilee spirituality in Luke's
Gospel, we cannot but conclude that he very intentionally carried that perspective into his story of the apostolic church. Sharing among the first believers was not simply a spontaneous, one-time response to an immediate
need, as some have surmised. As Luke had indicated in Luke 4:19, this was
"the year of the Lord's favor." God's reign was experienced by the early
church as a fundamental commitment to share not only in worship and fellowship but also at the common table and in the distribution of their possessions so that all would have enough and none would have too much.

Another similar summary paragraph, Acts 4:32–35, reemphasizes the
communion and the community of goods among the growing body of believers. Our observations concerning the previous text apply here. The *koi-*
nonía experienced by the believers was not just religious or charismatic but
socioeconomic. We note here a direct reference to another basic Sabbath
text, Deuteronomy 15:4, in the words "There was not a needy person
among them." This was the purpose of Sabbath economics and Jubilee
spirituality, that poverty would be overcome and all would be free, not just
through charity but through release from debts and slavery and the redistribution of possessions. "And great grace was upon them all" ties the grace of
sharing all things with the grace of God who provides for all. In fact the
passage begins with the extraordinary phrase that says literally that they
"were of one heart and soul." This was a profound experience of community based on a common experience of the Spirit. We believe it was a fulfillment of the Sabbath–Jubilee vision going back to Exodus, Deuteronomy,
Leviticus, the Prophets, and Jesus.

This passage is followed by the dramatic story of Ananias and Sapphira, which demonstrates the seriousness of commitment to community
and the necessity of truth and trust within community. They thought they
could deceive the others and hoard some of the proceeds from the sale of

their property. Like the rich fool of the parable, Luke 12:13–21, their greed led to death. They lost the opportunity to share fully God's grace through the full sharing of their goods among God's people.

Both the gift of the Spirit and the gift of sharing in community are essential and belong together. Spiritual life cannot be genuine without solidarity with all God's people, particularly those in need.

The Lord's Supper

No passage of the New Testament is more foundational than the words of the institution of the Lord's Supper in 1 Corinthians 11:23–26. Every pastor and every believer should know them by heart. This is the gospel in sacred word and sacred action. As Calvin said, "the Word without the Sacrament is like a head without a torso." We are invited and instructed to remember our Lord Jesus by participating in the communion of his body and blood. By sharing this bread and this cup we "proclaim the Lord's death until he comes." The Lord's Supper is a central focus of Christian worship.

We have found that this passage takes on new meaning when it is read in context; that is, in the context of the preceding and following paragraphs. The whole passage, 1 Corinthians 11:17–34, is a concentric construction typical of Paul and other writers of the Scriptures.

vv. 17–22	Abuses at the Lord's Supper
vv. 23–26	Institution of the Lord's Supper
vv. 27–34	Judgment for abuses at the Lord's Supper

The heart of the passage is, of course, the institution of the Lord's Supper, but the preceding and following paragraphs shed important light on the meaning of the Lord's Supper. These are serious reprimands by the Apostle upon the behavior of the Corinthian believers.

Irene Foulkes (1996, pp. 304–309) explains the first paragraph in this way. While there were various house churches in Corinth, there were occasions for the wider gathering of the believers to partake of the Lord's Supper. On these occasions a large house would be needed, so the host family would likely be one of the more wealthy families. These meetings would be held on Sunday evenings, as Sundays were working days like the rest of the week. The wealthier members would most likely arrive first, being able to dispose of their work and their time more freely, and they would most likely be friends with the host family. What happened, apparently, was that those who arrived early took advantage of the food and drink, even to excess, before the others arrived. The latter, being poor freedmen and spouses and slaves, would arrive late because they had to fulfill all the chores in their households and places of employment. Arriving late, tired, and hungry, they would find nothing to eat and drink, thus experiencing not only hunger but further humiliation for their inferior status. This, says Paul, is to "show contempt for the church of God and humiliate those who have nothing" (v. 22).

Paul's language in this first paragraph is devastating. It opens and closes with the words "I do not commend you." The believers gather as a church, but there are divisions or factions among them. Those who already have more take more than they need, and those who have nothing receive nothing. This is not really the Lord's Supper! (v. 20). It is a blatant denial of the gospel. It is a direct contradiction of God's rule, of Sabbath economics and Jubilee spirituality.

As in other societies, both ancient and modern, the people of Corinth were bound by grades of honor that determined how each should be treated. The shameful treatment of the poor at the Lord's table was, according to Paul, a grave dishonor to them and also a denial of Christ's body.

> Persons of precarious (slaves, the poor) or relatively low social condition (freedmen, women in general) had little of this intangible but essential property, honor. But believers belonging to those levels had been incorporated into the Christian community as equals with those considered more honorable. In that way the humble ones had been given a large quota of honor. They could say with heads held high that the Gospel of Jesus Christ dignifies people (cp. Galatians 3:28). But now . . . they were being humiliated by the wealthy members, covering them with shame and taking away the honor that they had recently acquired in that same group. (Foulkes, 1996, p. 312)

For Paul this is not just a matter of courtesy. It is so serious that he uses the occasion to set down the oldest and most sacred teaching that he has "received from the Lord."

The paragraph following the institution of the Lord's Supper is even more shocking. Those who eat the bread or drink the cup of the Lord in this unworthy manner, writes Paul, "will be answerable for the body and blood of the Lord" (v. 27). Furthermore, "all who eat and drink without discerning the body, eat and drink judgment against themselves" (v. 29). He then explains that "many of you are weak and ill, and some have died" because of such abuses at the Lord's Supper—an affirmation that reminds us of the death of Ananias and Sapphira.

Paul's logic here echoes the logic of the Sabbath–Jubilee mandates. Those mandates were based on God's gracious intervention on behalf of the Hebrew slaves in Egypt. It would be intolerable for the people of Yahweh to practice debt extortion and slavery; they were freed from Egypt and given the Promised Land so that they might create an alternative social possibility in covenant with Yahweh. Paul's instruction to the Corinthian believers is based on the sacrifice of their Lord, which they were celebrating at the Lord's table. It was intolerable for them to practice greed at the expense of the lesser brothers and sisters at that table; they were freed from such inhuman behavior and given this new covenant so that all would be respected as equal members of Christ's body.

How then should followers of Jesus eat the bread and drink the cup of the Lord? How are we to discern Christ's body? How are we to judge ourselves and avoid judgment? The final verses seem simple enough. We are to wait for one another and share with one another when we come together to eat—or stay at home. But Paul's warnings may have wider implications in keeping with the Sabbath–Jubilee mandates. If it is a grave failure to discern the body of Christ when we do not wait for our sisters and brothers at the Lord's table, surely it is an abuse to fill our stomachs and our homes and our investments to overflowing when millions of our brothers and sisters are starving anywhere in the world. Surely we must do everything in our power to provide equally for them. Here the Sabbath–Jubilee mandates take on new and concrete meaning, for we are now speaking about the central celebration of the Christian faith, the primary proclamation and enactment of the good news, the ultimate expression of Christian spirituality.

In first-century Corinth the polarities between Jews and Greeks, slaves and free, rich and poor, men and women were more powerful than any that we face today. The body of Christ had to confront and overcome those polarities through the power of the Holy Spirit in the lives of all the members. Debates among biblical scholars continue as to Paul's treatment of slaves and women, of the institution of slavery and the dominant bias against women. We know that the Pauline writings have been used to justify and reinforce structures and prejudices that marginalize and exclude. But we also know that Paul invoked powerful biblical–theological foundations, grounded upon Jesus' ministry and sacrifice, that have contributed to the full liberation and participation of women and slaves and other marginalized and excluded people.

In his Letter to the Galatians, Paul develops this theology even more. He tells the believers,

> *in Christ Jesus you are all children of God through faith. As many of you as were baptized into Christ have clothed yourselves with Christ. There is no longer Jew or Greek, there is no longer slave or free, there is no longer male and female; for all of you are one in Christ Jesus.*   Galatians 3:26–28

Traditionally, many Christians have read these and similar passages in terms of personal faith or privatistic religion: The gospel is proclaimed as personal faith in Christ and eternal life in heaven across these barriers, but little is done to change the realities of racial–ethnic, socioeconomic, and gender oppression. This is why it so important to connect Paul's theology with the Sabbath–Jubilee vision and with Jesus' application of that vision. We can see that Paul insisted dogmatically that Gentiles who received the gospel were to become members of Christ's body without becoming Jews, without being circumcised, without keeping other Hebrew laws and customs. This was a break with established Jewish religion and identity. From that point on

Christianity became a radical new faith and was no longer a Jewish sect. Likewise, slaves who received the gospel were to become full members of Christ's body with equal right to participate in the Lord's Supper, in worship, and in the life of the faith community. This explains Paul's violent reprimand in 1 Corinthians 11. The Corinthian church had not discerned that slaves were no longer slaves. They were to experience their socioeconomic freedom as an essential dimension of their spiritual freedom in Christ. Finally, we must conclude that Paul affirms here that women and men are fully and equally God's children, free from the gender structures and prejudices that any given society may try to impose.

The Collection for the Poor in Jerusalem

We now turn to Paul's appeal in 2 Corinthians 8–9, because it deals directly with economic matters and because it is based directly on Sabbath–Jubilee principles. Paul makes a similar appeal in Romans, 1 Corinthians, and Galatians, so this has an important place in Paul's missionary understanding. It is a practical matter—evidently the Christians in Jerusalem were facing serious economic need as Judea was moving toward its final confrontation with Rome. Paul was naturally concerned for their welfare, but Paul deals with this concrete need as a very serious spiritual–theological matter.

This section of 2 Corinthians begins and ends with references to God's grace (*cháris*). In 8:1–7 he refers to "the grace (*cháris*) of God" granted to the churches of Macedonia, who out of "their abundant joy and their extreme poverty have overflowed in a wealth of generosity" in response to his appeal, "begging us earnestly for the privilege (*cháris*) of sharing (*koinonía*) in this ministry (*diakonía*) to the saints." Paul hopes to "complete this generous undertaking (*cháris*)" among the believers of Corinth by persuading them "to excel also in this generous undertaking (*cháris*)." He ends this section of the letter with the exclamation, "Thanks (*cháris*) be to God for his indescribable gift!" (9:15).

In 8:9 Paul reinforces his appeal with an eloquent summary of the gospel:

> *For you know the generous act* [cháris] *of our Lord Jesus Christ, that though he was rich, yet for your sakes he became poor, so that by his poverty you might become rich.*

He then refers to the Corinthians' earlier promise to make their contribution, which evidently they had not fulfilled, and goes on to ask them to balance or equalize their abundance with others' need. And then in 8:15 he makes a direct reference to Sabbath economics by citing Exodus 16:18:

> *The one who had much did not have too much, and the one who had little did not have too little.*

The grace of God in Christ is the same grace that God required of the ancient tribes of Yahweh. They had been liberated from slavery and given the Promised Land so that they might create a different socioeconomic reality in which all would be free from poverty and oppression. This is what the believers in Jerusalem had experienced at Pentecost. They had been liberated from their sins/debts and filled with God's Spirit so that they might create a new community in which all shared their possessions and none were in need. This is the grace that Paul calls forth from the churches of Corinth, Macedonia, Rome, and Galatia. In Christ they too were freed from every form of bondage so that they could graciously give of their abundance to meet the need of the Christians of Jerusalem. This is what we have called Jubilee spirituality, which means that all God's people might have socioeconomic–spiritual fullness of life through sharing or solidarity.

Recent research on the ancient patronage system has shed new light on Paul's appeal in 2 Corinthians 8–9. As we have noted already, there was a code of honor in first-century Corinth and throughout the Roman Empire that paralleled and transcended class structures. Ultimately rooted in the emperor himself and his court, this system extended through pyramids of social, political, economic, and military power to the farthest reaches of the empire. Everyone was included in this pattern of asymmetrical relations in which persons of greater influence, power, or wealth extended favors to those below them in return for praise, honor, and service.

> In a society where banks did not loan money and in which there was not in most places an adequate social safety net, personal patronage was a practical necessity. A patronage relationship would be established by a gift or some other favor and by acceptance of the gift, which placed the recipient in the inferior role in the relationship and obligated him or her to respond with expressions of gratitude, praise, and honor. . . . These relationships were usually informal and supralegal, sometimes even involving actions that were not fully or strictly legal. In theory they were voluntary, but in practice social inferiors often had no choice but to engage in such relationships in order to be materially supported. (Witherington, 1995, p. 414)

Paul resisted and rejected this additional form of inequality and oppression, because it was a denial of liberty in Christ and it could endanger his freedom to carry out his mission. So in the matter of the collection for the Christians in Jerusalem, he is careful to persuade but not command the Corinthian believers to do their duty (8:1–15). He commends to them Titus, but indicates that he is going there of his own accord along with two other brothers in the faith to carry out this "generous undertaking" (*cháris*) (8:16–24). In fact Paul writes to them in anticipation so that they will be ready and eager and not be humiliated when the brothers arrive, so that their contribution will be ready "as a voluntary gift and not as an extortion" as in the predominant patronage system (9:1–5). He reasons that

God's blessings are abundant, so they must "share abundantly," "not reluctantly or under compulsion" as in the patronage system (9:6–9). The One who provides the seed and the bread will thus multiply their seed, providing for the needs of the saints, and increase their justice, enriching them and producing thanks (*eúcharistía*) to God. Through this ministry (*diakonía*) of sharing they confess the good news of Christ and glorify God. This is an expression of "the surpassing grace (*cháris*) of God" given to them (9:10–15). In this way Paul intends not only to meet urgent needs of the saints in Jerusalem, but also to launch a movement in direct opposition to the patronage system, that is, toward the periphery rather than the center of power, prestige, and economic benefits.

Paul himself took great care not to fall under the obligations of the patronage system. In 2 Corinthians 11:7–11 he explains that he did not accept the Corinthians' financial support, which would have exalted them and humbled him. Rather he accepted support from friends in Macedonia, which as we have seen was a poorer church. Also, Paul chose to support himself as a tentmaker. Now for his upcoming third visit to Corinth he reiterates his intention not to become dependent upon them.

> Divine reward was not normally considered in Greco-Roman reciprocity relationships, but Paul tries to force the Corinthians to rethink social relationships in the light of Christ. His rejection of personal patronage in Corinth is of a piece with his rejection of other status conventions of Greco-Roman antiquity. For the Corinthians to respond to what Paul says will involve them in seeing God in Christ as their ultimate patron or benefactor and Paul as the agent of that patron. . . . He wants them to see him as their benefactor, not as their client. (ibid., p. 418)

In this way Paul was able to continue his apostolic ministry free of pressures from the Corinthian believers and also to avoid entrapment by one or more of the divisions among them. This helps to explain the attacks he suffered at the hands of other "apostles" or "super-apostles" (11:5) who may have been directed by influential members of the Corinthian church who resented his independence or lack of submission.

All of the above helps to bring out the full meaning of Paul's central theological affirmations in 2 Corinthians 5:11–21. In Christ, God is creating a new world order, transforming not just religious faith but all relationships, including the social and the economic. God pardons sins/debts so that we will forgive others their sins/debts. We are ambassadors for Christ, as God brings about this new order through us, bringing about new relationships here in this life in conformity with God's justice.

To be in Christ is to be reconciled not only to God but to our neighbors. As we found in Galatians 3:28, it means to break down the walls that separate Jews and Greeks, slaves and free, men and women. Not to do so would be to violate the body of Christ, as we saw in 1 Corinthians 11:17–

34. This reading of Paul's theology corresponds closely with the Sabbath–Jubilee vision of an alternative socioeconomic–spiritual order based on God's act of liberation. It echoes the Johannine affirmation that it is not possible to love God and not to love a brother or sister (1 John 4:20) and Jesus' linking of love of God and neighbor in the Great Commandment (Mark 12:29–31). It holds out the possibility of fullness of life for all God's people.

Responsible Discipleship ◆ ◆ ◆ ◆ ◆

Once again we sense the grave limitation we bring to the task of bringing about real change in our approach to discipleship. So once again we shall simply select some examples as suggestive, provocative pointers to consider as we work out our own responses personally and with family and colleagues and friends. We do not presume to know where the path forward will lead, but we know that the longest journey necessarily begins with first steps. We must not be immobilized by the immensity of the challenge set before us by the Sabbath–Jubilee vision and the intransigence of our current national and global reality. We need to see examples of responsible discipleship within our reach.

Borders—Walls or Bridges?

Recently we attended a fascinating conference at Nogales straddling the Arizona–Mexico border. It was sponsored by BorderLinks, an ecumenical program based in Tucson that uses experiential education to help North Americans better understand the complexities of the U.S.–Mexico border. As preparation for the conference, mixed delegations of North Americans, Mexicans, and Central Americans had spent a week visiting the local border, Chiapas, or one of the Central American countries. On the opening night Bishop Thomas Gumbleton gave a stirring address about the sin of the global economy that is so beneficial to so few and so devastating to so many. The next day the 350 participants, mostly faith-oriented, socially concerned activists from all over the United States, traveled by bus to the twin cities of Nogales, which Rick Ufford-Chase, BorderLinks coordinator, describes as "the reality behind the world's corporate glitter . . . the scar tissue underlying today's Wall Street miracles" (Ufford-Chase, 1997, p. 12). The wall dividing the two cities, historically one city, now rises twelve feet and is patrolled by almost 400 U.S. agents "to ensure that this division will effectively perpetuate realities crucial to the globalization of the world's economies" (ibid., p. 13). In Nogales, Arizona, population 22,000, the minimum wage is $4.75 per hour; in Nogales, Mexico, a city of 350,000, it is less than $3.50 per day. One can easily extrapolate the differences in housing, schools, health care, nutrition, and basic necessities such as clean water, sewage disposal, and electricity.

On the way to the border, a member of the BorderLinks team shared his experience as "a border person" with family on both sides. Interestingly he was not bitter about the realities of that border but rather spoke of the challenge to build bridges rather than walls. As a BorderLinks brochure puts it, "our commitment is to cross borders—national borders, religious borders, racial borders, class borders, and ideological borders—and to test our perceptions against the reality of what we experience. We call that 'living our faith'!" The following day, back in Tucson, some of us worked in groups on issues arising out of our exposure to the border realities and our own struggles for fullness of life for all God's people.

The U.S.–Mexico border, which is almost 2,000 miles long, is only one symbol of the injustice and inequality of today's world, though it is perhaps the biggest and most dramatic one. The borders of nationality, race, ethnicity, class, and gender run right through every North American city and town, and the current tendency is, as we have seen throughout our studies, to build higher and stronger walls to divide us. The Sabbath–Jubilee challenge is to build bridges instead of walls so that we might all recover our humanity, to build communities instead of ghettos so that we might all live in peace, to build a new socioeconomic–spiritual reality in response to God's revealed purpose for humankind.

We have for many years participated in immersion experiences for North American church and solidarity groups who want to learn from the faith and hope and suffering of the peoples of Central America. Some who come are eager and open; others are resistant or fearful; almost all are impacted when they begin to look at our world through the eyes and lives of others whose experiences are so different. The U.S.–Mexico border is much closer, and much more could be made of it as a place of learning and challenge and even service. We wonder if the churches and other organizations might not be able to develop opportunities for similar learning and challenge right on their own doorsteps, in their own cities and towns, wherever those borders of class, race, ethnicity, and gender exist. The critical question is, no doubt: Do we realize that this is fundamental to our faith and our vocation?

Churches—Privileged Ghettos or Servant Communities?

One of the most powerful testimonies to the possibility of an alternative socioeconomic–spiritual way of life in the United States is the Catholic Worker movement. Founded in 1933 by Dorothy Day and Peter Maurin, this movement invites ordinary Christians, primarily but not only Catholics, to embrace poverty in solidarity with and service to the poor in their struggle for dignity and fullness of life as God's children. Larry Holben's new book, *All the Way to Heaven: A Theological Reflection on Dorothy Day, Peter Maurin, and the Catholic Worker*, puts it this way:

Certainly no element of Worker life has a more venerable history than its embrace of what St. Francis affectionately dubbed "Sister Poverty." The teaching of Jesus in the Gospels still has the power to profoundly disturb the comfortable hearer: "Woe to you who are rich . . . You cannot serve God and money . . . It is easier for a camel to pass through the eye of the needle than for a rich person to enter heaven . . . Do not lay up treasure for yourself on earth where moth and rust corrupt, or thieves break in and steal . . . If you want to be perfect, go and sell all you have and give the money to the poor. (Excerpted in *Catholic Agitator*, November, 1997, pp. 4–5)

There are now some 100 Catholic Worker houses across the United States, each autonomous to develop its own programs and personnel and resources. The Los Angeles community, for example, was founded in 1970 and operates a free soup kitchen, a hospitality house for the homeless, an AIDS ministry, a hospice for the dying, a monthly newspaper, and a "public prophetic witness in opposition to institutionalized war-making and injustice." Staff member Jeff Dietrich writes:

We believe that the Incarnation is the basis of the Christian message. We are called to make the Word of God flesh by responding to the suffering Christ incarnate among our poor and marginalized brothers and sisters. The homeless, the addict, the mentally ill, the AIDS victim, the infirm, the politically and culturally oppressed are the ones who Christ told us will be first in his Kingdom. If we too desire to become citizens of this Kingdom, then we must, in some measure, live our lives in proximity to and solidarity with those who are the least. (Dietrich, 1998, p. 4)

Their soup kitchen is located in Los Angeles' central city skid row and serves over 15,000 meals a month. Hennacy House, a fourteen-bedroom home in the working-class Latino neighborhood of Boyle Heights, provides housing for members of the staff, twelve to fourteen homeless guests, and hospice care for the dying. Full-time staff receive a stipend of $10 per week.

This is a remarkable example of discipleship in response to the biblical Jubilee and its concern for the vulnerable and marginalized. It offers good news and liberation not only to the poor and oppressed but also to any who choose to make a radical commitment to and with them. The difficult question that it raises for most of us is, however: How can the Catholic Worker example be made accessible to a much wider spectrum of Christians who are not yet ready to make a total break with "the American dream" as we know it? Many local churches and coalitions have some kind of outreach program—soup kitchens, shelters for the homeless and for battered women, food banks for the hungry, advocacy for human rights and against military spending, orphan sponsorship, or self-development programs for the poor. But somehow we generally do not take that more fundamental step, perhaps the biggest and most dramatic one, of choosing to be poor in order to be genuinely in solidarity with them.

We do not know the answer to this concern, this question. Each reader and study group will have to find their own answer on the basis of their own study and experience. They would no doubt be welcome to visit a local Catholic Worker house and other similar efforts in their city or town, and they can certainly pose this concern or question in their local church, working group, or organization. But there is no substitute for direct involvement and action with those who live at the margins of the dominant socioeconomic order in which we live. Our experience and our hope are that such involvement will impact our own lives, evangelize us, and empower us to make further commitments and lifestyle changes in faithfulness to God's rule, in response to the Jubilee challenge.

Globalization—Slavery or Liberation?

With the approach of the year 2000, many are using the name Jubilee as a rallying point for various causes, some of which reflect the concerns of the biblical Jubilee. One of these, "Jubilee 2000," is carrying out a massive, worldwide campaign for the cancellation of unpayable debt among the poorest countries of the world by the year 2000. Starting in the United Kingdom, strongly advocated by the Anglican Archbishop of Canterbury, and supported by all of Britain's mainline churches, this campaign is also being adopted by mainline churches in the United States and Canada. Organizers around the world hope to gather 24 million signatures, making this the biggest petition the world has ever seen. Surely this is a prophetic action that all of us can join as part of our response to the Sabbath–Jubilee mandates. (For more information, contact Jubilee 2000/USA Campaign for Global Debt Relief, 222 East Capitol St., N.E., Washington, D.C., 20003-1036.)

As we have seen in Central America, the poor countries of the world are entangled in the international debt crisis to such an extent that they must submit to the dictates of their creditors, principally the IMF and World Bank and governments of the rich countries, and subject their people to sharp reductions in education, health care, and other social programs. The debts are being used to impose free market policies in line with the ideology of our increasingly global domination system, which as we have seen is oriented primarily toward the accumulation of greater wealth for the rich and powerful nations and social sectors of the world. It is argued that debts must be repaid in order to maintain the stability of the world's economy, although it is increasingly recognized that the social cost of repayment through these policies is unconscionable, and some measures are now being applied to reduce debts of countries that are totally incapable of escaping from the downward spiral of indebtedness. Jubilee 2000 proposes to give wider relief to poor countries so that they can begin the new millennium free from the bondage that these debts have created and direct their resources and creativity toward the real needs of their people.

While this campaign is very much in keeping with the biblical concept of Jubilee, its appeal extends across all religious, cultural, and ideological lines. It may even spark other initiatives that will extend processes of humanization in our increasingly inhuman world—locally and nationally as well as globally. Debt relief for the poorest countries will not by itself solve their problems, but it can be a significant first step toward global commitment to fullness of life for all the people of the world, a struggle that will require many more steps and many more years.

There are of course related matters for responsible economic discipleship. With the rapid globalization of financial markets and the transnationalization of business, we must be concerned about our personal investments, our churches' influence in corporate boardrooms, and our government's trade and aid policies. Some of our churches have local, regional, and national committees for social witness and advocacy on a wide range of issues. If we are able to overcome the great divorce between spirituality and economics, we may be able to engage our local churches in serious dialogue about these very serious matters affecting the lives of millions. Gradually, if not more dramatically, we may begin to work out guidelines for actions in keeping with Sabbath economics, Jubilee spirituality, and the goal of liberty for all God's people.

8

Jubilee—Celebrating Life Together

In this final chapter we shall depart from our previous format. We shall focus on ways to celebrate our life together. We have noted repeatedly that the Sabbath–Jubilee vision is based on God's gracious intervention on our behalf, beginning with the liberation of the Hebrew slaves from the oppression of Egypt and leading to the proclamation of God's reign throughout Jesus' ministry. We have considered the mandates of the Sabbath Day, the Sabbath Year, and the Jubilee Year as fundamental principles for the creation of a new socioeconomic–spiritual possibility. Throughout these studies we have discovered much to celebrate as an affirmation of fullness of life for all God's people.

As we come to the end of an era and the dawn of the third millennium, we face devastating prognoses based on current, seemingly incurable, human propensities. As people of faith we look to the future with hope and realism. We are commited to the God who liberates and calls us to build the new possibility that we have discovered as Sabbath economics, Jubilee spirituality, and liberty for all. We know that conversion is possible. We now want to consider some concrete ways to proclaim and celebrate those changes that we hope to see in our own lives and faith communities and social contexts.

Our liturgical celebrations normally include elements of denunciation as well as proclamation, confession and repentance as well as rejoicing, praise to God as well as intercession before God. But perhaps they have lacked some of the fundamental perspectives that we have found in these studies. The following suggestions are intended to stimulate that wider reflection and experimentation for the integral human transformation that we all so desperately need.

Jubilee must become jubilation in order to empower God's people to take up the challenge and continue the long and difficult journey through the wilderness toward the Promised Land where liberty and justice are not only proclaimed but lived. We have all glimpsed that vision and sensed that jubilation in the midst of the struggle for life—during personal devotional times, sharing with close or distant companions on the way, demonstrating at city hall, worshiping on memorable dates, singing "We Shall Overcome" or portions of Nicaragua's "Peasant Mass," participating in meaningful Bible study, remembering the martyrs in our prayers with the affirmation "*Presente!*". We know and believe the good news that personal-ecclesial-social transformation is possible because it is actually taking place. We can celebrate Jubilee because this is how God reigns among us!

Recovering Times and Spaces to Be Human— The Promised Land ◆ ◆ ◆ ◆ ◆

Let's consider first some possibilities for *personal transformation*. What are some of the times and spaces that we can recover for our own humanization as well as for the humanization of those around us? In the Bible, seven is the number of perfection, so the seventh day, the seventh year, and the fiftieth year were hallowed in the Sabbath–Jubilee traditions. We may want to follow that pattern or create a different one to fit the cycles of our lives. The important thing is to break the routine of work and the domination of the systems of oppression that rule our lives through external and internal pressures. Some may choose a time each day or each week for personal or family "centering" on the real meaning and the many blessings of life in the midst of so much dehumanization. Some may look forward to times each year, such as the great liturgical seasons, for nurture and release from the struggles we face. And some may want to make plans for a "sabbatical year" or a shorter sabbatical time in which they can evaluate and recover basic goals and perspectives for their lives.

There are of course many spaces or areas of our personal and family lives that can be dedicated to the recovery of our full humanity. Daily times for meditation and for exercise can contribute enormously to our sense of well-being, our physical and emotional health, our work, and even our life expectancy. Relationships with partners and children, other close relatives and friends can be eased and strengthened through regular activities that carry the intention of mutual growth and healing as needs arise. Special experiences of gardening in the back yard or hiking in the mountains can renew our communion with nature. Regular times for reading together about critical issues of peace and justice, new expositions of biblical faith, and challenging experiences of others who struggle to be faithful to God's rule in today's world can widen the horizons and deepen the foundations of our vocation. Personal discipleship might well include a continuing commitment to visit the sick, aged, unemployed, handicapped, imprisoned, lonely.

Now let's consider some possibilities for *ecclesial transformation*. These studies have brought to our attention fundamental lessons about the Sabbath Day that most of us have never really thought through. We may want to explore new possibilities for our churches' practice of Sunday worship, for the liturgical calendar and the celebration of important dates, and for long-term planning and evaluation based on the Sabbath and Jubilee mandates.

What might Sundays dedicated to Sabbath economics and Jubilee spirituality look like? The members might go first to a nearby slum, ghetto, prison, reservation, or skid row to observe and meditate on the causes and effects of those realities in the lives of the men, women, and children who live there. Then they might consider together those particular realities and similar global realities in their study time and worship, in their time of confession and their preaching, in their intercessions and their time of dedication, in their subsequent witness and service. A church retreat might be organized as an immersion into such a reality in order to place at the center of the church's own life and mission fundamental questions about our discipleship. There might be opportunities for exchanges with faith communities very different from our own, including both worship and dialogue, to help us to see ourselves and others in new ways, and so to discover new possibilities across the many borders that separate us. In all of the above we would seek to strengthen both the inward journey and the outward journey, both contemplation and action, as essential dimensions of our vocation as God's people.

Finally, we can see that both the personal and the ecclesial dimensions are related to our concern for *social transformation*. The times and spaces for involvement in this dimension of our discipleship are as diverse and ubiquitous as life itself. The daily news brings innumerable issues that invite us to reflect on the human predicament, to remember our vocation as agents of God's justice and peace, and to act in accord with the Sabbath–Jubilee mandates. Periodic local, national, and global crises offer opportunities to discuss these issues with colleagues and friends and to share our concerns for the fullness of life for all God's people.

Every major denomination, many local churches, and ecumenical organizations as well as social action and solidarity groups offer lists of opportunities for involvement in areas of need and struggles for justice and the preservation of the environment. Every concerned person can subscribe to at least one alternative publication that presents news and critical analysis of current developments as well as reports of effective and creative responses to the many needs around us. Faced with the sea of demands and possibilities, each person, group, and faith community will have to make a selection that is reasonable and effective for them. Participation in these movements and programs should become not a burden or a guilt trip but a meaningful participation in and celebration of the struggle for life.

Respecting and Renewing Creation—New Heavens and a New Earth ◆ ◆ ◆ ◆ ◆

As the world's population becomes further removed from the land, we all need to find opportunities for the renewal of our *personal ties* to Mother

Earth and the God of creation. We need to be concerned about nature not only as a critical issue for the future of our planet but also as a fundamental part of our own spirituality. The Sabbath–Jubilee mandate for rest and recuperation is certainly as valid today as it ever was, so let us celebrate creation as God's great gift for the life for all God's people.

A good friend who teaches biology at the University of Costa Rica occasionally takes groups of theological students, church leaders, and others on walks through a local park or a biological reserve with the purpose of enabling them to restore very simple but almost mystical ties to God's creation. We stop to listen to the sounds of the wind and the birds, to breathe deeply the clean air, to watch the ants and other insects, to feel and smell the earth. We are led to imagine what the life of a butterfly or a spider is like, to talk to the flowers, to cherish the warmth of the sun, to commune with nature as part of it in harmony with all the rest. We read passages from the Bible that evoke the strength and beauty and trust and fruitfulness of nature. We take time to meditate upon the destruction of the environment and pray for its restoration. We play games and make up drama and sing music and read poetry to celebrate God's creation.

Our churches may be accomplices in the devastation of the Earth because of their almost total dedication to the salvation or liberation of humankind and their overall lack of concern for the preservation and renewal of nature. The Sabbath–Jubilee mandates should help the churches remember the importance of rest and to call into question the incessant drive toward ever greater quotas of production and profit. The churches themselves can become primary agents of education for environmental health because for us this is not just a political matter. It is an important part of our faith commitment and our spiritual development.

We need to be creative in order to bring these realities into our worship, into our devotional life, into our nurture and formation for service, into our daily lives. We need to learn from other religions, such as the Native American cosmovision and spirituality that we cited in Chapter 2, but we can do so only as we begin to know and respect others in their own reality. We have much to learn from our own Christian heritage, from mystics such as St. Francis of Assisi and from ecofeminists such as Rosemary Radford Ruether and Ivone Gebara. We can benefit greatly from poetry and art and music that take us beyond the narrow confines of intellectual reason and debate.

Personally and as churches we can join in *local, national, and global efforts* to save the environment, stop global warming, protect endangered species, recycle resources, reduce waste, and redirect the world's economy for the well-being of our planet and all its inhabitants. The Earth Charter mentioned in Chapter 2 offers material for study and an opportunity to join a worldwide campaign. All of these efforts can become a part of our Jubilee celebration of God's gift of life for all now and for future generations.

One of the great texts from our Judeo-Christian tradition is the vision of "new heavens and a new earth" in Isaiah 65:17–25, which we cited in

Chapter 4. That eloquent, poetic, passionate vision of our Earth can be used for meditation in our own devotional life, for study in our churches' educational programs, and for wider cultural and even political contexts. It begins as celebration of a new possibility of rejoicing over creation, then dramatizes the fruits of injustice and oppression, proffers a more just social reality, and ends with a portrayal of peace in which the animals themselves overcome their natural propensities and live in harmony. Such a vision must surely be a central part of our own and our churches' vision for the future.

Overcoming Poverty and Wealth—Enough Is Enough for All ◆ ◆ ◆ ◆ ◆

We often hear that "good news for the poor" is "bad news for the rich." That is a zero-sum argument. We have argued that the Sabbath economics of enough is really an appeal to the well-being of all, including those who are wealthy. Surely all of us are caught up in the current ideology and mechanisms of consumption and wealth accumulation, however rich or poor we may be. This is perhaps the most pervasive spiritual problem of our time. It condemns thousands of millions of our sisters and brothers to extreme poverty and hundreds of millions to wealth. Both extremes are deprived of their fundamental humanity, though in very different ways. The Sabbath–Jubilee vision calls us to build a socioeconomic–spiritual order in which we can all recover our full humanity through mutual service and equal participation in the means of life. Surely this is a matter for celebration—and for hard decisions at the personal, ecclesial, and social levels.

At the *personal level* we will have to work out such difficult questions as lifestyle, budget, use of disposable income, employment, savings, and investments. Some of those who signed the Shakertown Pledge, which we included in Chapter 2, worked out a formula to establish guidelines for a lifestyle that could reasonably be reached by all the world's population without exhausting the world's resources. It would have required North Americans to share their vehicles and housing, greatly reduce the wasting of energy and food, give up unnecessary appliances and luxury items, limit the buying of clothes and other apparent necessities. We must begin to turn from the suicidal rush for more wealth and take steps toward Jubilee (Finnerty, 1977).

We have assumed that almost no one can break the addiction of economic entitlement alone, as we indicated in Chapter 6, but we believe that at least some will be willing to adopt the Jubilee vision if they can find help in their faith communities. We believe that the life of our churches could be revitalized by adopting that vision and using something like the Twelve Step pattern of discipleship for those members who choose to follow Jesus along this path. This is not a challenge to be undertaken lightly. It can easily create tensions right within the churches, for there are enormous inequalities and injustices among us, even among church professionals and their staffs. But it may be a necessary part of the road to Jubilee spirituality.

Sooner or later we have to relate the Sabbath–Jubilee mandates to the wider *local, national, and global family*. We know that we cannot impose our values and beliefs, but we do have civic and political responsibilities that require us to work for the well-being of the human family. Every year vital issues of welfare, education, health care, social security, immigration, taxes, regulation of business and finance, police and prisons, child care, and military spending are discussed and decided by policy makers and representatives. Every year programs and movements of concern in all these areas need volunteers and support, expertise and advocacy. Every year millions more join the rolls of the unemployed and underpaid in all the regions of the world. There can be no celebration of Jubilee without firm commitment to seek fullness of life for all God's people.

Liberation from Debts, Slavery, Disease, and Sin ◆ ◆ ◆ ◆ ◆

In our study we have found that the biblical message, from the Law and the Prophets of the Hebrew Bible to Jesus and Paul in the New Testament, is concerned not only with the cultic liberation of sinners from punishment but also with the liberation of the poor, the oppressed, and the sick from every kind of bondage. We must consider the danger, today as in ancient times, that God's people might fall into false confidence in cultic worship without the practice of justice, which must be condemned for the sake of victims and oppressors alike. *Every* believer is called to honor God's covenant for human liberation at home and in the workplace, in the faith community and in the wider community, as an essential counterpart to faithful worship. The struggle for justice is an essential component of spirituality.

Interestingly the Greek word for liberation or release (*aphíemi*) appears in the Septuagint version of the Hebrew Scriptures and in the Christian Scriptures in key Sabbath and Jubilee passages such as Deuteronomy 15, Leviticus 25, Isaiah 58 and 61, and Luke 4. It refers to release from debts, liberation from slavery, release from captivity, liberation from oppression, release from disease, and release from sin. At some points, as we noted in the healing of the paralytic man and in the Lord's Prayer, it seems to refer to release both from debts and from sin, which is good news for both debtors and creditors, oppressed and oppressors, insofar as we all "hunger and thirst for justice." Only on this basis dare we approach God in worship. Only in this way can we truly celebrate God's reign as Jubilee.

In our study of the Lord's Supper and other passages from the Apostle Paul we found that *the body of Christ* is present among the members breaking down the walls of class, race, and gender. To deny any member of the body full participation is to deny Christ's body and so to fall into judgment. The challenge to our North American churches is frightening even today, for they are still to a great extent reflections of the economic, racial, and ethnic divisions of our society. In some of our denominations, great strides toward equality of gender have been made, but male dominance is still evident in many aspects of leadership and service. We recognize that God's gift of liberation includes the mandate and the possibility of bringing down the walls of prejudice, injustice, and inequality. These are grounds for Jubilee celebration and commitment for the future.

The witness and service of Christians, individually and collectively, in the *wider society* cannot be overemphasized, both in terms of release from disease and sin and in terms of liberation from class, race, and gender inequality and oppression. Together with people of other faiths and of no specific religious affiliation we must face the new millennium with a clear vision of the human family in which all are invited, encouraged, and enabled to seek fullness of life. This is the real meaning of God's reign, of liberty for all through Sabbath economics and Jubilee spirituality. This is the substance of what we can hope to celebrate in the year 2000 and beyond.

The churches have traditionally given primary importance to evangelism and Christian education, but they have also played an important role in education and health care and other dimensions of human development. They have not often fulfilled their true vocation, however, as agents of reconciliation and justice. Bishop Gumbleton put it this way, in his address at Tucson mentioned in Chapter 7: "The churches have down through history done immense works of charity for the poor, the sick, and the forgotten, but they have failed to recognize the sin of structural social injustice and our responsibility to do something about it." This is so because we are so wrapped up in those structures. May God enable us to recognize our sin and the sin of the whole world as we work toward Jubilee in the new millennium.

Discovering Others, Finding Ourselves ◆ ◆ ◆ ◆ ◆

In Chapter 6 we considered the terrible tragedy of the 500 years of European conquest of the Americas, which has encompassed the entire globe with military, political, economic, social, and racial imperialism buttressed by sexism and patriarchy. As we enter the new millennium and set goals for the future, we will want to consider personally and as churches the ongoing need to build bridges so that we can all discover "the other" across borders of nationality, race and ethnicity, gender, and generations. We have given primary importance to economics, which is more prominent than ever in today's global system of domination, and we can see that economics is intertwined with the other divisions. We speak of the feminization of poverty, as women are more affected than men. In many places around the world, economic inequality is closely related to race and ethnicity. Much more could be said about the marginalization of the very young and the very old, who are the first to suffer the effects of violence and injustice.

At the *personal level* we can all examine and evaluate our relationships to see whether we are bound by traditional patterns of power and privilege, whether we are increasingly open to others and appreciative of their otherness, whether we are growing toward fuller humanity through mutual discovery of each other's experience, perceptions, and values. This can be fundamental to our spirituality and our life's journey. Many of us can attest that the discovery of ourselves through intimacy and daily living with our partners can continue throughout our lives. As those of us who have had the privilege of living and working among people of different cultures and realities can recount, we receive far more blessing and understanding than we could ever give. So as we enter the new millennium we will want to be very intentional about the building of relationships across lines of gender, race, ethnicity, and generation as well as class.

Most of our *churches* will have to discover new ways to move beyond the prevalent class and racial–ethnic captivity in which they find themselves. Recently we attended worship in a church that was designed with Native American motifs; gathers people with very diverse economic and racial–ethnic backgrounds; includes readings and prayers in English, Spanish, and a local native language; is led in music by an extraordinary African American pianist; and gathers each Sunday prayers concerning not only personal needs and blessings but also local and global developments and crises. That service lasted two hours, and no one complained! Could not many more congregations become living expressions of Jubilee in their worship, in their programs of nurture and service, and in their vision for the future?

In recent years the United States has seen the failure of the Equal Rights amendment, which diminishes all of us; the reversal of Affirmative Action, which offends many of us; the growth of legislation and police reinforcements against undocumented immigrants, which reflects and promotes prejudice and xenophobia in our culture; and the dismantling of the welfare system, which further endangers the life and well-being of the poor, the weak, and the vulnerable, especially single mothers and children, the disturbed, and the elderly. These are symptoms of the moral and spiritual climate of our time. They are matters for which the Sabbath–Jubilee vision calls us to respond.

Going Home—Identity, Security, Peace ◆ ◆ ◆ ◆ ◆

The crowning achievement of the Sabbath–Jubilee mandates was to be the return of every family to their land at the fiftieth year, the Jubilee Year, when the trumpet heralded "liberty throughout the land to all its inhabitants" (Leviticus 25:10). For the tribes of Yahweh in Yahweh's Promised Land, this mandate gave all the people their identity and dignity as full participants in the life of their communities, their social and economic security in the face of ever-present dangers from natural and human disasters, and their sense of peace and well-being in the bosom of their families, clans, and tribes. All around the world today, people are suffering from a loss of identity and dignity, even the most affluent and the middle class, for we are all caught up in a domination system of individualism and competition. We face a loss of security, for we are all subject to impersonal economic and administrative decisions that can cut off our employment and erase our savings and take away our homes. We have lost any sense of peace, for we see no alternative but to continue down the frenetic path of competition and stress and alienation with little possibility of responding to the needs of others and increasing gloom about the future for our own children. We desperately need a vision of Jubilee.

At the *personal level* and in our families we can take concrete steps to recover times and spaces to rest from the pressures and the pace of modern urban life, to gain perspective as to our real values, to practice Sabbath, to be human, to recover the life-giving and life-sharing meaning of home and household. These times and spaces will no doubt enable us to make other decisions and take other steps toward our own freedom and the freedom of others. They should help us find physical, emotional, and socioeconomic well-being and to work for the well-being of those around us. This experience of Jubilee may be very modest, but it can free us from some of the stress and alienation of the domination system. This struggle may be as difficult and as important as any recovery from addiction.

As we explored in Chapter 7, the process of recovery requires the accompaniment of others who have made the same commitment and are dealing with the same struggle. Some within our *faith communities* will need to reorient our life of worship and nurture and caring in order to enable us to continue on the road to recovery, as we confront, in addition to the usual vicissitudes of daily living, the great frontiers of economic, racial–ethnic, and gender entitlements. The foundation for our recovery is the faith that God rules in our lives and among God's people in this present world.

Going home includes the possibility of helping *others* to recover their roots, their identity as human beings, to gain some semblance of security in a very insecure socioeconomic–spiritual order, and to build new possibilities for a sense of peace that is based not on material success or excess but on more durable values and relationships. None of the many books and videos on how to be successful will do. There is no established formula. But if we begin to work together in solidarity, we will discover answers day by day, enough to continue on that way. This is the promise of Jubilee that we celebrate.

Working for Justice, Celebrating Life Together ◆ ◆ ◆ ◆ ◆

When we examine the Sabbath and Jubilee texts and other prophetic passages from the Old Testament and the New, we find that the concern for justice is not a marginal addendum for God's people. It is central. Some of our Latin American biblical scholars and base community leaders have affirmed forthrightly, as did the prophets of Israel, that the only way to know God is to practice justice. Theologies of and movements for liberation not only call us out of bondage and oppression; they call us to build new socioeconomic–spiritual possibilities founded on God's rule of justice. In the Bible, God's justice is not a matter simply of objective fairness and equal opportunity; it requires a privileged place for those who have been marginalized or excluded. The Great Commandment is to love God and neighbor; it is impossible to do the former without the latter. Jubilee means to work together for justice and so to celebrate together the God of life.

The central agenda of God's mission "on earth as it is in heaven" runs right through *our own personal lives.* We all have the possibility of being instruments of God's grace, God's peace, God's justice, God's love. The Sabbath–Jubilee vision is no more the province of pastors than of laymen, of missionaries than of other believers, of public figures than of quiet witnesses, of mature members than of new or youthful members. We all face daily the great frontiers of human division and divine grace. We are endowed with gifts grounded in love that those around us need so greatly. We know that God loves us, so through God's Spirit we can love others whom God loves, not because they are especially lovely, but because the nature of God's love is to give of oneself and so to receive from the other.

Our churches are, at least potentially, spaces in which concerned people can begin to practice Sabbath economics, Jubilee spirituality, and liberty for all. Our churches are human institutions with all the temptations and foibles and troubles of other institutions. But they are grounded, at least in theory, upon biblical and confessional foundations that call us constantly to account. Part of that calling to account must be the challenge of the Sabbath–Jubilee vision that is so prominent in the history of Israel, in the life and ministry of Jesus, and also in the early church. Hopefully, the millenial celebrations will sound the trumpet call of God's Jubilee and hold up that vision of new possibilities in our world.

The peoples of the world will no doubt be looking for signs of hope, liberation, justice, and peace as we enter the new millennium. Every sector of the new global reality, from economics and politics to science and technology, from the United Nations to local city councils, from philosophers to journalists, from health workers to educators, from grandparents to grandchildren, will be called upon to articulate their hopes and fears for humankind and for our fragile planet. People of every faith will be expected to draw deeply from their spiritual wells in order to share fresh water of life for the refreshing of weary souls. As heirs of the Judeo-Christian tradition, we will be able to share our vision of a new socioeconomic–spiritual possibility in which all have enough and none too much, in which debts are forgiven and slaves liberated, in which divisions of race, ethnicity, gender, class, and generation become bridges to mutual growth, in which all of us can return home to genuine humanity in community with all humankind. How great might be this celebration of Jubilee!

References and Further Reading

Bermúdez, Enrique. (1986). *Death and Resurrection in Guatemala*. Maryknoll, NY: Orbis Books.

Brecher, Jeremy, and Tim Costello. (1994). *Global Village or Global Pillage: Economic Reconstruction from the Bottom Up*. Boston: South End Press.

Brueggemann, Walter. (1977). *The Land: Place as Gift, Promise, and Challenge in Biblical Faith*. Philadelphia: Fortress.

Brueggemann, Walter. (1987). *Hope within History*. Atlanta: John Knox Press.

Brueggemann, Walter. (1988). *Israel's Praise: Doxology against Idolatry and Ideology*. Philadelphia: Fortress.

Ceresko, Anthony. (1992). *Introduction to the Old Testament: A Liberation Perspective*. Maryknoll, NY: Orbis Books.

Comisión Evangélica Pentecostal Latinoamericana. (1999). *Jubileo: La Fiesta del Espíritu*. Maracaibo, Venezuela: CEPLA.

Deats, Richard. (1997). "People Power vs. the Power of Unbridled Wealth." *Fellowship* 63(7–8), 3.

Dietrich, Jeff. (1998). "Catholic Worker Community." *Catholic Agitator*, 4–5.

Duchrow, Ulrich. (1995). *Alternatives to Global Capitalism: Drawn from Biblical History, Designed for Political Action*. Utrecht, Holland: International Books.

Earth Council. Aparado 2323–1002. San José, Costa Rica.

Elliott, Neil. (1994). *Liberating Paul: The Justice of God and the Politics of the Apostle*. Maryknoll, NY: Orbis Books.

Episcopado Guatemalteco. (1988). *El Clamor por la Tierra: Carta Pastoral Colectiva*. Guatemala: Febrero.

Fager, Jeffrey. (1993). *Land Tenure and the Biblical Jubilee: Uncovering Hebrew Ethics through the Sociology of Knowledge*. Sheffield, UK: Journal for the Study of the Old Testament.

Finnerty, Adam Daniel. (1977). *No More Plastic Jesus: Global Justice and Christian Lifestyle*. Maryknoll, NY: Orbis Books.

Foulkes, Irene. (1996). *Problemas Pastorales en Corinto: Comentario Exegético-Pastoral a Corintios*. San José, Costa Rica: Departimento de Investigaciones and Seminario Bíblico Latinamericana.

Galeano, Eduardo. (1973). *Open Veins of Latin America: Five Centuries of the Pillage of a Continent.* New York: Monthly Review Press.

Girardi, Guilio. (1992). *La conquista permanente: El Cristianismo entre paz del imperio y paz de los pueblos.* Managua: Nicarao.

Gorostiaga, Xabier. (1991). "Latin America in the New World Order." Managua: *Envío* (Revista mensual de la Universidad Centroamericana [UCA] de Managua), August, 31–43.

Gottwald, Norman K. (1979). *The Tribes of Yahweh: A Sociology of the Religion of Liberated Israel,* 1250–1050 B.C.E. Maryknoll, NY: Orbis Books.

Gottwald, Norman K. (1985). *The Hebrew Bible: A Socio-Literary Introduction.* Philadelphia: Fortress.

Goudzwaard, Bob, and Harry de Lange. (1995). *Beyond Poverty and Affluence: Toward an Economy of Care.* Grand Rapids, MI: Eerdmans.

Hamilton, Jeffries M. (1992). *Social Justice and Deuteronomy: The Case of Deuteronomy 15.* Atlanta: Scholars Press.

Hanks, Thomas. (1983). *God so Loved the Third World: The Bible, the Reformation, and Liberation Theologies.* Maryknoll, NY: Orbis Books.

Harris, Maria. (1996). *Proclaim Jubilee! A Spirituality for the Twenty-First Century.* Louisville, KY: Westminster/John Knox.

Herzog, William R. (1994). *Parables as Subversive Speech: Jesus as Pedagogue of the Oppressed.* Louisville, KY: Westminster/John Knox.

Holben, Lawrence. (1997). *All the Way to Heaven: A Theological Reflection on Dorothy Day, Peter Maurin, and the Catholic Worker.* Marion, IN: Rose Hill Books.

Horsley, Richard A., ed. (1997). *Paul and Empire: Religion and Power in Roman Imperial Society.* Harrisburg, PA: Trinity Press.

Horsley, Richard A., and Neil Asher Silberman. (1997). *The Message and the Kingdom: How Jesus and Paul Ignited a Revolution and Transformed the Ancient World.* New York: Grosset/Putnam.

Kairos/USA. (1994). *On the Way: From Kairos to Jubilee.* Chicago: Kairos/USA (5757 Sheridan Road, #16A, Chicago, IL 60660).

Matul, Daniel. (1994). *Somos un Solo Corazón: Cultura Maya Contemporánea.* San José, Costa Rica: Liga Maya Internacional.

Meeks, Douglas. (1989). *God the Economist.* Minneapolis, MN: Augsburg Fortress.

Miranda, Jose Porfirio. (1974). *Marx and the Bible: A Critique of the Philosophy of Oppression.* Maryknoll, NY: Orbis Books.

Mulligan, Mary Jane. (1992). "¿Estamos Condenados?" *Pensamiento Propio X,* 95.

Myers, Ched. (1988). *Binding the Strong Man: A Political Reading of Mark's Story of Jesus.* Maryknoll, NY: Orbis Books.

Myers, Ched. (1996). *Interpreting the Lessons of the Church Year: Pentecost 1, Proclamation 6, Series B*. Minneapolis, MN: Fortress.

Phillips, Kevin. (1990). *The Politics of Rich and Poor*. New York: Random House.

Prior, Michael. (1995). *Jesus the Liberator: Nazareth Liberation Theology (Luke 4:16–30)*. Sheffield, UK: Sheffield Academic Press.

Richard, Pablo. (1996). "Interpretación bíblica de las culturas indígenas (mayas, kunas, y quichuas de América Latina)." *Pasos* 66(July–August), 4–11. San José, Costa Rica: Departimento de Investigaciones.

Ringe, Sharon. (1985). *Jesus, Liberation, and the Biblical Jubilee: Images for Ethics and Christology*. Philadelphia: Fortress.

Roberts, Tom. (1999). "Guatemala: Truth commission report details years of military abuses." *National Catholic Reporter* 35(19, March 12), 13–16.

Robertson, Laurel, Carol Flinders, and Brian Rupperthal. (1986). *The New Laurel's Kitchen: A Handbook for Vegetarian Cookery and Nutrition*. Berkeley: Ten Speed Press.

Ruether, Rosemary Radford, ed. (1996). *Women Healing Earth: Third World Women on Ecology, Feminism, and Religion*. Maryknoll, NY: Orbis Books.

de Santa Ana, Julio. (1991). *La práctica económica como religión: crítica teológica a la economía política*. San José, Costa Rica: Departimento de Investigaciones.

Schaef, Ann Wilson. (1988). *When Society Becomes an Addict*. San Francisco: Harper.

Schumacher, Edward. (1973). *Small Is Beautiful: Economics as if People Mattered*. London: Blond & Bridges.

Schlensky, Evely Laser. (1977). Interview in *The Witness*. October, 8–10.

Tovar, Antonio. (1983). "Las leyes agrarias de Levítico 25 (Año Sabático y Año de Jubileo): El derecho a la tierra como el derecho a la vida," *Tesis de Licenciatura en Teología*. San José, Costa Rica: Seminario Bíblico Latinoamericana.

Ufford-Chase, Rick. (1997). "Glimpsing the Future." *The Other Side*, January–February, 12–17, 55.

Wink, Walter. (1992). *Engaging the Powers: Discernment and Resistance in a World of Domination*. Minneapolis, MN: Fortress.

Winters, Alicia. (1994). "El Goel en el Antiguo Israel." *Ribla* 18, 19–29. San José, Costa Rica: Departimento Ecuménico de Investigaciones.

Witherington, Ben. (1995). *Conflict and Community in Corinth: A Socio-Rhetorical Commentary on 1 and 2 Corinthians*. Grand Rapids, MI: Eerdmans.

World Council of Churches. (1993). *Christian Faith and the World Economy Today*. Geneva: World Council of Churches.

Wright, Christopher. (1992). "Jubilee" in *The Anchor Bible Dictionary*, Vol. 3, pp. 1025–1030. New York: Doubleday.

Zinn, Howard. (1995). *A People's History of the United States, 1492–Present*, rev. ed. New York: HarperCollins.

Index